The Complete Instant Pot Cookbook for Beginners

800 Easy Pressure Cooker Recipes for Home Made Meals | to Help Beginners to Master Your Instant Pot

Donald S. Bey

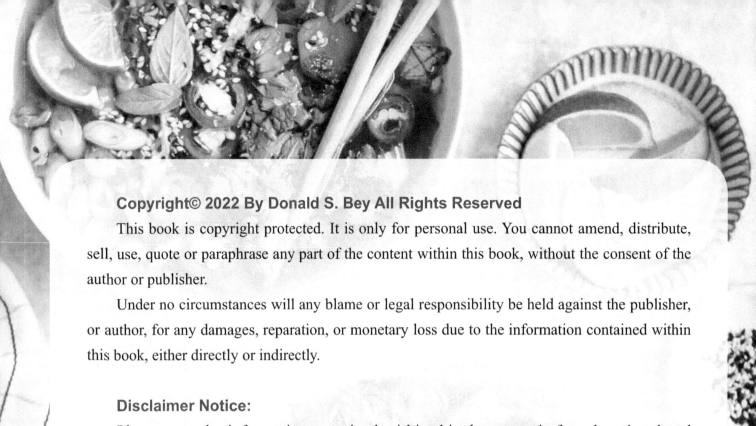

Copyright© 2022 By Donald S. Bey All Rights Reserved

This book is copyright protected. It is only for personal use. You cannot amend, distribute, sell, use, quote or paraphrase any part of the content within this book, without the consent of the author or publisher.

Under no circumstances will any blame or legal responsibility be held against the publisher, or author, for any damages, reparation, or monetary loss due to the information contained within this book, either directly or indirectly.

Disclaimer Notice:

Please note the information contained within this document is for educational and entertainment purposes only. All effort has been executed to present accurate, up to date, reliable, complete information. No warranties of any kind are declared or implied. Readers acknowledge that the author is not engaged in the rendering of legal, financial, medical or professional advice. The content within this book has been derived from various sources. Please consult a licensed professional before attempting any techniques outlined in this book.

By reading this document, the reader agrees that under no circumstances is the author responsible for any losses, direct or indirect, that are incurred as a result of the use of the information contained within this document, including, but not limited to, errors, omissions, or inaccuracies.

Contents

Introduction 1

Chapter 1 Beginner's Instant Pot Guide 2

Chapter 2 Breakfasts 6

Chapter 3 Beef, Pork, and Lamb 19

Chapter 4 Poultry 34

Chapter 5 Fish and Seafood 48

Chapter 6 Vegetables and Sides 60

Chapter 7 Stews and Soups 72

Chapter 8 Desserts 85

Chapter 9 Staples, Sauces, Dips, and Dressings 99

Appendix 1 Measurement Conversion Chart 111

INTRODUCTION

Cooking could be very tedious and unenjoyable, especially when you have to monitor the cooking gas or stove. It could easily become something you dread doing when you think about the stress involved, the time consumed over the stove, the splash of food particles all over the stove and wall of the kitchen; which takes a lot of time to wash off. Sometimes it is simply tiring to handle the children, work, cooking, and life itself.

These issues are enough to make you search out better ways to cook. We need something that would save us the several hours of cleaning after cooking due to the stains during cleaning.

And viola, there is! The Instant Pot. I came across the Instant pot when I visited a friend and decided to get one to see how seamless it could make my evening meals prepared.

At first, it was hard for me to understand all the buttons. Though it was spelled out in simple terms in the usual manual. But after using it to prepare meals twice, I got to grasp the use of the buttons, and since then, cooking has become easier and something I enjoy doing.

You do not have to be a person in tech to understand the instructions on the manual of the Instant pot cooker. Just by going through it, you can understand how to use it. I failed to go through the manual at first hence my initial difficulty in using the device. The Instant pot provides you with satisfying functions including a time scale for preparing each dish.

Chapter 1 Beginner's Instant Pot Guide

Chapter 1 Beginner's Instant Pot Guide

The Instant pot is an electric pressure cooker with many features to make cooking easier, faster, and better. Its features include the sauté pot for preparing brown meats and thickening soups, the pressure cooker manual, which set the cooker's pressure on a high or low level, and also the keep warm and cancel features.

At first use, this Instant pot seems complicated with many buttons, instructions, and precautions, but it becomes easy to handle and use if properly understood. As a career woman just like me, or a person who runs fast food, 'Instant Pot' can come in handy to help make your cooking a lot easier and get more meals prepared in a lesser time.

To get started, the user must ensure that the components of the pot are properly arranged. The inner pot must go into the Instant pot; here, you add your liquid, be it water or stock. Then place your trivet if needed for the meal about to be cooked.

After closing the pot with its lid, you must ensure that it is properly sealed by turning on the valve to the sealing position. Then select your cooking feature, push in the time and start to cook. Ensure that care is taken while releasing the pressure valve; preferably, a long kitchen utensil should be used.

Instant Pot Cooking Instructions

Sauté

The Sauté mode allows brown meat before cooking or thickening soups, stews, and sauces without using any other pan or pot on the stove. This feature allows you to cook without the Instant pot lid on. A glass lid can be used in its stead. It has a max time of 30 minutes when you click on the sauté mode, which does not change.

Within ten seconds, you need to press the adjust button to select the desired temperature setting. The pot will automatically start to heat. Push the cancel button to turn it off when you are done cooking.

Pressure cook | Manual

This function allows you to prepare food in large quantities but with the same timing as if you were preparing less, especially when cooking chicken. It is written as either a pressure cook or a manual button. To use the pressure cook or manual function, press the button to begin the pressure cooking cycle.

Pressure level | pressure

This button is either labeled pressure level or pressure, and it helps set the pressure cooker to either high pressure or low pressure. Although most food recipes provide for high-pressure levels while cooking, you have the liberty to choose which of the settings to use.

Keep warm

This function helps you keep your food warm. Rather than warm up meals with microwave hours after cooking with your pressure pot, all you need to do is cancel the cooking program and then click on the keep warm button.

This function also helps you cook your meal or meat when you feel it's not as cooked as you would have it. It automatically

comes on when meals are done cooking in the pressure pot. You can switch it off/on using the keep warm button.

Cancel

This button is used to end a cooking program. For instance, after pressure cooking your meal, you wish to keep it warm for a couple of hours before use. All you need to do is cancel the program before clicking on the keep warm button. It also comes to aid when you think your food is properly cooked before the timer goes off. It is used by clicking on the cancel button.

What foods are best for Instant pot?

The Instant Pot is used to cook a variety of food item. But I have created this special list of what I have used my Instant pot to prepare.

Chicken

The Instant Pot can be used to prepare all kinds of chicken parts, whether frozen or not. It takes about two to three minutes to defrost a chicken using the pressure cook function of the Instant pot. The Instant pot cooker gives you a perfectly cooked chicken, though the time for cooking a chicken breast may differ from cooking a chicken thigh. Getting a shredded chicken for your shawarma sauce or chicken pie sauce is made easy by simply putting a cup of water in your Instant pot, laying your chicken breast on the trivet insert that came with it, then adding your seasoning. When well cooked, shred.

Pork, Beef, Lamb, and other Meats

Meats produce protein and fat needed for the body, and a good quantity of it is needed for healthy living. The Instant Pot cooker helps get your meat properly cooked in a lesser time than cooking with other means. The sauté function is used to boil meats. It takes about 20 minutes to prepare beef.

Vegetables

Eating vegetables is healthy, and having them steamed before serving is even healthier. With the Instant Pot, you can steam up your vegetables before serving by placing them in the steamer basket.

Pour into your Instant pot a cup of water and arrange it in your steamer basket. Allow to pressure cook for 5 minutes, then allow the valve to release the pressure. Take off the lid and drain the water before adding your olive oil to your vegetable and any other seasoning or side dish if you wish to add any. Ensure to take your vegetable out of the Instant pot on time to prevent it from being overly cooked.

Instant Pot Safety Precautions

Safety precautions must be taken to effectively use the Instant pot without creating or getting yourself involved in a domestic accident. Amongst these precautions are:

♦ A long kitchen utensil should be used, preferably a wooden spoon, while turning on the steam release valve when you are ready to release pressure in your Instant pot.

♦ Putting on a kitchen hand glove will also be helpful.

♦ Never attempt to open the lid of the Instant pot while it is yet to release the pressure fully through the steam valve. Ensure that all the pressure has been released first before taking off the lid to avoid blowing in your face.

♦ Ensure that before you start cooking, you check and properly arrange the Instant pot as provided by the Instant pot manual. Also ensure the pot is plugged properly into a socket and placed in a well-ventilated place due to the pressure released.

♦ Do not overfill the cooker. Foods like beans and grains swell as they cook and should be given space to cook properly. Food of this kind should be half-filled in the Instant pot.

♦ Properly maintaining an Instant pot could be another issue; precautions should be taken. You need to unplug your Instant pot and allow it to cool down after use. Then, clean the Instant pot base with a damp cloth; note that this part should never be submerged in water or a dishwasher. However, the inner pot and steam rack can be washed in warm soapy water. Clean Instant pot lid, allow to dry and reassemble components.

The Instant Pot is a beautiful item to have in your kitchen, it saves time and make cooking seamless, you should try it out.

Chapter 2 Breakfasts

Chapter 2 Breakfasts

Hash Browns

Prep time: 5 minutes | Cook time: 15 minutes | Serves 4

2 tablespoons olive oil
2 tablespoons vegan margarine
4 cups peeled and grated russet potatoes
Pinch salt
Pinch freshly ground black pepper

1. Add the oil and margarine to the Instant Pot and press the Sauté button. Add the potatoes and sauté 5 minutes, stirring occasionally, until they just begin to brown. 2. Season with salt and pepper. Use a wide spatula to press down firmly on the potatoes in the pot. 3. Lock the lid into place. Press the Manual button and adjust time to 10 minutes. When the timer beeps, quick-release the pressure until the float valve drops and then unlock the lid. Serve warm.

Huevos Rancheros

Prep time: 10 minutes | Cook time: 12 minutes | Serves 4

1 cup dried pinto beans, picked over and soaked overnight or quick-soaked
4 teaspoons taco seasoning, plus more for garnish
1 cup tomato salsa
Salt and freshly ground black pepper
4 large eggs
4 (6-inch) corn tortillas, warmed, or 4 handfuls tortilla chips
Optional Garnishes:
Sour cream
Chopped fresh cilantro
Grated Pepper Jack cheese

1. Drain the beans and add them to the pot. Add 1½ cups water and the taco seasoning and stir to combine. Lock on the lid, select the Pressure Cook function, and adjust to High pressure for 7 minutes. Make sure the steam valve is in the Sealing position. 2. When the cooking time is up, quick-release the pressure. Drain off most of the cooking liquid from the beans (about ⅔ cup) and discard. Return the beans in the pot to the appliance. Stir in the salsa. Season with salt and pepper. Use a wooden spoon to create four indentations in the beans (it's okay if liquid rushes back in; you're just creating a little space for the eggs). 3. Carefully crack the eggs into the indentations. Sprinkle the eggs with a few pinches of taco seasoning. Cover with a regular pot lid or a glass Instant Pot lid. Select Sauté, adjust to Normal/Medium, and adjust the time to at least 5 minutes. Cook, keeping a close eye on the pot, until the egg whites are just set, 5 minutes. The yolks will be runny. Press Cancel. 4. Remove the pot from the appliance. If you prefer well-set egg whites, let the pot stand, covered, for a few more minutes. (The yolks will still be runny.) Place the tortillas or tortilla chips on plates. With a large serving spoon, carefully scoop up the eggs and beans and place them on top of the tortillas or chips. Serve immediately, with garnishes, if desired.

Mexican Eggs in Purgatory with Chorizo

Prep time: 10 minutes | Cook time: 25 minutes | Serves 4 to 6

1 tablespoon extra-virgin olive oil
1 small russet potato, diced
2 tomatillos, husked, washed and diced
1 yellow onion, diced
1 jalapeño pepper, minced
8 ounces (227 g) ground pork
chorizo
½ teaspoon ground cumin
½ teaspoon smoked paprika
Salt, to taste
Freshly ground black pepper
1 cup store-bought salsa verde
1 cup low-sodium chicken stock
4 to 6 large eggs

1. Place the olive oil in the Instant Pot. Press Sauté. Wait 1 minute for the oil to heat up and then add the potato, tomatillos, onion, jalapeño and chorizo. Sauté for 5 minutes, stirring occasionally. 2. Stir in the cumin, paprika and salt and black pepper to taste. Sauté for an additional minute. 3. Press Cancel. Stir in the salsa verde and stock and be sure to scrape up any browned bits from the bottom of the pot. 4. Secure the lid with the steam vent in the sealed position. Press Pressure Cook and use the plus and minus buttons to adjust the timer until the display reads 4 minutes on high. 5. When the timer sounds, quick release the pressure. Remove the lid. 6. Give the mixture a quick stir. Press Sauté until the display light is beneath normal. 7. Crack the eggs into the salsa verde mixture, leaving about an inch between each egg. Season the top of each egg with a little bit of salt and pepper. Sauté for about 10 minutes, or until the white part of the egg is no longer translucent.

Buckwheat and Bulgur Porridge

Prep time: 10 minutes | Cook time: 21 minutes | Serves 6

4½ cups water
½ cup bulgur wheat
½ cup raw buckwheat groats
⅓ cup packed raisins or dried cranberries, chopped
¼ cup granulated white sugar
1 teaspoon vanilla extract
½ teaspoon ground cinnamon
¼ teaspoon table salt
½ cup heavy cream or half-and-half

1. Mix the water, bulgur, buckwheat, raisins, sugar, vanilla, cinnamon, and salt in 3-, 6-, or 8-quart cooker. Secure the lid with the steam vent in the sealed position. 2. Select Pressure Cook or Manual, and cook on high for 16 minutes with the Keep Warm setting off. 3. When the machine has finished cooking, turn it off and let the pressure return to normal naturally, about 15 minutes. Unlatch the lid and open the cooker. 4. Press the Sauté button, set on Medium or Normal for 5 minutes. 5. Stir often as the porridge comes to a bubble. Stir in the cream or half-and-half and continue stirring. Turn off the Sauté function and remove the hot insert from the machine to stop the cooking. Serve warm.

Chickpea-Flour Egg Bites with Roasted Red Peppers

Prep time: 10 minutes | Cook time: 10 minutes | Makes 7 bites

1 cup almond milk	¼ teaspoon fine sea salt
¾ cup chickpea flour	⅛ teaspoon ground turmeric
2 tablespoons egg replacer powder	½ cup chopped roasted red bell pepper
1 tablespoon nutritional yeast	1 tablespoon chopped fresh flat-leaf parsley
1 tablespoon coconut oil, plus more for greasing	

1. Grease a silicone egg bite mold generously with coconut oil. Pour 1 cup water into the Instant Pot. 2. In a blender, combine the almond milk, chickpea flour, egg replacer, nutritional yeast, coconut oil, salt, and turmeric. Blend at medium speed for about 1 minute, until smooth, then transfer to a bowl and let the batter rest for 10 minutes to thicken. 3. Stir in the bell pepper and parsley, then pour ¼ cup of the batter into each cup of the egg bite mold (they will be about three-quarters full). Place the filled mold on a wire metal steam rack, then cover the mold with a round of parchment paper to keep condensation from dripping onto the egg bites as they cook. Grasping the handles of the steam rack, lower the egg bites into the Instant Pot. 4. Secure the lid and set the pressure release to Sealing. Select the Steam setting and set the time for 10 minutes at high pressure. (The pot will take about 10 minutes to come up to pressure before the cooking program begins.) 5. When the cooking program ends, let the pressure release naturally for 10 minutes, then move the pressure release to Venting to release any remaining steam. Open the pot and, wearing heat-resistant mitts, grab the handles of the steam rack and lift the egg bite mold out of the pot. 6. Let the bites cool in the mold for 5 minutes, then invert the mold onto a plate and lift off the mold. You may have to jiggle the mold a bit to release the bites. 7. Transfer the egg bites to plates and serve warm. You can also store them in an airtight container, refrigerated, for up to 3 days.

Creamy Eggs Florentine

Prep time: 10 minutes | Cook time: 28 minutes | Serves 4

1 tablespoon olive oil	1½ cups cottage cheese
2 medium garlic cloves, chopped	5 large eggs
5 ounces (142 g) baby spinach	¼ to ½ cup crumbled feta cheese
Salt and freshly ground black pepper	2 tablespoons chopped fresh dill

1. Place a trivet with handles in the pot and add 1½ cups water. Spray a 7 × 3-inch metal baking pan well with cooking spray; set aside. 2. Put the oil in the pot, select Sauté, and adjust to Normal/Medium heat. When the oil is hot, add the garlic and cook, stirring frequently, until fragrant, 30 seconds. Add the spinach, 2 teaspoons water, a few pinches of salt, and several grinds of pepper. Cook, stirring occasionally, until wilted, 2 minutes. Press Cancel. 3. Transfer the spinach and garlic to a mesh strainer and press with a wooden spoon to extract as much liquid as possible. Place the spinach mixture in a large bowl. Add the cottage cheese and stir to combine. Add the eggs, feta cheese, and dill and whisk to combine. Add ½ teaspoon salt and a few grinds of pepper and stir to combine. 4. Pour the egg mixture into the prepared baking pan and cover tightly with foil. Place the baking pan on the trivet. Lock on the lid, select the Pressure Cook function, and adjust to High pressure for 25 minutes. Make sure the steam valve is in the Sealing position. 5. When the cooking time is up, quick-release the pressure. Blot the excess water from the top of the foil with paper towels. Remove the baking pan from the pot and carefully uncover. The eggs are done when a knife inserted into the center comes out clean with no liquid egg clinging to the knife. (If the casserole is not done, lock on the lid and return to High pressure for 1 minute more and then quick-release the pressure.) Let the dish sit for 5 minutes and then cut into wedges and serve.

Butter-Toasted Steel-Cut Oats with Dried Apples

Prep time: 5 minutes | Cook time: 15 minutes | Serves 6

2 tablespoons salted butter	½ teaspoon kosher salt
1½ cups steel-cut oats	Maple syrup or brown sugar, to serve
½ teaspoon ground allspice	
½ cup dried apples, chopped	Milk or cream, to serve

1. On a 6-quart Instant Pot, select More/High Sauté. Add the butter and cook, stirring often, until it begins to smell nutty and the milk solids at the bottom begin to brown, about 3 minutes. 2. Stir in the oats and allspice, then cook, stirring occasionally, until fragrant and toasted, about 3 minutes. Add 5½ cups water, the apples and salt; stir to combine, then distribute in an even layer. 3. Press Cancel, lock the lid in place and move the pressure valve to Sealing. Select Pressure Cook or Manual; make sure the pressure level is set to High. Set the cooking time for 5 minutes. When pressure cooking is complete, quick-release the steam by moving the pressure valve to Venting. Press Cancel, then carefully open the pot. 4. Stir the mixture well, then re-cover without locking the lid in place. Let stand for 10 minutes. Stir vigorously until thick and creamy, about 30 seconds. Serve with maple syrup and milk.

Cinnamon Roll Oatmeal

Prep time: 5 minutes | Cook time: 4 minutes | Serves 4

2 cups old-fashioned rolled oats	1 teaspoon ground cinnamon
4 cups milk	2 tablespoons unsalted butter (at room temperature)
¼ cup light brown sugar	
1 teaspoon pure vanilla extract	¼ cup pure maple syrup, for drizzling
½ teaspoon salt	

1. In the Instant Pot, combine the oats, milk, brown sugar, vanilla, salt and cinnamon and stir well. 2. Secure the lid with the steam vent in the sealed position. Press Manual and immediately adjust the timer to 4 minutes. Check that the display light is beneath high pressure. 3. Once the timer sounds, allow the pressure to release naturally for 20 minutes. Open the lid of the Instant Pot and stir in the butter. 4. Serve immediately in bowls and drizzle the oatmeal with maple syrup.

Zesty Egg White Bites

Prep time: 10 minutes | Cook time: 23 minutes | Makes 7 egg bites

1 tablespoon unsalted butter
½ yellow onion, sliced
Salt, to taste
Freshly ground black pepper
3 ounces (85 g) thick-cut ham, diced
1 cup water
½ cup shredded Swiss and Gruyère cheese blend
6 large egg whites
1 tablespoon heavy cream
½ teaspoon prepared ground horseradish
¼ teaspoon dried thyme

1. Press Sauté until the display light is beneath less. Once the pot is hot, add the butter. When the butter melts, add the onion. Sauté for about 10 minutes, or until caramelized, stirring occasionally. 2. Season with salt and pepper to taste. Stir in the diced ham and sauté for 5 more minutes. 3. Transfer the ham and caramelized onion to a plate to cool. Clean out the inside of the Instant Pot and return it to the device. 4. Place the water in the Instant Pot and insert the steam trivet. 5. Place some caramelized onion and ham along with cheese in the bottom of each well of a silicone egg bite mold. 6. In a small bowl, whisk together the egg whites, cream, horseradish, salt, pepper and thyme. Pour the egg mixture over the ham mixture, filling each mold about three-quarters of the way full. 7. Carefully insert the silicone egg bite mold into the Instant Pot on top of the steam trivet. Secure the lid with the steam vent in the sealed position. Press Steam and then use the plus and minus buttons to adjust the timer until the display reads 8 minutes. 8. When the timer sounds, let the pressure naturally release for 10 minutes. Quick release any remaining pressure. 9. Remove the lid and, using the steam trivet handles, carefully lift the trivet and egg bite mold out of the pot. 10. Use a butter knife to cut around the edges and release the egg bites from the mold. Flip the egg bites out onto a plate. Season with more salt and pepper, if needed.

Ham and Caramelized Onion Home Fries

Prep time: 10 minutes | Cook time: 16 minutes | Serves 4 to 6

1 tablespoon extra-virgin olive oil
2 tablespoons unsalted butter
2 yellow onions, diced
¾ cup diced thick-cut ham
½ teaspoon chopped fresh rosemary
3 sprigs thyme
3 large russet potatoes, cut into 1-inch cubes
Salt, to taste
Freshly ground black pepper
¼ cup chicken stock

1. Press Sauté and make sure the display light is beneath normal. Wait a minute or two for the pot to heat. Add the olive oil and butter. Once the butter melts, add the onions. Cook for about 9 minutes, or until the onions start to caramelize. 2. Add the ham, rosemary and thyme. Stir to combine. Sauté for another 3 minutes. 3. Press Cancel. Stir in the potatoes, salt and pepper to taste and the stock. Using a wooden spoon, scrape up any bits from the bottom of the pan. 4. Secure the lid with the steam vent in the sealed position. Press Pressure Cook until the display light is beneath high pressure. Use the plus and minus buttons to adjust the time until the display reads 3 minutes. When the timer sounds, quick release the pressure. 5. Remove the lid, stir and add more salt or pepper if needed.

Coddled Eggs with Garlicky Kale

Prep time: 10 minutes | Cook time: 10 minutes | Serves 4

1 tablespoon extra-virgin olive oil
½ yellow onion, diced
2 cups trimmed and chopped kale
Salt, to taste
Freshly ground black pepper
1 clove garlic, grated
1 cup water
Unsalted butter, for ramekins
4 large eggs
2 teaspoons heavy cream

1. Set the Instant Pot to Sauté. Once hot, add the olive oil. Let the oil heat for 1 minute, then add the onion. Sauté for 2 minutes. Mix in the kale along with a little salt and pepper. Sauté for 3 to 4 minutes, or until tender and slightly wilted. Add the garlic, stir to combine and sauté for an additional minute. 2. Press Cancel. Remove the kale mixture and transfer to a small plate. 3. Clean the Instant Pot and return it to the device. Pour the water into the Instant Pot and insert the steam trivet. 4. Butter four small soufflé ramekins with unsalted butter. Place a little bit of the kale mixture in the bottom of each ramekin. Crack an egg into each ramekin, then top each egg with ½ teaspoon of the heavy cream, plus salt and pepper. 5. Place the ramekins on top of the trivet. 6. Secure the lid with the steam vent in the sealed position. Press Steam. Use the plus and minus buttons to adjust the timer until the display reads 3 minutes. 7. When the timer sounds, allow the pressure to naturally release for 2 minutes. Quick release any remaining pressure.

Peanut Butter Bread Pudding

Prep time: 10 minutes | Cook time: 12 minutes | Serves 4 to 6

1½ cups water
Butter for greasing the baking dish
2 large eggs (at room temperature)
¾ cup whole or low-fat milk
½ cup half-and-half or heavy cream
½ cup creamy natural-style peanut butter
¼ cup maple syrup
2 tablespoons light brown sugar
2 teaspoons vanilla extract
8 ounces (227 g) white bread, cut into 1-inch squares (do not remove the crusts)

1. Pour the water into a 6- or 8-quart cooker. Set a heat- and pressure-safe trivet in the pot. 2. Generously butter the inside of a 2-quart, high-sided, round soufflé dish. Make an aluminum foil sling and set the baking dish in the center of it. 3. Whisk the eggs, milk, half-and-half or cream, peanut butter, maple syrup, brown sugar, and vanilla in a large bowl until the peanut butter dissolves and the mixture is uniform, about 2 minutes. Add the bread cubes and toss well to soak up the egg mixture. 4. Pile the bread cubes into the prepared baking dish in a fairly even layer, pouring any additional liquid in the bowl over them. Cover the baking dish tightly with foil, then use the sling to pick up and lower the baking dish onto the trivet. Fold down the ends of the sling so they fit in the pot. Lock the lid onto the cooker. 5. Select Pressure Cook or Manual and cook on high for 12 minutes with the Keep Warm setting off. 6. Use the quick-release method to bring the pressure back to normal. Unlatch the lid and open the cooker. Use the sling to transfer the hot baking dish to a wire rack. Uncover and cool for 5 minutes before serving by the big spoonful.

Blueberry Cinnamon Coffee Cake

Prep time: 10 minutes | Cook time: 40 minutes | Serves 6

Streusel Topping:
¼ cup Bisquick
¼ cup lightly packed brown sugar
½ teaspoon ground cinnamon
2 tablespoons canola oil
Cake:
2 cups Bisquick
¼ cup lightly packed brown sugar
⅔ cup milk
1 egg, beaten
1 cup frozen blueberries

1. Spray an 8-inch springform pan that will fit into the Instant Pot with cooking spray. Set a tall trivet in the pot and add 1½ cups hot water. (The trivet should sit high enough in the pot that the bottom of the cake pan does not touch the water; a trivet with 2-inch-high legs is ideal.) 2. Make the streusel topping: In a medium bowl, mix the topping ingredients together; set aside. 3. Make the cake: In a large bowl, whisk together the Bisquick and brown sugar. In a small bowl or measuring cup, whisk together the milk and egg. Pour the wet ingredients into the dry ingredients and stir until there are no traces of flour. (Do not overmix; it's okay if there are a few small lumps.) 4. Scrape the batter into the prepared pan. Sprinkle the blueberries and then the streusel over the top. Place the cake, uncovered, on the trivet in the pot. Lock on the lid, select the Pressure Cook function, and adjust to High pressure for 40 minutes. Make sure the steam valve is in the Sealing position. 5. When the cooking time is up, quick-release the pressure. Test the cake with a butter knife; it should come out mostly clean with a few moist crumbs when inserted into the center of the cake. The top of the cake may look a bit moist; this is fine. Remove the pan from the Instant Pot with tongs. Run a sharp knife around the sides of the pan, then unlock and release the sides of the pan. Let the cake stand for 10 minutes. Serve warm.

Spanish Tortilla with Red Bell Pepper Sauce

Prep time: 15 minutes | Cook time: 18 minutes | Serves 4

2 tablespoons olive oil
½ medium yellow onion, thinly sliced
1 large (12-ounce / 340-g) russet potato, peeled and cut into 1/16-inch slices, or 1½ cups hash browns such as Simply Potatoes brand
Salt and freshly ground black pepper
8 large eggs
½ teaspoon smoked paprika
1 cup drained jarred roasted red peppers

1. Spray a 7 × 3-inch round metal baking pan with cooking spray and line the bottom with a round of parchment paper; spray the parchment, too. 2. Put the oil in the pot, select Sauté, and adjust to Normal/Medium heat. When the oil is hot, add the onion and cook, stirring frequently, until beginning to soften, 3 minutes. Add the potato, 1 teaspoon salt, and several grinds of pepper and stir to combine. Cover loosely with the lid set to Venting and cook, stirring frequently, until the potatoes are barely tender when pierced with a fork, 4 to 5 minutes. Press Cancel. 3. Scrape the onion and potato into the prepared pan. In a small bowl, whisk together the eggs with ¼ teaspoon of the paprika. Pour the egg mixture into the baking pan over the potato mixture. 4. Pour 1½ cups water into the pot and set a trivet with handles in the pot. Place the baking pan, uncovered, on the trivet. Lock on the lid, select the Pressure Cook function, and adjust to High pressure for 10 minutes. Make sure the steam valve is in the Sealing position. 5. While the tortilla is cooking, blend the roasted peppers with the remaining ¼ teaspoon smoked paprika and a few grinds of pepper until smooth. Set aside. 6. When the cooking time is up, let the pressure come down naturally for 10 minutes and then quick-release the remaining pressure. Carefully remove the pan from the pot. Run a knife around the edges of the pan, place a dinner plate over the pan, and carefully invert the tortilla onto the plate. Discard the parchment paper. Cut the tortilla into wedges and serve with the sauce.

Peanut Butter Crunch Granola Bars

Prep time: 5 minutes | Cook time: 20 minutes | Makes 10

1 cup quick-cooking oats
⅓ cup pure maple syrup
½ cup all-natural peanut butter
1 tablespoon extra-virgin olive oil
¼ teaspoon fine sea salt
⅓ cup dried cranberries or raisins
½ cup raw pumpkin seeds (pepitas)

1. Line a 7-inch round pan with parchment paper. 2. In a large bowl, combine the oats, maple syrup, peanut butter, olive oil, and salt and stir well. Fold in the dried fruit and pumpkin seeds, then pour the batter into the prepared pan, using a spatula to press the mixture evenly into the bottom of the pan. 3. Pour 1 cup water into the Instant Pot and arrange the handled trivet on the bottom. Place the pan on top of the trivet. Cover the pan with an upside-down plate or another piece of parchment to protect the granola bars from condensation. Secure the lid, moving the steam release valve to Sealing. Select Manual or Pressure Cook to cook on High pressure for 20 minutes. 4. Let the pressure naturally release for 10 minutes, then move the steam release valve to Venting. When the floating valve drops, remove the lid. Use oven mitts to lift the trivet and the pan out of the pot. Let the granola cool completely in the pan, at least 1 hour. 5. Cut the cooled granola into 10 pieces. The round pan will make the bars uneven in size, but you can cut them into uniform wedges if you'd prefer. Wrap them individually in plastic wrap or place them in an airtight container and store in the fridge for 2 weeks.

Cozy Fruit Compote

Prep time: 5 minutes | Cook time: 3 minutes | Makes 2½ cups

1 (12-ounce / 340-g) package fresh or 3 cups frozen cranberries
⅔ cup packed brown sugar
¼ cup thawed orange juice concentrate
2 tablespoons raspberry vinegar
½ cup chopped dried apricots
½ cup golden raisins
½ cup chopped walnuts, toasted

1. In a 6-quart electric pressure cooker, combine cranberries, brown sugar, orange juice concentrate and vinegar. Lock lid; make sure vent is closed. Select Manual setting; adjust pressure to High, and set time for 3 minutes. When finished cooking, allow pressure to naturally release for 5 minutes, then quick-release any remaining pressure according to manufacturer's directions. 2. Stir in apricots, raisins and walnuts. Refrigerate leftovers.

Ham and Egg Casserole

Prep time: 2 minutes | Cook time: 20 minutes | Serves 2 to 4

6 beaten eggs
½ cup plain Greek yogurt
1 cup Cheddar cheese, shredded
1 cup ham, diced
¼ cup chives, chopped
½ teaspoon black pepper
1 cup water

1. In a medium bowl, whisk together eggs and yogurt until combined. 2. Add the cheese, ham, chives, and pepper. Stir well. 3. Prepare the Instant Pot by adding the water to the pot and placing the trivet in it. 4. Pour the mixture into the heatproof bowl or cup. 5. Place the bowl on the trivet and secure the lid. 6. Close and lock the lid. Select the Manual setting and set the cooking time for 20 minutes at High pressure. 7. When the timer beeps, use a quick release. Carefully unlock the lid. 8. Serve the dish warm.

Lower-Sugar Strawberry Chia Jam

Prep time: 2 minutes | Cook time: 4 minutes | Makes about 1½ cups

12 ounces (340 g) fresh or frozen strawberries
2 tablespoons fresh lemon juice
1 tablespoon pure maple syrup
1 tablespoon water
1 tablespoon arrowroot starch
1 tablespoon chia seeds

1. Add the strawberries, lemon juice, and maple syrup to the inner pot. Lock the lid and ensure the steam release valve is set to the Sealing position. Select Pressure Cook (High), and set the cook time for 1 minute. 2. Once the cook time is complete, allow the pressure to release naturally. Carefully remove the lid—it will look very watery with soft strawberries. Mash the strawberries with a wooden spoon. 3. Make a slurry by whisking together 1 tablespoon water and arrowroot in a small bowl. Stir the slurry into the pot. Simmer on Sauté (Medium) until thickened, 2 to 3 minutes, stirring with a wooden spoon. Stir in the chia seeds. 4. Transfer the jam to a glass storage container and let cool to room temperature. Secure the lid and store in the refrigerator for up to 5 days.

Crustless Crab Quiche

Prep time: 10 minutes | Cook time: 10 minutes | Serves 6

6 large eggs
¼ cup unsweetened almond milk
2 teaspoons fresh thyme leaves
½ teaspoon sea salt
¼ teaspoon ground black pepper
½ teaspoon hot sauce
½ pound (227 g) crab meat
¼ cup crumbled goat cheese
2 thick slices bacon, diced
¼ cup peeled and diced onion
¼ cup seeded and diced green bell pepper
2 cups water

1. In a medium bowl, whisk eggs, milk, thyme leaves, salt, pepper, and hot sauce. Stir in crab meat and goat cheese. Set aside. 2. Grease a 7-cup glass dish. Set aside. 3. Press the Sauté button on Instant Pot. Add diced bacon and brown for 2 minutes, rendering some fat. Add onion and bell pepper and stir-fry with bacon until tender. Transfer mixture to the glass container. Pour in egg mixture. 4. Place trivet in Instant Pot. Pour in water. Place dish with egg mixture onto trivet. Lock lid. 5. Press the Manual button and adjust time to 5 minutes. When timer beeps, let pressure release naturally for 10 minutes. Quick-release any additional pressure until float valve drops and then unlock lid. 6. Remove dish from Instant Pot. Let cool for 10 minutes to allow eggs to set. Slice and serve.

Bacon and Chive Egg Muffins

Prep time: 10 minutes | Cook time: 5 minutes | Serves 4

4 large eggs
2 tablespoons whole milk
¼ teaspoon salt
⅛ teaspoon black pepper
2 slices cooked bacon, crumbled
2 tablespoons diced chives
2 tablespoons sharp Cheddar cheese
1½ cups water

1. Spray four silicone muffin cups with cooking spray and set aside. 2. In a small bowl, whisk together eggs, milk, salt, and pepper. Evenly distribute egg mixture into muffin cups. 3. Evenly divide up bacon and chives and drop equal amounts onto each egg muffin. 4. Top each with ½ tablespoon cheese. 5. Pour water into Instant Pot. Place trivet inside. 6. Place filled muffin cups inside of a 7-inch cake pan. Top pan with a paper towel and a piece of foil crimped around the edges. Create a foil sling and gently lower pan into Instant Pot so it sits on top of trivet. Fold foil sling over pan. 7. Close lid and set pressure release to Sealing. 8. Press Manual or Pressure Cook button and adjust time to 5 minutes. 9. When the timer beeps, let pressure release naturally for 2 minutes and then quick release remaining pressure. Unlock lid and remove it. Remove pan from Instant Pot using foil sling. 10. Remove foil from the top of muffin cups and then carefully remove egg muffins. Enjoy immediately and refrigerate any leftovers.

Southwestern Breakfast Casserole

Prep time: 20 minutes | Cook time: 20 minutes | Serves 4

2 large eggs
4 large egg whites
⅔ cup fat-free milk
1½ teaspoons chili powder
¼ teaspoon ground cumin
¼ teaspoon cayenne pepper
¼ teaspoon pepper
¾ cup canned black beans, rinsed and drained
½ cup frozen corn, thawed
½ cup cubed fully cooked ham
½ cup shredded extra-sharp cheddar cheese
¼ cup canned chopped green chiles
3 slices whole wheat bread, lightly toasted and cubed

1. In a large bowl, whisk together the first 7 ingredients. Stir in beans, corn, ham, cheese and chiles. Stir in toasted bread cubes to moisten. 2. Transfer to a greased 1½-quart baking dish. Place trivet insert and 1 cup water in pressure cooker. Cover baking dish with foil. Fold a (18 x 12 inch) piece of foil lengthwise into thirds to make a sling. Use the sling to lower the dish onto the trivet. 3. Lock lid; close pressure-release valve. Adjust to Pressure Cook on high for 20 minutes. Let pressure release naturally for 10 minutes; quick-release any remaining pressure. Using foil sling, carefully remove baking dish. Uncover and let stand 10 minutes before serving.

Denver Omelet Frittata

Prep time: 25 minutes | Cook time: 35 minutes | Serves 6

1 tablespoon olive oil
1 medium Yukon Gold potato, peeled and sliced
1 small onion, thinly sliced
1 cup water
12 large eggs
1 teaspoon hot pepper sauce
½ teaspoon salt
¼ teaspoon pepper
8 ounces (227 g) sliced deli ham, chopped
½ cup chopped green pepper
1 cup shredded Cheddar cheese, divided

1. Select Sauté setting on a 6-quart electric pressure cooker and adjust for high heat; then heat oil. Add potato and onion; cook and stir 4 to 6 minutes or until potato is lightly browned. Transfer to a greased 1½-quart (6- or 7-inch) souffle or round baking dish. Wipe pressure cooker clean. Pour in water. 2. In a large bowl, whisk eggs, pepper sauce, salt and pepper; stir in ham, green pepper and ½ cup cheese. Pour over potato mixture. Top with remaining cheese. Cover baking dish with foil and place on a trivet with handles; lower into pressure cooker. Lock lid; make sure vent is closed. 3. Select Manual setting; adjust pressure to High and set time for 35 minutes. When finished cooking, allow pressure to naturally release for 10 minutes; quick-release any remaining pressure according to manufacturer's instructions.

Caramelized Onion, Mushroom and Spinach Strata

Prep time: 20 minutes | Cook time: 38 minutes | Serves 6 to 8

3 tablespoons grass-fed butter or ghee, plus more for casserole
1 large yellow onion, thinly sliced
8 ounces (227 g) white button or cremini mushrooms, cleaned and thinly sliced
3 cloves garlic, finely chopped
1 tablespoon chopped fresh thyme
3 large eggs
1 cup milk
1 (16-ounce / 454-g) loaf day-old gluten-free bread, cut into 1-inch cubes
1 cup shredded sharp or mild cheddar cheese
½ cup shredded Parmesan cheese
1 cup frozen chopped spinach, thawed and moisture squeezed out
¼ cup chopped fresh flat-leaf parsley, plus more for garnish
Zest of 1 lemon
1 teaspoon sea salt
1½ cups water

1. Place your healthy fat of choice in the Instant Pot and press Sauté. Once the fat has melted, add the onion and mushrooms and cook, stirring occasionally, for 7 minutes, or until the onion and mushrooms are light golden brown and caramelized. 2. Add the garlic and thyme and stir with a wooden spoon for 1 minute until fragrant, making sure to scrape up any browned bits at the bottom of the pot. Press Keep Warm/Cancel. Transfer the onion mixture to a bowl and set aside. 3. Butter a 1½-quart casserole dish that fits inside the Instant Pot. Set aside. 4. In a very large bowl, whisk together the eggs and milk until fully incorporated. Add the bread cubes, shredded cheeses, onion mixture, spinach, parsley, lemon zest and salt, then gently fold to combine. 5. Pour the mixture into the prepared casserole dish and cover the dish with its glass lid. If your casserole dish doesn't come with a glass lid, you can cover the top of the dish with unbleached parchment paper, then top it with foil and secure it around the edges. 6. Pour the water into the Instant Pot and insert the steam trivet. Carefully set the covered casserole dish on top of the trivet. Secure the lid with the steam vent in the sealed position. Press Manual and set on High Pressure for 30 minutes. 7. Once the timer sounds, press Keep Warm/Cancel. Allow the Instant Pot to release pressure naturally for 15 minutes. Using an oven mitt, do a quick release. If there is any steam left over, allow it to release until the silver dial drops, then carefully open the lid. 8. Carefully lift the trivet and the casserole dish out of the Instant Pot. Use oven mitts or towels because the Instant Pot and dish will be extremely hot. Carefully remove the hot lid. Allow to rest at room temperature for 10 minutes before serving.

Peanut Butter and Jelly Oatmeal

Prep time: 5 minutes | Cook time: 7 minutes | Serves 2

1 cup old-fashioned oats
1¼ cups water
⅛ teaspoon salt
2 teaspoons smooth peanut butter
2 tablespoons strawberry jelly
¼ cup whole milk

1. Add oats, water, and salt to the Instant Pot. Lock lid. 2. Press the Porridge button and adjust cook time to 7 minutes. When timer beeps, let pressure release naturally for 5 minutes. Manually release any additional pressure and unlock lid. 3. Transfer oatmeal to two bowls. Stir in peanut butter and jelly. Add milk. Serve warm.

Eggs in a Boat

Prep time: 5 minutes | Cook time: 4 minutes | Serves 4 to 6

½ cup water
3 to 4 demi baguettes
½ cup mixed fresh baby spinach and arugula
6 grape tomatoes, halved
6 to 8 large eggs
Salt, to taste
Freshly ground black pepper
Crushed red pepper flakes

1. Pour the water into the Instant Pot and insert the steam trivet. 2. Cut each demi baguette to create a lid and well in the bread. Slice length-wise from end to end at a 45 degree angle about three-quarters of the way through the bread. Use your fingers to pull the "lid" off the baguette. Remove any stray pieces of bread from inside the well. Ensure there is enough room for the eggs. 3. To each demi baguette, add a few leaves of spinach and arugula along with a few tomato halves. Crack 2 eggs into each bread boat. Top with salt, black pepper and a tiny pinch of red pepper flakes. 4. Arrange up to three bread boats inside the Instant Pot on top of the trivet. 5. Secure the lid with the steam vent in the sealed position. Press Pressure Cook until the display light is beneath high pressure. Use the plus and minus buttons to adjust the timer until the display reads 4 minutes. 6. When the timer sounds, allow the pressure to naturally release for 3 minutes. After 3 minutes, quick release any remaining pressure. 7. Remove the boats with tongs and transfer to a plate. Allow the boats to cool for a minute or two so the bread will harden up a bit again, before slicing and serving.

Tex-Mex Breakfast

Prep time: 15 minutes | Cook time: 10 minutes | Serves 4

6 large eggs	potatoes, grated
½ teaspoon sea salt	2 cups cubed cooked ham
¼ teaspoon ground black pepper	1 small onion, peeled and diced
⅛ teaspoon chili powder	1 small jalapeño, seeded and diced
½ cup shredded Cheddar cheese	
1 small Roma tomato, diced	½ cup sliced button mushrooms
2 tablespoons butter	2 cups water
2 small (or 1 large) Yukon gold	

1. In a medium bowl, whisk together eggs, salt, pepper, and chili powder. Stir in cheese and tomato. Set aside. 2. Press the Sauté button on Instant Pot. Heat the butter and stir-fry potatoes, ham, onion, jalapeño, and mushrooms for approximately 5 minutes until the potatoes are tender and onions are translucent. 3. Transfer cooked mixture to a 7-cup greased glass dish. Pour whisked eggs over the potato mixture. 4. Place trivet in Instant Pot. Pour in water. Place dish with egg mixture onto trivet. Lock lid. 5. Press the Manual button and adjust time to 5 minutes. When timer beeps, quick-release pressure until float valve drops and then unlock lid. 6. Remove dish from the Instant Pot. Let sit at room temperature for 5 to 10 minutes to allow the eggs to set. Slice and serve warm.

Cornmeal Mush

Prep time: 5 minutes | Cook time: 15 minutes | Serves 6

1 cup yellow cornmeal	½ teaspoon salt
4 cups water, divided	1 tablespoon vegan margarine

1. In a medium bowl, whisk together the cornmeal, 1 cup water, and salt. Set aside. 2. Add the remaining water to the Instant Pot, press the Sauté button, and adjust to High. Bring to a boil. Stir the cornmeal and water mixture into the boiling water. Add the margarine and stir continuously until the mixture returns to a boil. 3. Lock the lid into place. Press the Manual button and adjust time to 10 minutes. When the timer beeps, quick-release the pressure until the float valve drops and then unlock the lid. 4. Spoon into serving bowls and serve warm.

Chipotle Huevos-Less Rancheros

Prep time: 5 minutes | Cook time: 35 minutes | Serves 4

2 teaspoons extra-virgin olive oil, divided	8 ounces (227 g) extra-firm tofu, drained
½ yellow onion, diced	Pinch of ground turmeric
2 cups water	8 small corn tortillas, warmed in the microwave or lightly charred in a skillet
½ cup dry black beans, rinsed	
1 chipotle pepper in adobo sauce	1 cup baby spinach
½ teaspoon garlic powder	1 avocado, sliced
¾ teaspoon sea salt, plus more to taste	1 cup pico de gallo
	2 radishes, thinly sliced
1 teaspoon adobo sauce	1 cup fresh cilantro

1. Select Sauté (Medium), and heat 1 teaspoon oil (optional), in the inner pot until hot. (Otherwise, you can dry sauté in the hot pot or add a bit of water in the bottom of the pot.) Add the onion and sauté until softened and golden, 3 to 5 minutes. Press Cancel. Add 2 cups water, beans, chipotle pepper, and garlic powder. 2. Lock the lid and ensure the steam release valve is set to the Sealing position. Select Pressure Cook (High), and set the cook time for 27 minutes. 3. Once the cook time is complete, allow the pressure to release naturally for 10 minutes, then quick release any remaining pressure. Carefully remove the lid. Stir in the salt, and remove and discard the chipotle pepper. Transfer to a medium bowl. Add the adobo sauce ¼ teaspoon at a time to add heat to taste, if desired. 4. Rinse out the inner pot and place back into the Instant Pot. Select Sauté (High), and heat the remaining 1 teaspoon oil. Pat the tofu with paper towels to soak up as much water as possible. Crumble the tofu into the pot with the hot oil. Season with turmeric and salt. Sauté until hot, about 2 minutes. Drain the beans and add them into the tofu scramble, or keep them separate. Press Cancel. 5. To assemble the dish, place the warm tortillas on plates. Top with a few spinach leaves and the bean and tofu scramble, avocado, pico de gallo, radish, and cilantro. Enjoy immediately.

Ham and Swiss Muffin Frittatas

Prep time: 10 minutes | Cook time: 15 minutes | Serves 3

1 tablespoon olive oil	4 large eggs
¼ cup small-diced ham	½ teaspoon sea salt
¼ cup diced red bell pepper, seeded	½ teaspoon ground black pepper
	¼ cup shredded Swiss cheese
	1 cup water

1. Press the Sauté button on Instant Pot. Heat olive oil. Add ham and bell pepper and stir-fry 3 to 5 minutes until peppers are tender. Transfer mixture to a small bowl to cool. 2. In a medium bowl, whisk together eggs, salt, pepper, and Swiss cheese. Stir in cooled ham mixture. 3. Place trivet into Instant Pot. Pour in water. Place steamer basket on trivet. 4. Distribute egg mixture evenly among 6 silicone muffin cups. Carefully place cups on steamer basket. Lock lid. 5. Press the Manual button and adjust time to 8 minutes. When timer beeps, quick-release pressure until float valve drops and then unlock lid. 6. Remove frittatas and serve warm.

Maple Pecan Breakfast Risotto with Chia Seeds

Prep time: 5 minutes | Cook time: 10 minutes | Serves 4

1 cup Arborio rice	1 vanilla bean
3 cups coconut milk	¼ cup pure maple syrup
2 tablespoons chia seeds	½ cup pecans, chopped

1. Add the coconut milk to the Instant Pot and select the Sauté setting. 2. Heat the coconut milk, stirring occasionally, until it boils. 3. Add in the Arborio rice and stir. 4. Seal the lid of the cooker and select the Pressure Cook setting. 5. Cook on high for 5 minutes. 6. Release the steam naturally from the cooker. 7. Carefully remove the lid from the cooker. Scrape the inside of the vanilla bean into the cooker, along with the maple syrup, and stir. 8. Let sit for 5 minutes before serving. 9. Serve garnished with chopped pecans.

Sausage and Cheddar Egg Muffins

Prep time: 10 minutes | Cook time: 5 minutes | Serves 4

4 large eggs
2 tablespoons whole milk
¼ teaspoon salt
⅛ teaspoon black pepper
2 precooked breakfast sausage links, sliced
2 tablespoons sharp Cheddar cheese
1½ cups water

1. Spray four silicone muffin cups with cooking spray and set aside. 2. In a small bowl, whisk together eggs, milk, salt, and pepper. Evenly distribute egg mixture into four muffin cups. 3. Evenly divide sausages and drop into egg mixture. Top each with ½ tablespoon cheese. 4. Pour water into Instant Pot and add trivet. 5. Place filled muffin cups inside of a 7-inch cake pan. Top pan with a paper towel and a piece of foil crimped around the edges. 6. Create a foil sling and gently lower pan into Instant Pot so it sits on top of trivet. Fold foil sling over pan. 7. Close lid and set pressure release to Sealing. 8. Press Manual or Pressure Cook button and adjust time to 5 minutes. 9. When the timer beeps, let pressure release naturally for 2 minutes and then quick release remaining pressure. Unlock lid and remove it. Remove pan from Instant Pot using foil sling. 10. Remove foil from the top of muffin cups and then carefully remove egg muffins. Enjoy immediately.

Double Chocolate Banana Bread

Prep time: 10 minutes | Cook time: 55 minutes | Serves 8 to 10

8 tablespoons grass-fed butter, ghee or avocado oil, melted
½ cup pure maple syrup
3 small ripe bananas, quartered
2 large eggs (at room temperature)
1 teaspoon pure vanilla extract
1 cup cassava flour
¼ cup unsweetened cocoa powder
¼ cup grass-fed hydrolyzed collagen
1 teaspoon baking soda
½ teaspoon sea salt
1 cup chopped quality chocolate
1 cup water

1. Use your healthy fat of choice to grease a 1½-quart casserole dish that fits inside the Instant Pot. Line the bottom of the casserole dish with a circle of parchment paper. Set aside. 2. In a blender, in the order listed, place all the ingredients, except the chopped chocolate and water. Mix on low speed until smooth and fully combined, about 20 seconds, scraping down the sides, if needed. 3. Add the chopped chocolate to the blender and give it a stir with a spatula to fold in. Pour the batter into the prepared casserole dish. Cover the casserole dish with its glass lid. If your casserole dish doesn't come with a glass lid, you can cover the top of the dish with unbleached parchment paper, then top it with foil and secure it around the edges. 4. Pour the water into the Instant Pot and insert the steam trivet. Carefully set the covered casserole dish on top of the trivet. Secure the lid with the steam vent in the sealed position. Press Manual and set on High Pressure for 55 minutes. 5. Once the timer sounds, press Keep Warm/Cancel. Allow the Instant Pot to release pressure naturally for 20 minutes. Using an oven mitt, do a quick release. If there is any steam left over, allow it to release until the silver dial drops, then carefully open the lid. 6. Carefully lift the trivet and the casserole dish out of the Instant Pot. Use oven mitts or towels because the Instant Pot and dish will be extremely hot. Carefully remove the hot lid, taking care not to drip any of the condensation on the top of the bread. Test with a toothpick to make sure the center is fully cooked; no more than a few moist crumbs should be on the toothpick. If it needs more time, re-cover with the lid (make sure to wipe off any condensation first) and return to the Instant Pot to cook on Manual for another 5 minutes, then do a quick pressure release. 7. Allow the bread to cool at room temperature sitting on top of the trivet (as a cooling rack) for 45 minutes. Gently run a knife around the edges of the bread to loosen it when you're ready to remove it from the dish. Turn the dish upside down on a plate to release the banana bread. Cut the banana bread into thick slices and serve immediately.

Sausage and Egg Sandwiches

Prep time: 10 minutes | Cook time: 9 minutes | Serves 4

4 large eggs
2 tablespoons whole milk
¼ teaspoon salt
⅛ teaspoon black pepper
1½ cups water
4 English muffins
2 teaspoons butter
4 breakfast sausage patties
4 slices Cheddar cheese

1. Spray four ramekins with cooking spray and set aside. 2. In a small bowl, whisk together eggs, milk, salt, and pepper. Pour evenly into four ramekins. Wrap ramekins tightly in foil. 3. Pour 1½ cups water into Instant Pot. 4. Place foil-wrapped ramekins into Instant Pot, stacked two by two. Close lid and set pressure release to Sealing. 5. Press Manual or Pressure Cook button and adjust time to 8 minutes. 6. While eggs are cooking, toast English muffins and spread with butter. 7. When the timer beeps, let pressure release naturally for 2 minutes and then quick release the remaining pressure. Unlock lid and remove it. 8. Carefully remove ramekins from Instant Pot. Pour out water from inner pot and put inner pot back into Instant Pot. 9. Press Sauté button and place sausage patties inside Instant Pot. Heat sausage patties, turning once, 1 minute. Remove from Instant Pot. 10. Remove each egg from its ramekin and place on one half of English muffin. Top each egg with a sausage patty and a slice of cheese. Place other half of the English muffin on top to create a sandwich.

Sweet Potato Spice Breakfast Oat Groats

Prep time: 5 minutes | Cook time: 60 minutes | Serves 8

Pressure Cooker:
3 cups water
2 cups oat groats, rinsed and drained
2 cups chopped sweet potatoes
2 teaspoons ground cinnamon
1 teaspoon ground ginger
¾ teaspoon ground allspice
⅛ teaspoon ground cloves
Toppings (optional):
Sweetener of choice, to taste
Toasted pecans
Toasted coconut
Chopped dates

1. Add the water, oat groats, sweet potatoes, cinnamon, ginger, allspice and cloves to your Instant Pot. Cook on High Pressure for 60 minutes. Manually release the pressure. Mash the sweet potatoes with a potato masher. The oat groats should still stay whole. 2. Serve with your favorite toppings (if using). You can freeze extra servings for a grab-and-go breakfast another time.

Mushroom and Goat Cheese Frittata

Prep time: 10 minutes | Cook time: 14 minutes | Serves 4

6 large eggs
¼ cup chopped fresh basil leaves
½ cup crumbled goat cheese
½ teaspoon salt
¼ teaspoon ground black pepper
1 tablespoon olive oil
2 cups sliced baby bella mushrooms
1 small yellow onion, peeled and diced
1 cup water

1. In a medium bowl, whisk together eggs, basil, goat cheese, salt, and pepper. Set aside. 2. Press the Sauté button on the Instant Pot. Heat oil for 30 seconds and stir-fry mushrooms and onions for 5 minutes, until onions are translucent. 3. Transfer cooked mushroom mixture to a 7-cup glass bowl greased with either oil or cooking spray and set aside to cool for 5 minutes. Pour whisked eggs over the cooked mixture and stir to combine. 4. Add water to the Instant Pot and insert steam rack. Place glass bowl with egg mixture on steam rack. Lock lid. 5. Press the Manual or Pressure Cook button and adjust cook time to 8 minutes. When timer beeps, let pressure release naturally until float valve drops and then unlock lid. 6. Remove dish from pot and set aside 10 minutes to allow the eggs to set. Slice and serve warm.

Breakfast Hash

Prep time: 10 minutes | Cook time: 27 minutes | Serves 4 to 6

3 tablespoons butter
1 medium yellow onion, chopped
1 medium green bell pepper, stemmed, cored, and chopped
1 medium red bell pepper, stemmed, cored, and chopped
1 pound (454 g) smoked deli ham, any coating removed, diced
2 medium garlic cloves, peeled and minced
1 teaspoon dried sage
1 teaspoon dried thyme
½ teaspoon celery seeds (optional)
¼ teaspoon table salt
¼ teaspoon ground black pepper
1 pound (454 g) yellow potatoes, diced
1½ cups chicken broth

1. Press the Sauté button, and set on Medium or Normal for 5 minutes. 2. Melt the butter in a 6-quart cooker. Add the onion and both bell peppers. Cook, stirring occasionally, until softened, about 4 minutes. Add the ham, garlic, sage, thyme, celery seeds (if using), salt, and pepper. Cook, stirring often, until fragrant, about 1 minute. 3. Turn off the Sauté function. Stir in the potatoes and broth, scraping up any browned bits on the pot's bottom. Lock the lid onto the cooker. 4. Select Pressure Cook or Manual, and cook on high for 12 minutes with the Keep Warm setting off. 5. Use the quick-release method to bring the pressure back to normal. Unlatch the lid and open the cooker. Stir well. 6. Press the Sauté button, and set on High or More for 10 minutes. 7. Bring the mixture to a simmer, stirring often. Continue without stirring until the liquid boils off and the hash touching the hot surface starts to brown, 3 to 4 minutes. Turn off the Sauté function and remove the hot insert from the machine to stop the cooking. Some of the potatoes may have fused to the surface. Use a metal spatula to get them up. The point is to have some browned bits and some softer bits throughout the hash.

Chocolate-Covered-Strawberry Breakfast Quinoa

Prep time: 5 minutes | Cook time: 12 minutes | Serves 2

½ cup uncooked quinoa
¾ cup unsweetened coconut milk, plus more for serving
½ cup water
2 tablespoons maple syrup
1 tablespoon unsweetened cocoa powder
½ teaspoon vanilla extract (optional)
Pinch kosher salt

1. Thoroughly rinse the quinoa in a fine-mesh strainer for 2 minutes, using your hands to sort through and pick out any discolored pieces or pebbles. 2. Put the quinoa in the bowl of your cooker and stir in the coconut milk, water, maple syrup, cocoa powder, vanilla (if using), and salt. Seal the lid with the vent shut and press the button for the Rice setting to cook on Low pressure for 12 minutes. 3. Allow the pressure to naturally release, about 10 minutes, then open the vent at the top and remove the lid. 4. Fluff the quinoa with a fork and spoon it into two cereal bowls. Add more coconut milk, and top with strawberries and chocolate shavings.

Berries and Cream Breakfast Cake

Prep time: 10 minutes | Cook time: 35 minutes | Serves 8

1 cup (2 sticks) unsalted butter (at room temperature), plus extra for greasing
2 cups all-purpose flour, plus extra for preparing the pan
2½ teaspoons baking powder
1 teaspoon fine sea salt
¾ cup granulated sugar
1 large egg
¾ cup milk
2 cups fresh berries
1 cup water, for steaming
1 (16-ounce / 454-g) container cream cheese frosting

1. Butter and flour a 7-inch round cake pan. 2. Combine the flour, baking powder, and salt in a medium mixing bowl. In a large mixing bowl, use an electric mixer to cream together the butter, sugar, and egg. 3. In ½-cup increments, mix the flour mixture into the butter mixture. Gently stir in the milk and berries. Pour the batter into the prepared pan. Place a paper towel over it and then cover tightly with aluminum foil. 4. Pour the water into the inner cooking pot and place a trivet on the bottom. Using a sling, lower the foil-covered pan onto the trivet. Lock the lid into place and turn the valve to Sealing. Select Manual or Pressure Cook and adjust the pressure to High. Set the time to 35 minutes. When cooking ends, let the pressure release naturally. 5. Unlock and remove the lid. Use the sling to remove the pan from the pot. Remove the aluminum foil and paper towel. Using a fork, check to ensure that the cake is done. The fork's tines should come out clean. If not, replace the paper towel and aluminum foil and return the pan to the pot, lock the lid back into place, and cook for a few more minutes. 6. Place the cake pan on a cooling rack for 10 minutes to cool. Run a knife around the edge of the cake and then invert it onto a plate. Allow to cool completely. 7. Open the container of frosting and scoop ½ cup of it into a microwave-safe container. Microwave it for 15 seconds. Stir the frosting and drizzle over the cake, then cut into 8 slices. Warm and drizzle more frosting, if desired.

Pumpkin Spiced Latte Oats

Prep time: 5 minutes | Cook time: 4 minutes | Serves 6

- 1 cup strong brewed coffee
- 1 cup water
- 1 cup coconut milk
- 1½ cups oats
- 2 tablespoons chia seeds
- 1 teaspoon pure vanilla extract
- ½ teaspoon allspice
- ½ teaspoon ground ginger
- ½ teaspoon cinnamon
- ½ cup walnuts, chopped

1. In a heat-resistant bowl, combine all the ingredients except for the walnuts. Mix well and set aside. 2. Place about 1 cup of water in the bottom of the Instant Pot and place in the steaming rack. 3. Place the bowl with the oat mixture on the steaming rack. 4. Seal the cooker and using the Pressure Cook option. Cook on high for 4 minutes. 5. Use the natural release method to release the steam from the cooker. 6. Stir the oats and top with chopped walnuts before serving.

Steel-Cut Oats Cooked with Earl Grey Tea

Prep time: 2 minutes | Cook time: 3 minutes | Serves 4

- Pressure Cooker:
- 3 cups brewed Earl Grey Tea (you can use black, decaf or rooibos)
- 1 cup steel-cut oats
- For Serving:
- 1 teaspoon rosewater, vanilla extract or a few drops of lavender extract
- Sweetener of choice, to taste
- Nondairy milk

1. Add the brewed tea and oats to your Instant Pot. Cook on the Manual/Pressure Cooking setting for 3 minutes. Allow the pressure to release naturally. 2. Open and mix in an extra flavoring and your choice of sweetener. Serve topped with nondairy milk.

Smoked Salmon and Pumpernickel Egg Casserole

Prep time: 10 minutes | Cook time: 20 minutes | Serves 4

- 2 slices dense pumpernickel bread (5 ounces / 142 g)
- 4 ounces (113 g) hot-smoked wild salmon, broken into bite-size chunks
- 7 large eggs
- 1 cup half-and-half
- 3 tablespoons roughly chopped fresh dill, or 1 teaspoon dried
- Finely grated zest of ½ lemon
- Salt and freshly ground black pepper
- Optional Garnishes:
- Sour cream
- Capers
- Thinly sliced red onion

1. Thoroughly coat a 7- or 8-inch round metal baking pan with 3½-inch-high sides with cooking spray. Pour 1½ cups cold water into the pot and set a trivet with handles in the bottom. 2. Place the bread in the baking pan, tearing pieces to fit evenly over the base of the pan. Sprinkle the salmon over the bread and press down gently; set aside. 3. In a medium bowl, whisk together the eggs, half-and-half, dill, lemon zest, ½ teaspoon salt, and several grinds of pepper until smooth. Pour the egg mixture into the baking pan. Cover tightly with foil. 4. Set the baking pan on the trivet. Lock on the lid, select the Pressure Cook function, and adjust to High pressure for 20 minutes. Make sure the steam valve is in the Sealing position. 5. When the cooking time is up, let the pressure come down naturally for 10 minutes and then quick-release the remaining pressure. Blot the foil with paper towels to remove excess moisture. Carefully remove the trivet-pan setup from the pot and remove the foil. Insert a butter knife into the center of the casserole; it should come out with no liquid custard coating the knife. (If the casserole is not done, lock on the lid and return to High pressure for 1 minute more and then quick-release the pressure.) 6. Let the casserole stand for a few minutes before cutting into wedges. Serve with the optional garnishes, if desired.

Peaches and Cream Steel-Cut Oatmeal

Prep time: 5 minutes | Cook time: 4 minutes | Serves 4

- 2 cups steel-cut oats
- 4 cups water
- 1 pound (454 g) frozen sliced peaches
- ½ teaspoon ground cinnamon, plus more for serving (optional)
- ¼ cup pure maple syrup
- ½ cup full-fat coconut milk, plus more for serving (optional)

1. Combine the steel-cut oats and water in the Instant Pot and give them a stir, then add the peaches, cinnamon, and maple syrup. Secure the lid and move the steam release valve to Sealing. Select Manual or Pressure Cook to cook on High pressure for 4 minutes. 2. When the cooking cycle has completed, let the pressure naturally release for 15 minutes to finish cooking the oatmeal. (This method prevents the oatmeal from sticking to the bottom of the pot.) Move the steam release valve to Venting to release any remaining steam pressure. When the floating valve drops, remove the lid. 3. Stir in the coconut milk, then taste and adjust any seasonings. Serve warm, with additional cinnamon or coconut milk, if desired. Leftover oats can be stored in an airtight container in the fridge for 5 days. You can serve them chilled, or quickly reheat them using the Sauté function of your Instant Pot. (You may need to add a splash of water as you reheat, since oats tend to thicken when chilled.)

Savory Oat Porridge

Prep time: 10 minutes | Cook time: 3 minutes | Serves 4

- 1 cup rolled oats (not instant)
- ¼ cup steel-cut oats
- 1 tablespoon amaranth
- ¼ cup pepitas (pumpkin seeds), plus more for garnish
- ¼ cup almond slivers
- 2 tablespoons nutritional yeast flakes
- 1¼ cups low-sodium vegetable broth
- 1¼ cups unflavored flaxseed milk (or other plant-based milk)
- Herbamare or sea salt, to taste

1. Add the rolled oats, steel-cut oats, amaranth, pepitas, almonds, nutritional yeast, broth, and milk to the pressure cooker. Stir to combine. 2. Cover and bring to pressure and cook at high pressure for 3 minutes. Allow for a normal release. 3. Add Herbamare to taste and garnish with additional pepitas.

Pull-Apart Cinnamon Bread

Prep time: 5 minutes | Cook time: 20 minutes | Serves 6

1½ cups water
⅓ cup granulated white sugar
⅓ cup packed light brown sugar
1½ teaspoons ground cinnamon
¼ teaspoon table salt (optional)
1 (16-ounce / 454-g) can regular or buttermilk home-style biscuits
¼ cup (½ stick) butter, plus additional for greasing

1. Pour the water into a 6- or 8-quart cooker. Place a heat- and pressure-safe trivet inside the pot. Generously butter the inside of a 7-inch round springform pan. Make an aluminum foil sling and set the prepared baking dish in the middle of it. 2. Mix the white sugar, brown sugar, cinnamon, and salt (if using) in a large, microwave-safe bowl. Cut the raw biscuits into quarters, then add them to this bowl and toss well to coat. Lightly pack the biscuits into the springform pan. (Much of the sugar mixture will stay behind in the bowl.) 3. Add the butter to the sugar mixture. Microwave on high in 15-seconds bursts, stirring after each, until the butter melts and the mixture bubbles. Pour and scrape this mixture over the biscuits in the pan. 4. Use the sling to pick the pan up and lower it onto the trivet in the pot. Lay a piece of aluminum foil or parchment paper over the top of the pan without crimping or sealing it to the pan. Fold down the ends of the sling so they fit inside the machine. Lock the lid onto the cooker. 5. Select Meat/Stew, Pressure Cook or Manual, and cook on high for 20 minutes with the Keep Warm setting off. 6. When the machine has finished cooking, turn it off and let its pressure return to normal naturally for 10 minutes. Then use the quick-release method to get rid of any residual pressure in the pot. Unlatch the lid and open the cooker. 7. Use the sling to transfer the hot baking dish to a wire rack. Uncover and cool for 10 minutes, then run a flatware knife around the inside perimeter of the pan (or a nonstick-safe knife if the pan has a nonstick finish). Unlatch the sides and remove the ring. Serve by pulling apart the warm bread.

Vegan Yogurt

Prep time: 3 minutes | Cook time: 8 hours | Makes 4 cups

1 quart unsweetened nondairy milk (soy, almond, cashew, or coconut)
¼ teaspoon arrowroot
¼ teaspoon xanthan gum
2 tablespoons agave nectar
2 tablespoons nondairy yogurt with active live cultures, at room temperature

1. Add the nondairy milk, arrowroot, xanthan gum, and agave nectar to the Instant Pot and whisk to combine. Do not cover the pot. Select the Yogurt program and adjust it to its high setting. 2. When the cooking program ends, wearing heat-resistant mitts, lift the inner pot out of the Instant Pot housing and place it on a trivet. Let the milk mixture cool in the pot until it reaches 110ºF (43ºC) to 115ºF (46ºC). Once the milk has cooled, add the nondairy yogurt and whisk to combine. 3. Ladle or pour the mixture into two widemouthed pint jars and cover the jars with their lids. Rinse out the pot and return it to the housing. 4. Add 1 cup water to the pot and place the wire metal steam rack inside. Place the jars on the steam rack. Secure the lid and set the pressure release to Venting. Select the Yogurt program once more, this time adjusting it to its normal setting. Leave the time at the setting's default 8 hours for a mildly tangy yogurt, increase to 10 hours for a tangier yogurt, or set to 12 hours for a very tangy yogurt. 5. When the cooking program ends, transfer the jars of yogurt to the refrigerator. Let chill for at least 8 hours before using. The yogurt will keep, refrigerated, for up to 1 week.

Raspberry-Almond Breakfast Cake

Prep time: 10 minutes | Cook time: 30 minutes | Serves 2

¼ cup unsalted butter, at room temperature, plus more for greasing
1 cup all-purpose flour, plus more for dusting and coating
1 teaspoon baking powder
¼ teaspoon salt
⅓ cup granulated sugar
1 egg, at room temperature
½ teaspoon vanilla extract
½ teaspoon almond extract
¼ cup buttermilk
1 cup fresh raspberries
Powdered sugar, for garnish (optional)

1. Add 1 cup of water to the pressure cooker and place the trivet or egg rack in the bottom. 2. Coat a 7-inch cake pan with butter and then with flour. Set aside. 3. In a small bowl, mix 1 cup of flour, the baking powder, and the salt. Reserve 2 tablespoons of the flour mixture in another small bowl for Step 5. 4. In a large bowl, using an electric hand mixer, mix the granulated sugar and ¼ cup of butter until thoroughly combined, scraping down the sides of the bowl as necessary. Add the egg, vanilla, and almond extract and mix to combine. 5. Add the flour mixture and the buttermilk in alternating batches to the batter, mixing well after each addition. 6. In a medium bowl, lightly toss the raspberries with some flour to coat. Gently fold the berries into the cake batter. Pour the batter into the prepared pan and put the pan on the trivet in the pressure cooker. 7. Secure the lid and cook on High pressure for 30 minutes. Quick release the pressure in the pot, then remove the lid and immediately transfer the cake to a cooling rack. 8. Let cool for 10 to 15 minutes, then dust with powdered sugar (if desired). Serve warm.

Soft-Boiled Eggs with Truffle San and Prosciutto

Prep time: 2 minutes | Cook time: 3 minutes | Serves 2

1 cup water
4 large eggs
1 teaspoon truffle salt
8 slices prosciutto

1. Pour the water into the Instant Pot and insert the steam trivet. Carefully place the eggs on the trivet. 2. Secure the lid with the steam vent in the sealed position. Press Manual and immediately adjust the timer to 3 minutes. Check that the display light is beneath high pressure. 3. When the timer sounds, quick release the pressure and carefully remove the lid. Run the eggs under cold water until cool, then peel. 4. Sprinkle the eggs with truffle salt. Serve with the prosciutto slices.

Tofu or Chickpea Shakshuka

Prep time: 5 minutes | Cook time: 20 minutes | Serves 4

Sauté:
1 tablespoon oil (or water sauté to make oil-free)
1 cup minced onion
1 teaspoon minced garlic
1 cup chopped bell pepper
Pressure Cooker:
1 (28-ounce / 794-g) can crushed tomatoes
½ cup water
1 (1-pound / 454-g) package super firm tofu, cut into cubes (or 3 cups cooked chickpeas)
1 cup chopped carrots
1 teaspoon ground cumin
1 teaspoon ground coriander
1 teaspoon dried oregano
1 teaspoon smoked paprika
2 packed cups chopped kale
Salt and pepper, to taste
Cayenne pepper or other hot pepper powder, to taste
For Serving:
Chopped parsley
Vegan feta cheese (optional)
Toasted gluten-free bread

1. Turn your Instant Pot to Sauté. Add the oil and cook the onion until translucent, 3 to 5 minutes. Add the garlic and bell pepper, and sauté for 5 minutes. 2. Turn the Sauté off. Add the tomatoes, water, tofu, carrots, cumin, coriander, oregano and paprika to your Instant Pot. Cook on High Pressure for 10 minutes and manually release the pressure. 3. Stir in the kale; it will cook from the heat of the stew. Add the salt, pepper and cayenne pepper until it's just right for you. Top with parsley and crumbled vegan cheese (if using), and serve with toasted gluten-free bread to soak up all the broth.

Cheesy Hash Brown Casserole

Prep time: 10 minutes | Cook time: 20 minutes | Serves 4

8 ounces (227 g) frozen hash browns
6 precooked breakfast sausage patties
6 large eggs
¼ cup whole milk
½ teaspoon hot sauce
¼ teaspoon salt
⅛ teaspoon black pepper
½ cup shredded sharp Cheddar cheese
1½ cups water

1. Grease a 7-inch cake pan with cooking spray. Arrange frozen hash browns on the bottom of cake pan. 2. Place sausage patties in a single layer on top of hash browns with one in the center and five around edges. 3. In a small bowl, whisk together eggs, milk, hot sauce, salt, and pepper. Pour egg mixture over hash browns and sausage. Sprinkle cheese over top of hash brown casserole. 4. Place a paper towel on top of cake pan and tightly cover with foil. 5. Pour water into Instant Pot and add trivet. 6. Create a foil sling with a long piece of foil folded lengthwise into thirds. Place it underneath cake pan. Use foil sling to gently lower pan into Instant Pot so it sits on top of trivet. Fold foil sling over pan. 7. Close the lid and set pressure release to Sealing. 8. Press the Manual or Pressure Cook button and adjust the time to 20 minutes. 9. When the timer beeps, allow the pressure to release naturally for 5 minutes and then quick release the remaining pressure. Unlock lid and remove it. 10. Carefully remove the casserole using the foil sling. Remove the foil and paper towel from the top of the pan. Serve immediately.

Raisin Nut Oatmeal

Prep time: 10 minutes | Cook time: 5 minutes | Serves 6

3 cups vanilla almond milk
¾ cup steel-cut oats
¾ cup raisins
3 tablespoons brown sugar
4½ teaspoons butter
¾ teaspoon ground cinnamon
½ teaspoon salt
1 large apple, peeled and chopped
¼ cup chopped pecans

1. In a 6-quart electric pressure cooker, combine first 7 ingredients. Lock lid; close pressure-release valve. Adjust to Pressure Cook on high for 5 minutes. Let pressure release naturally. 2. Stir in apple. Let stand 10 minutes before serving (oatmeal will thicken upon standing). Spoon oatmeal into bowls; sprinkle with pecans.

Chapter 3 Beef, Pork, and Lamb

Chapter 3 Beef, Pork, and Lamb

Smoked Pork Shoulder

Prep time: 5 minutes | Cook time: 1 hour 20 minutes | Serves 4 to 6

3 pounds (1.4 kg) pork shoulder, cut into half
2 tablespoons vegetable oil
3 cloves garlic, chopped
Salt and ground black pepper, to taste
1 cup water or bone broth
2 tablespoons liquid smoke
Steamed green beans, for serving

1. Select the Sauté setting on the Instant Pot and heat the oil. 2. Add the garlic and sauté for 1 minute. 3. Season the meat with salt and pepper to taste. 4. Add the pork shoulder to the pot and cook for 5 minutes on both sides, until browned. 5. Pour in the water and liquid smoke and deglaze the pot by scraping the bottom to remove all of the brown bits. Close and lock the lid. 6. Press the Cancel button to reset the cooking program, then select the Manual setting and set the cooking time for 70 minutes at High pressure. 7. Once cooking is complete, let the pressure release naturally for 10 minutes. Release any remaining steam manually. Uncover the pot. 8. Transfer the pork to a plate and shred the meat. 9. Serve with the sauce and green beans.

Sauerbraten-Style Pot Roast

Prep time: 15 minutes | Cook time: 1⅔ hours | Serves 4 to 6

1 tablespoon butter
1 tablespoon vegetable, corn, or canola oil
2½ pounds (1.1 kg) beef bottom round roast
½ teaspoon table salt
½ teaspoon ground black pepper
1 large yellow onion, chopped
2 medium carrots, chopped
2 medium garlic cloves, peeled and minced
½ cup dry but fruit-forward red wine
½ cup beef broth
½ cup red wine vinegar
1 teaspoon granulated sugar
½ teaspoon caraway seeds
½ teaspoon ground allspice
4 bay leaves
1 tablespoon tomato paste

1. Press the Sauté button, and set on Medium or Normal for 20 minutes. 2. Melt the butter in the oil in a 6- or 8-quart cooker. Season the beef with the salt and pepper, get it in the pot, and brown it well, turning a couple of times, about 10 minutes. Transfer the beef to a nearby cutting board. 3. Add the onion and carrot; cook, stirring often, until the onion just begins to soften, about 2 minutes. Add the garlic and stir until aromatic, just a few seconds. Pour in the wine and scrape up any browned bits on the pot's bottom. 4. Turn off the Sauté function. Stir in the broth, vinegar, sugar, caraway seeds, allspice, and bay leaves. Return the meat and any juices to the pot, nestling the meat into the sauce. Secure the lid with the steam vent in the sealed position. 5. Select Meat/Stew, Pressure Cook or Manual, and cook on high for 1 hour 15 minutes with the Keep Warm setting off. 6. When the machine has finished cooking, turn it off and let its pressure return to normal naturally, about 40 minutes. 7. Unlatch the lid and open the cooker. Using a large, metal spatula and a big cooking spoon (mostly for balance), transfer the meat to a clean cutting board. Find and discard the bay leaves. 8. Press the Sauté button, and set on Medium or Normal for 5 minutes. 9. When the sauce comes to a simmer, stir in the tomato paste and cook, stirring often, until the sauce has thickened slightly, 2 to 3 minutes. Turn off the Sauté function, then remove the hot insert from the machine to stop the cooking. Slice the meat against the grain into ½-inch-thick slices. Serve in bowls with lots of the sauce.

Korean Short Ribs

Prep time: 10 minutes | Cook time: 25 minutes | Serves 6

½ cup soy sauce
½ cup pure maple syrup
½ cup rice wine
1 tablespoon sesame oil
1 teaspoon white pepper
½ teaspoon ground ginger
½ teaspoon garlic powder
½ teaspoon gochujang
3 pounds (1.4 kg) beef short ribs
1 cup beef broth
2 green onions, sliced
1 tablespoon toasted sesame seeds

1. In a small bowl, combine soy sauce, maple syrup, rice wine, sesame oil, white pepper, ground ginger, garlic powder, and gochujang. Using your hands, rub this mixture into the rib sections. Refrigerate covered for 60 minutes up to overnight. 2. Add beef broth to Instant Pot. Insert trivet. Arrange ribs standing upright with the meaty side facing outward. Lock lid. 3. Press the Manual button and adjust time to 25 minutes. When the timer beeps, let pressure release naturally until float valve drops and then unlock lid. 4. Transfer ribs to a serving platter and garnish with green onions and sesame seeds.

Southern Pork-Sausage Gravy

Prep time: 2 minutes | Cook time: 15 minutes | Serves 4

1 pound (454 g) pork sausage
½ tablespoon olive oil
4 cloves garlic, minced
2 cups whole milk
¼ cup flour
Salt and ground black pepper, to taste

1. To preheat the Instant Pot, select Sauté. Once hot, add the oil to the pot. 2. Add the garlic and sauté until fragrant. 3. Add the pork sausage, stir and break into chunks with a spatula. Cook until brown. 4. Pour in 1½ cups of milk, stir. 5. Press the Cancel button to stop the Sauté function. 6. Close and lock the lid. Select Manual and cook at High pressure for 5 minutes. 7. When the timer goes off, do a quick release. Allow a 5-minute rest time and then carefully open the lid. 8. Add the flour and remaining milk to the pot, stir until smooth. 9. Season with salt and pepper to taste. 10. Select Sauté and cook, stirring occasionally, until thickened. 11. Serve warm.

Beef and Pasta Casserole

Prep time: 10 minutes | Cook time: 25 minutes | Serves 4

1 pound (454 g) ground beef
2 tablespoons butter
1 yellow onion, chopped
1 carrot, chopped
1 celery stalk, chopped
1 teaspoon kosher salt
½ teaspoon ground black pepper
1 tablespoon red wine
16 ounces (454 g) tomato purée
17 ounces (482 g) pasta (of your choice)
Water, as needed
1½ cups Mozzarella cheese, shredded

1. Add the butter to the Instant Pot and select Sauté. 2. Once the butter has melted, add the onion, carrot and celery. Stir until well coated and sauté for 5 minutes. 3. Raise the heat to High. Add the ground beef, ½ teaspoon of salt, and ground pepper. Stir well. 4. Cook, stirring occasionally, for 8 to 10 minutes until nicely browned. 5. Add red wine, stir well and cook for another 1 minute, or until the wine has evaporated. 6. Press the Cancel button to stop the Sauté function. 7. Add the tomato purée, pasta and ½ teaspoon of salt. Pour enough water into the pot to cover the pasta. Stir well. 8. Close and lock the lid. Select Manual and cook at High pressure for 5 to 6 minutes. 9. When the timer beeps, use a quick release. Carefully unlock the lid. 10. Carefully drain off most of the cooking liquid, reserving ½ cup. 11. Add the cheese to the pot, stir and close the lid. Let the dish sit for 10 to 15 minutes. 12. Serve with the remained sauce.

Italian Sausage and Peppers Hoagies

Prep time: 15 minutes | Cook time: 20 minutes | Serves 6

2 tablespoons olive oil, divided
1 pound (454 g) sweet Italian sausage links, uncooked, divided
1 large onion, peeled and sliced
1 small red bell pepper, seeded and sliced
1 small green bell pepper, seeded and sliced
1 small yellow bell pepper, seeded and sliced
4 cloves garlic, minced
½ cup chicken broth
1 (15-ounce / 425-g) can diced stewed tomatoes, including juice
¼ cup chopped fresh basil
2 tablespoons fresh oregano leaves
1 teaspoon cayenne pepper
1 teaspoon sea salt
½ teaspoon ground black pepper
6 hoagie rolls

1. Press the Sauté button on the Instant Pot. Heat 1 tablespoon olive oil. Add half of the sausage links and brown all sides for about 4 to 5 minutes. Remove and set aside. Add the remaining 1 tablespoon olive oil and remaining sausages. Brown all sides for another 4 to 5 minutes. Remove from Instant Pot and set aside. 2. Add onions and bell peppers to Instant Pot and stir-fry for 3 to 5 minutes until onions are translucent. Add garlic. Cook for an additional minute. Add broth and deglaze Instant Pot by scraping the sides and bottom of the Instant Pot. Add tomatoes, basil, oregano, cayenne pepper, salt, and pepper. Lock lid. 3. Press the Manual button and adjust time to 5 minutes. When timer beeps, quick-release the pressure until float valve drops and then unlock the lid. 4. Using a slotted spoon, transfer pot ingredients to a serving platter. Slice sausages. Serve on hoagie rolls.

Pork Belly Braised in Ginger Beer

Prep time: 15 minutes | Cook time: 1 hour | Serves 6

1 tablespoon vegetable, corn, or canola oil
2 pounds (907 g) skinless pork belly, cut into 6 pieces
1 (12-ounce / 340-g) bottle non-alcoholic ginger beer
⅓ cup soy sauce, preferably reduced-sodium
⅓ cup fresh orange juice
4 medium scallions, trimmed and cut into 1-inch pieces
2 tablespoons finely minced orange zest
1 medium garlic clove, peeled and minced
2 tablespoons minced peeled fresh ginger
½ teaspoon ground cinnamon
2 star anise pods

1. Press the Sauté button, and set on High or More for 25 minutes. 2. Warm the oil in a 6- or 8-quart cooker for a minute or two. Add half the pork belly pieces and brown well on all sides, turning occasionally, about 10 minutes. Transfer these to a nearby bowl and brown the remaining pieces the same way before transferring them into that bowl. 3. Pour the ginger beer into the cooker and scrape up any browned bits on the pot's bottom. Turn off the Sauté function, then stir in the soy sauce, orange juice, scallions, orange zest, garlic, ginger, cinnamon, and star anise pods. Return the pork belly pieces and any juices to the cooker. Secure the lid with the steam vent in the sealed position. 4. Select Meat/Stew, Pressure Cook or Manual, and cook on high for 35 minutes with the Keep Warm setting off. 5. Use the quick-release method to bring the pressure back to normal. Unlatch the lid and open the cooker. Transfer the pork belly to a serving platter or serving bowls. Find and discard the star anise pods. Use a flatware tablespoon to skim the excess surface fat from the sauce. Chunk up the meat, then spoon the sauce and scallions over it in bowls.

Beef Bourguignon

Prep time: 15 minutes | Cook time: 40 minutes | Serves 4 to 6

1 pound (454 g) flank steak
1 tablespoon olive oil
1 large red onion, sliced
3 cloves garlic, minced
1½ cups shiitake mushroom caps
4 medium-sized carrots, sliced
8 ounces (227 g) bacon slices
1 cup beef broth
1 cup red wine
1 teaspoon sea salt
2 tablespoons fresh parsley, finely chopped
2 tablespoons fresh thyme, finely chopped
1 tablespoon maple syrup

1. Preheat the Instant Pot by selecting Sauté. Add the oil. 2. Add the steak and cook for 3 to 4 minutes on each side, until browned. 3. Transfer the beef to a plate. 4. Add the onion, garlic, mushroom caps, carrots, and bacon. Stir and cook for 4 to 5 minutes, until the onion is translucent. 5. Pour the broth and wine, stir. Return the steak to the pot. 6. Add the salt, parsley and thyme, stir. Pour the maple syrup. 7. Press the Cancel button to stop the Sauté function. 8. Close and lock the lid. Select Manual and cook at High pressure for 30 minutes. 9. Once timer goes off, allow to naturally release for 10 minutes, then release any remaining pressure manually. Open the lid. 10. Serve.

Color Beef and Potato Curry

Prep time: 15 minutes | Cook time: 50 minutes | Serves 6

1 tablespoon vegetable, corn, or canola oil
2 tablespoons wet red, yellow, green, massaman, Penang, or sour vegetable curry paste
3 pounds (1.4 kg) beef bottom round, cut into 2-inch pieces
1 (4-inch) cinnamon stick
6 green or white cardamom pods
10 whole cloves
1 cup regular or low-fat coconut milk
½ cup beef or chicken broth
2 tablespoons dark brown sugar
1½ pounds (680 g) small white potatoes, halved

1. Press the Sauté button, and set on Medium or Normal for 5 minutes. 2. Warm the oil in a 6- or 8-quart cooker for a minute or two. Add the curry paste and stir until toasty, about 1 minute. Add the beef, cinnamon stick, cardamom pods, and cloves. Stir until the beef is well coated in the curry paste. 3. Turn off the Sauté function. Stir in the coconut milk and brown sugar until the brown sugar dissolves. Secure the lid with the steam vent in the sealed position. 4. Select Meat/Stew, Pressure Cook or Manual, and set on High for 40 minutes with the Keep Warm setting off. 5. When the machine has finished cooking, turn it off and let its pressure return to normal naturally, about 25 minutes. Unlatch the lid and open the cooker. Stir in the potatoes. Lock the lid back onto the pot. 6. Select Meat/Stew, Pressure Cook or Manual, and set on High for 5 minutes with the Keep Warm setting off. 7. Use the quick-release method to bring the pressure back to normal. Unlatch the lid and open the cooker. Remove and discard the cinnamon stick, cardamom pods, and whole cloves. Stir again before serving.

Memphis-Style Ribs

Prep time: 15 minutes | Cook time: 20 minutes | Serves 6

½ cup white vinegar
½ cup water
3 tablespoons smoked paprika
2 tablespoons brown sugar
2 teaspoons salt
2 teaspoons coarsely ground pepper
1 teaspoon garlic powder
1 teaspoon onion powder
1 teaspoon ground cumin
1 teaspoon ground mustard
1 teaspoon dried thyme
1 teaspoon dried oregano
1 teaspoon celery salt
¾ teaspoon cayenne pepper
2 racks pork baby back ribs (about 5 pounds / 2.3 kg)

1. Combine vinegar and water; brush over ribs. Pour the remaining vinegar mixture into a 6-quart electric pressure cooker. Mix together next 12 ingredients, reserving half. Sprinkle ribs with half of the seasoning blend. Cut ribs into serving-size pieces; transfer to pressure cooker. 2. Lock lid; make sure vent is closed. Select Manual setting; adjust pressure to High and set time for 20 minutes. When finished cooking, allow pressure to naturally release for 10 minutes and then quick-release any remaining pressure according to the manufacturer's instructions. Remove ribs; skim fat from cooking juices. Using a clean brush, brush ribs generously with the skimmed cooking juices; sprinkle with the reserved seasoning. Serve ribs with the remaining juices.

Mole Carnitas

Prep time: 20 minutes | Cook time: 1¼ hours | Serves 4 to 8

3½ pounds (1.6 kg) bone-in pork shoulder, cut into 3 pieces
1 tablespoon salt
1 teaspoon freshly ground black pepper
1 tablespoon ground cumin
1 tablespoon extra-virgin olive oil
Mole:
1 tablespoon extra-virgin olive oil
¼ cup diced red onion
3 cloves garlic, grated
1 teaspoon ground cinnamon
2 tablespoons tomato paste
2 tablespoons creamy peanut butter
1 canned chipotle pepper
1½ cups low-sodium beef stock
1 (10-ounce / 280-g) can red enchilada sauce
5 tablespoons dark unsweetened Dutch-processed cocoa powder

1. Liberally season all 3 pieces of pork shoulder with salt, black pepper and cumin. Rub the seasonings into the meat. 2. Place the oil in the Instant Pot. Press Sauté and then add the seasoned pork shoulder pieces. Sear on multiple sides for about 10 minutes total. After 10 minutes, press Cancel. 3. While the meat sears, combine the olive oil, red onion and garlic in a small saucepan. Sauté for 2 minutes over medium heat. Stir in the cinnamon, tomato paste, peanut butter, chipotle pepper, beef stock and enchilada sauce. Whisk to combine. Bring the mixture to a simmer and let cook for about 4 minutes. 4. Stir the cocoa powder into the sauce and then use an immersion blender to purée the sauce until smooth. 5. Add about half of the sauce directly on top of the seared pork. 6. Secure the lid with the steam vent in the sealed position. Press Pressure Cook until the display light is beneath high pressure. Use the plus and minus buttons to adjust the time until the display reads 60 minutes. 7. When the timer sounds, quick release the pressure. Remove the lid. Remove all the bones and large pieces of fat from the pork. Use two forks to shred the pork and mix it into the sauce. 8. The pork can be served right from the Instant Pot or can be transferred to a foil-lined baking sheet with some extra mole sauce and crisped up under a high broiler for 5 minutes.

Simple Shredded Beef

Prep time: 5 minutes | Cook time: 1 hour 25 minutes | Serves 4 to 6

3½ pounds (1.6 kg) beef chuck roast
2 tablespoons olive oil
1 teaspoon sea salt
2½ cups beef broth

1. Preheat the Instant Pot by selecting Sauté. Add the oil. 2. Season the meat with salt. 3. Add the beef roast to the pot and sauté for 8 to 10 minutes on both sides, until browned. 4. Close and lock the lid. Press the Cancel button to reset the cooking program, then select the Manual setting and set the cooking time for 75 minutes at High pressure. 5. Once cooking is complete, select Cancel and let naturally release for 10 minutes. Release any remaining steam manually. Uncover the pot. 6. Remove the beef roast from the pot and shred the meat with 2 forks. 7. Return to the Instant Pot and stir with remaining liquid. 8. Serve with cooked rice, potato or pasta. Also you can use the meat in sandwiches, burrito bowls, tacos, and more.

Easy Taco Casserole

Prep time: 10 minutes | Cook time: 10 minutes | Serves 4

- 1 tablespoon extra-virgin olive oil
- 1 pound (454 g) lean ground beef or turkey
- 1 red onion, chopped
- 1 teaspoon fine sea salt
- 1 clove garlic, minced
- 1 teaspoon chili powder
- 1½ teaspoons ground cumin
- 1 cup water
- 1½ cups prepared salsa
- ¾ cup bulgur (or quinoa, to make it gluten-free)
- 1 green bell pepper, seeded and chopped
- 1½ cups cooked black beans, or 1 (15-ounce / 425-g) can black beans, rinsed and drained
- Avocado slices, chopped fresh cilantro, chopped lettuce, chopped tomatoes, chopped green onions, and shredded Cheddar cheese, for topping (optional)

1. Press Sauté and add the olive oil, beef, onion, and salt to the Instant Pot. Sauté until the meat is browned and cooked through, breaking it up with a wooden spoon as you stir, about 8 minutes. Add the garlic, chili powder, and cumin and stir until fragrant, about 1 minute. Press Cancel to stop the cooking cycle. 2. Add the water and salsa and stir well, making sure that nothing is stuck in the bottom of the pot. Without stirring, sprinkle the bulgur over the top, making sure it doesn't touch the bottom of the pot (which might give you a "Burn" error). Scatter the bell pepper and black beans over the bulgur to help it cook evenly, then secure the lid and move the steam release valve to Sealing. Select Manual or Pressure Cook to cook on High pressure for 1 minute. 3. When the cooking cycle is complete, let the pressure naturally release for 10 minutes, then move the steam release valve to Venting to release any remaining pressure. When the floating valve drops, remove the lid. Stir the mixture well, then taste and adjust the seasonings as needed. 4. To serve, transfer the mixture to a serving platter and top as desired. Serve warm. Store leftovers in an airtight container in the fridge for 3 or 4 days.

Best-Ever Pot Roast

Prep time: 15 minutes | Cook time: 1¼ hours | Serves 4 to 6

- 2 teaspoons black pepper
- 1½ teaspoons kosher salt
- 1½ teaspoons seasoned salt
- 1½ teaspoons dried parsley
- 1 teaspoon dried thyme
- 1 teaspoon dried rosemary
- 1 teaspoon onion powder
- 1 teaspoon garlic powder
- 1 (3-pound / 1.4-kg) chuck roast
- 3 tablespoons extra-virgin olive oil
- 1 tablespoon salted butter
- 2 medium yellow onions, sliced into thick wedges
- 3 cloves garlic, sliced
- 2 tablespoons Worcestershire sauce
- 1 cup dry red wine
- 6 to 8 ounces (170 to 227 g) portobello mushrooms, sliced
- 2 cups beef broth
- 8 ounces (227 g) fresh baby carrots
- 1 pound (454 g) baby white potatoes
- 3 tablespoons cornstarch
- 1 packet beef gravy mix

1. Mix together the pepper, kosher salt, seasoned salt, parsley, thyme, rosemary, onion powder, and garlic powder and rub the mix into the roast on all sides. 2. On the Instant Pot, hit Sauté and adjust to the More or High setting. Pour in the oil and heat for 3 minutes, then sear the seasoned roast in the pan without moving it for about 1 to 2 minutes on each side. Remove the roast from the pot and set aside. 3. Without wiping out the liner pot, put the butter in the Instant Pot, and as it melts use a wooden spoon to scrape up any spices stuck to the bottom. Add the onions and cook for 2 minutes, continuing to stir and scrape up any browned bits. Add the garlic and Worcestershire sauce and continue to stir and scrape for another minute until the bottom of the pot is smooth. 4. Place the trivet over the onions with the handles facing upward, then add the wine and place the roast on top of the trivet, fat side up(so the juices will run through the meat as it cooks), and fill in the mushrooms around the sides. Pour the beef broth on top. 5. Wrap the potatoes and carrots each in their own foil pouches and place in the pot on top of the roast. It's okay if you have to move things around to make room. 6. Secure the lid, move the valve to the sealing position, hit Keep Warm/Cancel and then hit Pressure Cook or Manual on High Pressure for 60 minutes. When done, use a natural release for 15 minutes, and then a quick release. 7. Meanwhile, make a cornstarch slurry by mixing the cornstarch with 3 tablespoons of cold water and set aside. 8. Once the pot has finished cooking, remove the foil-wrapped veggies and set aside. Carefully remove the roast and the trivet and let the meat rest on a cutting board. 9. Press Keep Warm/Cancel and then Sauté and Adjust so it's on the More or High setting and bring the sauce to a simmer. Unwrap the veggies and stir them into the sauce along with the cornstarch slurry and gravy packet. Let simmer for 30 seconds and then turn the pot to the Keep Warm setting. 10. Using a sharp knife, slice the pot roast against the grain in strips about ¼ inch thick (or make thicker or bite-size cuts if you wish). Then, add them into the sauce (still on the Keep Warm setting). Make sure you toss in any remaining little strands of meat from your cutting board and give everything a final stir, then serve.

Beef Burgundy in a Pinch

Prep time: 15 minutes | Cook time: 28 minutes | Serves 4

- 2 tablespoons gluten-free all-purpose flour
- 1 teaspoon salt
- 1 teaspoon ground black pepper
- 2 pounds (907 g) boneless beef-round steak, cut into 1-inch pieces
- 4 tablespoons olive oil, divided
- 3 shallots, peeled and diced
- 3 cloves garlic, peeled and minced
- 1 cup dry red wine
- 2 cups sliced white mushrooms
- 2 medium carrots, peeled and thinly sliced
- 2 tablespoons fresh thyme leaves
- 1 cup beef broth
- 2 tablespoons tomato paste
- ¼ cup chopped fresh parsley

1. In a small bowl, combine flour, salt, and pepper. Dredge steak pieces in mixture until well coated. 2. Press the Sauté button on the Instant Pot and heat 2 tablespoons of oil 30 seconds. Add half of steak to pot. Sear 4 minutes, browning all sides of steak. Transfer to a plate. Heat remaining oil and sear remaining steak 4 minutes. Transfer steak to plate. Add shallots and garlic to pot. Stir-fry 2 minutes. 3. Deglaze pot by adding red wine, scraping any bits from the bottom or sides of pot. Cook for an additional 2 minutes to allow alcohol to cook off. 4. Add mushrooms, carrots, thyme, beef broth, and tomato paste to pot. Lock lid. 5. Press the Manual or Pressure Cook button and adjust cook time to 15 minutes. When timer beeps, let pressure release naturally until float valve drops and then unlock lid. 6. Transfer mixture to a serving dish and garnish with parsley. Serve warm.

Jewish Brisket

Prep time: 5 minutes | Cook time: 1¼ hours | Serves 4 to 6

1 (4- to 5-pound / 1.8- to 2.3-kg) beef brisket
Kosher salt
1½ cups water
1½ cups ketchup
¾ cup dark-brown sugar
¾ cup white vinegar
1 clove garlic, minced or pressed
4 yellow onions, coarsely chopped
3 tablespoons cornstarch

1. Take the brisket and cut it in half against the grain so it fits into your Instant Pot. Rub the brisket all over with kosher salt. 2. On the Instant Pot, hit Sauté and Adjust so it's on the More or High setting. Once hot, working with one piece at a time, sear the brisket for 2 minutes on each side, or until browned. When done, hit Keep Warm/Cancel, move the brisket to a plate, and clean and dry the liner pot. 3. Make the sauce by whisking together the water, ketchup, brown sugar, vinegar, and garlic in a mixing bowl. 4. With the liner pot and the trivet in the Instant Pot, place one half of the brisket on top of the trivet, fat-side up, and cover with about half of the onions and sauce. Then, in crisscross fashion, layer the other half of the brisket (also fat-side up) on top of the onions. Cover the brisket with the remaining onions and sauce. 5. Secure the lid, move the valve to the sealing position, and hit Manual or Pressure Cook on High Pressure for 75 minutes if you want it super tender (shredding apart) or 65 minutes if you want it a little firmer. When done, allow a 20-minute natural release followed by a quick release. 6. Very carefully transfer the brisket halves to a carving board (placing them fat side up) and let cool for 15 minutes. If you decide to carve it up into strips right away before it's done cooling, it will shred apart. While you wait, you may carefully shave off any undesired fat and discard (or keep it on if you wish). 7. Meanwhile, as the brisket's cooling, mix the cornstarch with 3 tablespoons cold water to form a slurry and set aside. 8. Hit Keep Warm/Cancel and then Sauté and adjust to the High or More setting to bring the sauce to a simmer. Add the slurry, stir immediately, and allow it to simmer for 30 seconds before turning the pot to the Keep Warm setting. The sauce will thicken as the brisket cools. 9. Once the brisket has cooled, use a carving knife to cut it into strips or chunks, slicing against the grain (meaning the opposite direction that the strings of meat are going in). 10. Carefully return the slices of meat to the Instant Pot and allow to marinate in the sauce (on the Keep Warm setting) for 5 to 10 minutes, so it stays tender until ready to serve.

Shredded Beef Burritos

Prep time: 20 minutes | Cook time: 40 minutes | Serves 6

2½ pounds (1.1 kg) boneless beef chuck roast, cut into 4 pieces
1 tablespoon chili powder
1½ teaspoons ground cumin
Dash salt
1 tablespoon canola oil
1 small onion, finely chopped
1 jalapeño pepper, seeded and finely chopped
1 garlic clove, minced
1 (14½-ounce / 411-g) can crushed tomatoes in purée
1 cup (8 ounces / 227 g) salsa verde
¼ cup beef broth
Tortillas
Optional toppings: shredded Cheddar cheese, sour cream, guacamole, salsa and fresh cilantro leaves

1. Season the roast with chili powder, cumin and salt. Select Sauté setting on a 6-quart electric pressure cooker; adjust for high heat. Add oil; brown roast on all sides. Top with onion, pepper and garlic. Add tomatoes, salsa verde and beef broth. Lock lid; make sure vent is closed. Select Manual setting; adjust pressure to High and set time for 40 minutes. 2. When finished cooking, allow pressure to naturally release for 10 minutes and then quick-release any remaining pressure according to manufacturer's instructions. Remove roast; shred with two forks. Skim fat from cooking juices. Return meat to pressure cooker; heat through. Wrap beef in tortillas with adding toppings as desired.

Teriyaki Pork Roast

Prep time: 10 minutes | Cook time: 30 minutes | Serves 10

¾ cup unsweetened apple juice
2 tablespoons sugar
2 tablespoons reduced-sodium soy sauce
1 tablespoon white vinegar
1 teaspoon ground ginger
¼ teaspoon garlic powder
⅛ teaspoon pepper
1 boneless pork loin roast, halved
8 teaspoons cornstarch
3 tablespoons cold water

1. Combine the first 7 ingredients in a 6-quart electric pressure cooker. Add roast and turn to coat. Lock lid; close pressure-release valve. Adjust to Pressure Cook on high for 25 minutes. Let pressure release naturally for 10 minutes; quick-release any remaining pressure. A thermometer inserted in pork should read at least 145°F (63°C). Press Cancel. 2. Remove pork to a serving platter; keep warm. In a small bowl, mix the cornstarch and water until smooth; stir into pressure cooker. Select Sauté setting and adjust for low heat. Simmer, stirring constantly, until thickened, 1 to 2 minutes. Serve with the pork.

Asian Lettuce Wraps

Prep time: 10 minutes | Cook time: 8 minutes | Serves 4

2 tablespoons olive oil
1 pound (454 g) ground pork
2 medium carrots, diced
1 medium bunch green onions, sliced
½ cup water
1 cup hoisin sauce
1 cup soy sauce
2 teaspoons minced ginger
½ teaspoon red pepper flakes
1 (8-ounce / 227-g) can water chestnuts, drained
1 small head Bibb lettuce

1. Press Sauté button on Instant Pot. Add oil, ground pork, carrots, and green onions to Instant Pot. Cook, stirring occasionally, 5 minutes. 2. Pour in water and deglaze bottom of pot. Turn Instant Pot off. 3. In a small bowl, mix hoisin sauce, soy sauce, ginger, and red pepper flakes together. Pour sauce and water chestnuts over pork. Do not stir. 4. Close lid and set pressure release to Sealing. 5. Press Manual or Pressure Cook button and adjust time to 2 minutes. 6. When the timer beeps, allow pressure to release naturally and then unlock lid and remove it. 7. Mix ingredients together. Scoop pork into lettuce leaves and serve.

Beef Gyro Bowls

Prep time: 10 minutes | Cook time: 14 minutes | Serves 4

2 pounds (907 g) flank steak, thinly sliced
1 medium onion, thinly sliced
3 cloves garlic, minced
1¼ cups uncooked long-grain white rice, rinsed
1¼ cups chicken stock
Juice of ½ lemon
Optional Toppings:
Tzatziki sauce
Lettuce
Tomato
Sliced onion
Crumbled feta cheese

1. Press Sauté to preheat the Instant Pot. Once hot, add the flank steak, onion and garlic. Cook for about 5 minutes, or until the meat is browned. 2. Add the rice, stock and lemon juice, taking care that the rice is completely submerged in the liquid. 3. Secure the lid with the steam vent in the sealed position. Press Manual and immediately adjust the timer to 9 minutes. Check that the display light is beneath high pressure. 4. When the timer sounds, quick release the pressure and carefully remove the lid. Serve in bowls and add your desired toppings.

Chinese Braised Pork and Eggplant

Prep time: 10 minutes | Cook time: 10 minutes | Serves 4

1 medium (1-pound / 454-g) Japanese eggplant, cut crosswise into 1½-inch-thick slices, or globe eggplant cut into 2-inch chunks
Salt and freshly ground black pepper
¼ cup canned chicken broth, or homemade
3 tablespoons soy sauce
1 tablespoon balsamic or red wine vinegar
1 tablespoon sambal oelek (chili garlic paste)
1½ pounds (680 g) thin-cut boneless pork chops, frozen for 15 minutes
1 tablespoon canola oil
1 tablespoon finely chopped fresh ginger
1 tablespoon cornstarch
Optional Garnish:
1 cup chopped dry-roasted peanuts

1. If using globe eggplant, toss the cubes with ¾ teaspoon salt and set aside in a colander for 20 minutes to draw out the bitter juices. Pat the eggplant dry with paper towels. (Skip this step if you're using Japanese eggplant.) 2. In a medium bowl, combine the broth, soy sauce, vinegar, and sambal oelek; set aside. Trim the fat from the chops and discard. Chop the pork into roughly ½-inch pieces. Season with salt and pepper. 3. Put the oil in the pot, select Sauté, and adjust to More/High heat. When the oil is hot, add the pork and ginger and cook, stirring frequently, until the pork is opaque and white all over, 3 minutes. Press Cancel. 4. Add the broth mixture and stir. Add the eggplant to the pot, but do not stir it into the sauce. Select the Pressure Cook function and adjust to High pressure for 3 minutes. Make sure the steam valve is in the Sealing position. 5. When the cooking time is up, quick-release the pressure. Using a slotted spoon, gently transfer the eggplant and most of the pork to a large serving bowl; set aside. In a small bowl, mix the cornstarch and 1 tablespoon cold water. Add the cornstarch mixture to the pot, select Sauté, and adjust to More/High heat. Simmer until thickened and bubbly, 1 minute. Press Cancel. Pour the sauce over the pork and eggplant, stir gently to combine, and serve immediately, garnished with peanuts, if desired.

Coconut Ginger Pork

Prep time: 10 minutes | Cook time: 57 minutes | Serves 4 to 6

3 pounds (1.4 kg) boneless pork butt or shoulder roast, trimmed of excess fat
1 teaspoon kosher salt
1 teaspoon black pepper
1 teaspoon ground cumin
1 teaspoon garam masala (or coriander)
1 tablespoon avocado oil or olive oil
1 onion, peeled and cut into 8 chunks
4 cloves garlic, finely chopped
2-inch piece ginger, peeled and thinly sliced
1 (14-ounce / 397-g) can coconut milk
Lime wedges, for garnish

1. In a bowl, combine the salt, pepper, cumin, and garam masala. 2. Rub all sides of the pork with the spice mix. 3. Select the Sauté setting on the Instant Pot and heat the oil. 4. Add the onion and garlic, sauté for 2 minutes. 5. Add the meat and ginger. Pour in the coconut milk. 6. Close and lock the lid. Press the Cancel button to reset the cooking program, then select the Manual setting and set the cooking time for 55 minutes at High pressure. 7. Once timer goes off, allow to naturally release for 15 minutes, then release any remaining pressure manually. 8. Slice the meat and serve with lime wedges.

Sicilian Meat Sauce

Prep time: 30 minutes | Cook time: 40 minutes | Serves 12

3 tablespoons olive oil, divided
2 pounds (907 g) boneless country-style pork ribs
1 medium onion, chopped
3 to 5 garlic cloves, minced
2 (28-ounce / 794-g) cans crushed or diced tomatoes
1 (6-ounce / 170-g) can Italian tomato paste
3 bay leaves
2 tablespoons chopped fresh parsley
2 tablespoons chopped capers, drained
½ teaspoon dried basil
½ teaspoon dried rosemary, crushed
½ teaspoon dried thyme
½ teaspoon crushed red pepper flakes
½ teaspoon salt
½ teaspoon sugar
1 cup beef broth
½ cup dry red wine or additional beef broth
Hot cooked pasta
Grated Parmesan cheese, optional

1. Select Sauté setting on a 6-quart electric pressure cooker and adjust for high heat; add 2 tablespoons olive oil. In batches, brown the pork on all sides. Set aside. 2. Add remaining oil to pressure cooker; sauté onion for 2 minutes. Add garlic; cook 1 minute more. Add the next 11 ingredients. Transfer meat to pressure cooker. Pour in broth and red wine; bring to a light boil. Lock lid; make sure vent is closed. Select Manual setting; adjust pressure to High and set time for 35 minutes. When finished cooking, allow pressure to naturally release for 10 minutes and then quick-release any remaining pressure according to manufacturer's instructions. 3. Discard bay leaves. Remove meat from pressure cooker; shred or pull apart, discarding bones. Return meat to sauce. Serve over pasta; if desired, sprinkle with Parmesan cheese.

Beef Roast with Asian Black Bean Sauce

Prep time: 25 minutes | Cook time: 1¼ hours | Serves 10

1 boneless beef chuck roast
½ teaspoon salt
½ teaspoon pepper
1 tablespoon olive oil
1 cup reduced-sodium beef broth
1 medium onion, cut into 1-inch pieces
½ pound (227 g) sliced fresh mushrooms
8 ounces (227 g) fresh snow peas, trimmed
¾ cup Asian black bean sauce
2 tablespoons cornstarch
2 tablespoons cold water
Hot cooked rice
4 green onions, sliced

1. Halve roast; sprinkle with salt and pepper. Select Sauté setting on a 6-quart electric pressure cooker. Adjust for medium heat; add 1½ teaspoons oil. When oil is hot, brown a roast half on all sides. Remove; repeat with remaining beef and 1½ teaspoons oil. 2. Add beef broth to pressure cooker. Cook 2 minutes, stirring to loosen browned bits from the pan. Press Cancel. Return all to pressure cooker; add onion. 3. Lock the lid and close pressure-release valve. Adjust to Pressure Cook on high for 60 minutes. Let the pressure release naturally for 10 minutes; quick-release any remaining pressure. Press Cancel. A thermometer inserted in beef should read at least 160°F (71°C). 4. Remove roast; keep warm. Add mushrooms, snow peas and black bean sauce to pressure cooker. Select Sauté setting and adjust for low heat. Cook and stir until the vegetables are tender; 6 to 8 minutes. 5. In a small bowl, mix the cornstarch and cold water until smooth; stir into pressure cooker. Simmer, stirring constantly, until thickened, 1 to 2 minutes. Serve with roast, hot cooked rice and green onions.

Carnitas Tacos with Avocado Crema

Prep time: 15 minutes | Cook time: 30 minutes | Serves 2

Carnitas:
1 pound (454 g) boneless pork shoulder roast, cut into 2-inch chunks
Kosher salt
Freshly ground black pepper
1 cup chicken stock
½ cup freshly squeezed orange juice
Juice of 1 lime
1 cup sliced onion
2 garlic cloves, crushed
½ teaspoon ground cumin
Avocado Crema:
1 medium avocado, halved and pitted, and cubed
½ cup coarsely chopped fresh cilantro
¼ cup sour cream
Juice of 1 lime
½ teaspoon kosher salt

1. Place the pork shoulder meat in the pressure cooker. Season generously with salt and pepper. Add the stock, orange juice, lime juice, onion, garlic, and cumin. Mix well and let the pork marinate for 20 minutes. 2. Secure the lid and cook on High pressure for 30 minutes, then allow the pressure to naturally release, about 10 minutes. Open the vent at the top and remove the lid. Press Cancel. 3. Preheat the oven broiler. Line a baking sheet with aluminum foil. 4. Transfer the pork to a plate. Carefully strain the juices from the pot through a fine-mesh sieve into a bowl, reserving the cooked onions. Use two forks to shred the meat, discarding any extra fat. Place the pork and onion in a single layer on the prepared baking sheet. 5. Broil for 4 to 5 minutes, or until the edges are crispy, then flip the meat, spoon on some of the reserved liquid if necessary, and broil for another 4 to 5 minutes. Make the Avocado Crema: 1. Scoop the avocado from the skin into the bowl of a food processor fitted with the blade attachment (or into a blender) and add the cilantro, sour cream, lime juice, and salt. Process until smooth, stopping to scrape down the side of the bowl with a rubber spatula as needed. 2. Transfer the crema to a small bowl. Cover with plastic wrap and store in the refrigerator for up to 2 hours if not using immediately.

Beef and Beans

Prep time: 10 minutes | Cook time: 15 minutes | Serves 8

1½ pounds (680 g) boneless round steak
1 tablespoon prepared mustard
1 tablespoon chili powder
½ teaspoon salt
¼ teaspoon pepper
1 garlic clove, minced
2 (14½-ounce / 411-g) cans diced tomatoes, undrained
1 medium onion, chopped
½ cup water
1 teaspoon beef bouillon granules
1 (16-ounce / 454-g) can kidney beans, rinsed and drained
Hot cooked rice

1. Cut steak into thin strips. Combine mustard, chili powder, salt, pepper and garlic in a bowl; add steak and toss to coat. Transfer to a 6-quart electric pressure cooker; add tomatoes, onion, water and bouillon. 2. Lock lid; close pressure-release valve. Adjust to Pressure Cook on high for 15 minutes. Quick-release pressure. Stir in the beans; heat through. Serve with rice.

Beefy Mexican Casserole

Prep time: 20 minutes | Cook time: 20 minutes | Serves 4

2 teaspoons olive oil
1 medium onion, chopped
3 cloves garlic, minced
1 pound (454 g) ground beef
1 tablespoon chipotle chili powder
1 tablespoon ancho chili powder
1 tablespoon ground cumin
½ cup water
1 cup uncooked long-grain white rice
1 red bell pepper, seeded and chopped
1 poblano pepper, chopped
1 jalapeño pepper, minced
1 (16-ounce / 454-g) jar red salsa
1 (14½-ounce / 411-g) can fire-roasted diced tomatoes
2 cups Mexican-blend shredded cheese
2 green onions, chopped
¼ cup chopped fresh cilantro

1. Press Sauté to preheat the Instant Pot. Once hot, add the oil and onion to the pot. Cook, stirring occasionally, until the onion is soft, about 5 minutes. Add the garlic, ground beef, chili powders and cumin. Cook the beef until no pink remains. 2. Add the water, taking care to scrape up any browned bits from the bottom of the pot. In this order, without stirring, add the rice, the bell, poblano and jalapeño peppers, and the salsa and tomatoes. 3. Secure the lid with the steam vent in the sealed position. Press Manual and immediately adjust the timer to 9 minutes. Check that the display light is beneath high pressure. 4. When the timer sounds, quick release the pressure and carefully remove the lid. Stir in the cheese, then top with green onions and cilantro.

Garlic-Herb Pork Loin

Prep time: 10 minutes | Cook time: 25 minutes | Serves 4

2 teaspoons olive oil
3 cloves garlic, minced
2 teaspoons Italian seasoning
1 teaspoon coarse salt
½ teaspoon freshly ground black pepper
1½ pounds (680 g) pork tenderloin
1 cup water or chicken stock

1. In a small bowl, mix together the olive oil, garlic, Italian seasoning, salt and pepper. Rub the mixture all over the outside of the pork loin. 2. Pour the water or stock into the Instant Pot and insert the steam trivet. Place the pork loin on the trivet. Secure the lid with the steam vent in the sealed position. Press Manual and immediately adjust the timer to 25 minutes. Check that the display light is beneath high pressure. 3. Once the timer sounds, allow the pressure to release naturally for 5 minutes, then quick release the pressure and carefully remove the lid. Remove the pork and allow it to rest on a carving board for 5 minutes, then slice and serve.

Coriander-Braised Pork with Oregano and Feta

Prep time: 15 minutes | Cook time: 50 minutes | Serves 4 to 6

3 tablespoons extra-virgin olive oil, plus more to serve
1 medium yellow onion, halved and thinly sliced
3 tablespoons ground coriander
1 cup dry red wine
3 pounds (1.4 kg) boneless pork shoulder, trimmed and cut into 1-inch chunks
Kosher salt and ground black pepper
6 bay leaves
1 tablespoon cornstarch
3 tablespoons minced fresh oregano
1 tablespoon lemon juice
2 ounces (57 g) feta cheese, crumbled
¼ cup finely chopped fresh flat-leaf parsley

1. On a 6-quart Instant Pot, select More/High Sauté. Add the oil and heat until shimmering. Add the onion and cook, stirring occasionally, until beginning to brown, about 7 minutes. 2. Add the coriander and cook, stirring, until fragrant, about 1 minute. Pour in the wine and cook, stirring occasionally, until most of the moisture has evaporated, 2 to 3 minutes. Add the pork, 1 teaspoon salt, ½ teaspoon pepper and the bay; stir to combine, then distribute in an even layer. Fast: 3. Press Cancel, lock the lid in place and move the pressure valve to Sealing. Select Pressure Cook or Manual; make sure the pressure level is set to High. Set the cooking time for 25 minutes. When pressure cooking is complete, allow the pressure to reduce naturally for 15 minutes, then release the remaining steam by moving the pressure valve to Venting. Press Cancel, then carefully open the pot. Slow: 4. With the pot still on More/High Sauté, bring the mixture to a boil. Press Cancel, lock the lid in place and move the pressure valve to Venting. Select Slow Cook and set the temperature to More/High. Set the cooking time for 4 to 5 hours; the pork is done when a skewer inserted into a piece meets no resistance. Press Cancel, then carefully open the pot. 5. Using a slotted spoon, transfer the pork to a medium bowl. Using a large spoon, skim off and discard the fat from the surface of the cooking liquid. Remove and discard the bay leaves. 6. Select More/High Sauté and bring to a boil. Cook, stirring occasionally, until the liquid is reduced to about 1 cup (or ½-inch depth in the pot), about 10 minutes. 7. In a small bowl, whisk the cornstarch and 2 tablespoons water, then stir into the pot. Cook, stirring constantly, until lightly thickened, about 1 minute. 8. Press Cancel to turn off the pot. Stir in the pork, oregano and lemon juice. Taste and season with salt and pepper. 9. Transfer to a serving dish and sprinkle with feta and parsley, then drizzle with additional oil.

Beef and Broccoli Casserole

Prep time: 15 minutes | Cook time: 25 minutes | Serves 4

1 cup water
1 pound (454 g) ground beef
2 large red potatoes, cut into ¼-inch-thick slices
1 medium head broccoli, chopped
1 (10½-ounce / 298-g) can cream of mushroom soup
½ cup beef broth
1 teaspoon Italian seasoning
½ teaspoon salt
¼ teaspoon black pepper
1 cup shredded Cheddar cheese

1. Pour water into Instant Pot and add trivet. 2. Spread ground beef on bottom of a 7-inch cake pan. Arrange sliced potatoes over beef. Sprinkle broccoli over potatoes. 3. In a small bowl, whisk together cream of mushroom soup, broth, Italian seasoning, salt, and pepper. Pour sauce over casserole and top with cheese. 4. Spray a piece of foil with cooking spray and cover cake pan. Create a foil sling and carefully lower pan into Instant Pot. 5. Close lid and set pressure release to Sealing. 6. Press Manual or Pressure Cook button and adjust time to 25 minutes. 7. When the timer beeps, allow pressure to release naturally and then unlock lid and remove it. 8. Remove cake pan from Instant Pot using foil sling. Serve hot.

Mama's Meatballs

Prep time: 15 minutes | Cook time: 30 minutes | Serves 4

½ pound (227 g) ground beef
½ pound (227 g) ground pork
2 large eggs
1 tablespoon Italian seasoning
1 teaspoon garlic powder
1 teaspoon celery seed
½ teaspoon onion powder
½ teaspoon smoked paprika
½ cup old-fashioned oats
2 tablespoons plus 2 cups marinara sauce, divided
3 tablespoons avocado oil, divided
2 cups water

1. In a medium bowl, combine beef, pork, eggs, Italian seasoning, garlic powder, celery seed, onion powder, smoked paprika, oats, and 2 tablespoons marinara sauce. Form into 20 meatballs. Set aside. 2. Press the Sauté button on the Instant Pot and heat 2 tablespoons oil. Place 10 meatballs around the edge of the pot. Sear all sides of the meatballs for about 4 minutes. Remove the first batch and set aside. Add another tablespoon of oil and add remaining meatballs and sear them. Remove meatballs. 3. Discard extra juice and oil from the Instant Pot. Add seared meatballs to a 7-cup glass dish. Top with remaining 2 cups marinara sauce. 4. Add water to the Instant Pot. Add trivet. Place the glass dish on top of the trivet. Lock lid. 5. Press the Manual button and adjust time to 20 minutes. When the timer beeps, let pressure release naturally for 10 minutes. Quick-release any additional pressure until float valve drops and then unlock lid. 6. Transfer meatballs to a serving dish.

Chi-Town Italian Beef and Peppers

Prep time: 20 minutes | Cook time: 1 hour | Serves 8

- ¼ cup olive oil
- 1 tablespoon Italian seasoning
- 1 teaspoon garlic powder
- 1 teaspoon smoked paprika
- ½ teaspoon red pepper flakes
- 1 teaspoon salt
- ½ teaspoon ground black pepper
- 1 green bell pepper, seeded and sliced
- 1 red bell pepper, seeded and sliced
- 1 yellow bell pepper, seeded and sliced
- 1 large yellow onion, peeled and sliced
- 1 (3-pound / 1.4-kg) boneless chuck roast, quartered
- 4 cups beef broth
- 1 cup chopped jarred giardiniera, drained

1. In a large bowl, combine oil, Italian seasoning, garlic powder, smoked paprika, red pepper flakes, salt, and black pepper. Add sliced bell peppers, onion, and quartered roast and toss. Refrigerate roast covered at least 30 minutes or up to overnight. 2. Press the Sauté button on the Instant Pot and add in meat, veggies, and marinade. Sear meat 5 minutes, making sure to brown each side. Add beef broth. Lock lid. 3. Press the Manual or Pressure Cook button and adjust cook time to 55 minutes. When timer beeps, let pressure release naturally for 5 minutes. Quick-release any additional pressure until float valve drops and then unlock lid. Strain all but ¼ cup of liquid from pot. Set strained liquid aside. 4. Transfer meat to a cutting board. Let meat rest 5 minutes, then thinly slice and add back to pot with veggies and liquid to moisten meat. 5. Using a slotted spoon, transfer meat and veggies to eight bowls, gluten-free buns, or lettuce wraps. Garnish with giardiniera and serve.

All-American Pulled Beef

Prep time: 10 minutes | Cook time: 2 hours | Serves 8

- 2 tablespoons vegetable, corn, or canola oil
- 1 (3-pound / 1.4-kg) boneless beef chuck roast, cut into 2 chunks and fat removed
- ½ teaspoon table salt
- ½ teaspoon ground black pepper
- 1 cup water
- 1 cup ketchup
- ¼ cup apple cider vinegar
- 2 tablespoons Dijon mustard
- 2 tablespoons Worcestershire sauce
- 2 tablespoons mild paprika
- 2 teaspoons celery seeds
- 1 teaspoon garlic powder
- 1 teaspoon onion powder

1. Press the Sauté button, and set on Medium or Normal for 20 minutes. 2. Warm the oil in a 6- or 8-quart cooker for a minute or two. Meanwhile, season the beef with the salt and pepper. Set one piece of chuck in the pot and brown well, turning once or twice, about 7 minutes. Transfer this piece of beef to a bowl and brown the second piece just as well before transferring it to the bowl. 3. Pour the water into the pot and scrape up the browned bits on the pot's bottom. Turn off the Sauté function and stir in the ketchup, vinegar, mustard, Worcestershire sauce, paprika, celery seed, garlic powder, and onion powder. Return both pieces of meat and any juices in the bowl to the pot; turn the meat on all sides to coat it in the sauce. Secure the lid with the steam vent in the sealed position. 4. Select Meat/Stew, Pressure Cook or Manual, and set on High for 1 hour 20 minutes with the Keep Warm setting off. 5. When the machine has finished cooking, once the machine has finished cooking, turn it off and let its pressure return to normal naturally, about 30 minutes. 6. Unlatch the lid and open the pot. Use a meat fork and a large slotted spoon to transfer the pieces of meat to a nearby cutting board. Use a flatware tablespoon to skim any excess surface fat from the sauce in the pot. 7. Press the Sauté button, and set on Medium or Normal for 15 minutes. 8. Bring the sauce to a simmer, stirring often. Simmer until thickened, about like a loose wet barbecue sauce, stirring almost all the while, 5 to 10 minutes. Meanwhile, shred the beef into bits with two forks. Once the sauce has reached the desired consistency, stir the meat into it and cook for 1 minute, stirring often, until well coated. Turn off the Sauté function and remove the hot insert from the pot. Set the lid askew over the insert and set aside for 5 minutes to blend the flavors and let the meat absorb more sauce.

Pork Ragu with Green Olives and Warm Spices

Prep time: 10 minutes | Cook time: 40 minutes | Serves 4 to 6

- 2 tablespoons extra-virgin olive oil
- 8 ounces (227 g) cremini mushrooms, trimmed and roughly chopped
- 3 bay leaves
- Kosher salt and ground black pepper
- ¾ cup dry red wine
- 4 medium garlic cloves, smashed and peeled
- 1 teaspoon ground cinnamon
- ¼ teaspoon ground allspice
- 1 (14½-ounce / 411-g) can crushed tomatoes
- 3 medium carrots, halved and cut into ½-inch pieces
- 2 medium celery stalks, sliced ½ inch thick
- ½ cup chopped pitted green olives
- 2 pounds (907 g) boneless pork shoulder, trimmed and cut into 1-inch chunk

1. On a 6-quart Instant Pot, select More/High Sauté. Add the oil and heat until shimmering. Add the mushrooms, bay and 1 teaspoon salt, then cook, stirring occasionally, until the liquid released by the mushrooms has evaporated, about 7 minutes. 2. Stir in the wine, garlic, cinnamon and allspice, scraping up any browned bits, then bring to a simmer. Cook, stirring occasionally, until the wine has reduced to a syrup, 5 to 7 minutes. 3. Press Cancel, then stir in the tomatoes, carrots, celery, half of the olives and ½ teaspoon pepper. Add the pork and stir to combine, then distribute in an even layer. Fast: 4. Lock the lid in place and move the pressure valve to Sealing. Select Pressure Cook or Manual; make sure the pressure level is set to High. Set the cooking time for 25 minutes. When pressure cooking is complete, allow the pressure to reduce naturally for 15 minutes, then release the remaining steam by moving the pressure valve to Venting. Press Cancel, then carefully open the pot. Slow: Select More/High Sauté and bring the mixture to a boil. Press Cancel, lock the lid in place and move the pressure valve to Venting. Select Slow Cook and set the temperature to More/Normal. Set the cooking time for 5 to 6 hours; the pork is done when a skewer inserted into a chunk meets no resistance. Press Cancel, then carefully open the pot. 5. Remove and discard the bay. Using a large spoon, skim off and discard the fat from the surface. Stir in the remaining olives, slightly breaking up the meat and carrots to lightly thicken the sauce. Taste and season with salt and pepper.

Sweet and Sour Pork

Prep time: 20 minutes | Cook time: 15 minutes | Serves 6

2 tablespoons plus 1½ teaspoons paprika
1½ pounds (680 g) boneless pork loin roast, cut into 1-inch strips
1 tablespoon canola oil
1 (20-ounce / 567-g) can unsweetened pineapple chunks
1 medium onion, chopped
1 medium green pepper, chopped
¼ cup cider vinegar
3 tablespoons packed brown sugar
3 tablespoons reduced-sodium soy sauce
1 tablespoon Worcestershire sauce
½ teaspoon salt
2 tablespoons cornstarch
¼ cup cold water
Thinly sliced or chopped green onions, optional
Hot cooked rice, optional

1. Place paprika in a large resealable plastic bag. Add pork, a few pieces at a time, and shake to coat. Select Sauté setting on a 6-quart electric pressure cooker and adjust for medium heat; add oil. Brown the pork in batches, then return all pork to pressure cooker. 2. Drain pineapple, reserving juice; refrigerate the pineapple. Add the pineapple juice, onion, green pepper, vinegar, brown sugar, soy sauce, Worcestershire sauce and salt to the pressure cooker. Lock lid; make sure vent is closed. Select Manual; adjust pressure to High and set time for 10 minutes. When finished cooking, quick-release pressure according to the manufacturer's instructions. 3. Select Sauté setting and adjust for high heat; bring liquid to a boil. In a small bowl, mix cornstarch and water until smooth; gradually stir into pork mixture. Add pineapple. Cook and stir until sauce is thickened, 1 to 2 minutes. If desired, sprinkle with green onions and serve over rice.

Spice-Rubbed Apricot-Glazed Ribs

Prep time: 15 minutes | Cook time: 50 minutes | Serves 3 to 4

Spice Rub:
1½ teaspoons garlic granules or garlic powder
1½ teaspoons onion powder
1½ teaspoons chili powder
1 teaspoon smoked paprika
1½ teaspoons dried thyme
1 teaspoon maple sugar
1 teaspoon sea salt
½ teaspoon freshly ground black pepper
Zest of 1 medium orange
1 rack baby back pork ribs (about 12 to 14 ribs)
1 cup water
½ cup cider vinegar
Glaze:
9 ounces (255 g) sugar-free all-fruit apricot jam
¼ cup pure maple syrup or honey
1 tablespoon coconut aminos
1 teaspoon finely minced or grated peeled fresh ginger
½ teaspoon finely chopped fresh thyme leaves
½ teaspoon finely chopped fresh rosemary leaves

1. Prepare the spice rub. In a small bowl, combine the garlic granules, onion powder, chili powder, smoked paprika, thyme, maple sugar, salt, black pepper and orange zest, then stir well. Set aside. 2. Remove the outer membrane on the ribs and discard. Rub the spice rub all over both sides of the ribs. Cut the rib rack in half to fit in the Instant Pot. Set aside. 3. Pour the water and cider vinegar into the Instant Pot and insert the steam trivet. Transfer the spice-rubbed ribs into the Instant Pot on top of the trivet, with the meat side facing outward. 4. Secure the lid with the steam vent in the sealed position. Press Manual and set on High Pressure for 25 minutes. 5. While the ribs are cooking, prepare the glaze: In a medium bowl, combine all the glaze ingredients, then stir well and set aside. 6. Preheat the oven to 400ºF (205ºC) and have ready a baking sheet. 7. Once the Instant Pot timer sounds, press Keep Warm/Cancel. Allow the Instant Pot to release pressure naturally for 15 minutes. Using an oven mitt, do a quick release. If there is any steam left over, allow it to release until the silver dial drops, then carefully open the lid. 8. With tongs, carefully place the rib racks on the baking sheet. Using a basting brush, evenly distribute the apricot glaze mixture all over the tops of the ribs. Bake in the preheated oven for 25 minutes. 9. Serve immediately.

Mexican Shredded Brisket Salad

Prep time: 15 minutes | Cook time: 50 minutes | Serves 4

6 tablespoons extra-virgin olive oil, divided
1 medium yellow onion, halved and thinly sliced
5 medium garlic cloves, smashed and peeled
Kosher salt and ground black pepper
3 bay leaves
2 teaspoons dried oregano, divided
2 pounds (907 g) beef brisket, trimmed and cut into 2- to 2½-inch pieces
½ cup lime juice, plus lime wedges to serve
½ cup pitted green olives, chopped
1 medium head romaine lettuce, roughly chopped
6 radishes, halved and thinly sliced
1 cup lightly packed fresh cilantro, roughly chopped
1 ripe avocado, halved, pitted, peeled and diced

1. On a 6-quart Instant Pot, select Normal/Medium Sauté. Add 1 tablespoon oil and heat until shimmering, then add the onion and cook, stirring occasionally, until softened, about 5 minutes. Add the garlic and cook, stirring often, until the onion is golden brown, another 2 to 3 minutes. 2. Stir in 1½ teaspoons salt, 1 teaspoon pepper, the bay, 1 teaspoon oregano and 1 cup water, scraping up any browned bits. Add the beef in an even layer, slightly overlapping the pieces if needed. 3. Press Cancel, lock the lid in place and move the pressure valve to Sealing. Select Pressure Cook or Manual; make sure the pressure level is set to High. Set the cooking time for 45 minutes. 4. When pressure cooking is complete, allow the pressure to reduce naturally for 15 minutes, then release the remaining steam by moving the pressure valve to Venting. Press Cancel, carefully open the pot and let the contents cool for 5 to 10 minutes. 5. While the beef is cooking, in a large bowl whisk together the lime juice, the remaining 5 tablespoons oil, the remaining 1 teaspoon dried oregano and 1 teaspoon each salt and pepper. Set aside. 6. Once the meat is done, use a slotted spoon to transfer the meat and onion to a medium bowl; do not discard the liquid remaining in the pot. With two forks, shred the beef into bite-size pieces. 7. Whisk the dressing to recombine. Add ½ cup of the dressing, the olives and ¼ cup of the reserved cooking liquid to the shredded meat, then toss to coat. Let cool to room temperature. 8. Whisk the remaining dressing once again. Add the lettuce, radishes and cilantro to it, then toss to coat. Transfer to a platter and top with the beef and the avocado. 9. Serve with lime wedges.

Pork Chops

Prep time: 15 minutes | Cook time: 5 minutes | Serves 4

½ cup all-purpose flour, divided
½ teaspoon ground mustard
½ teaspoon garlic-pepper blend
¼ teaspoon seasoned salt
4 (4-ounce / 113-g) boneless pork loin chops
2 tablespoons canola oil
1 (14½-ounce / 411-g) can chicken broth, divided

1. In a shallow bowl, mix ¼ cup flour, mustard, garlic pepper and seasoned salt. Add 1 pork chop at a time, and toss to coat; shake off excess. 2. Select Sauté setting on a 6-quart electric pressure cooker. Adjust for medium heat; add canola oil. When oil is hot, brown pork in batches. Add 1½ cups broth to pressure cooker. Cook for 30 seconds, stirring to loosen browned bits from pan. Press Cancel. Return all to pressure cooker. 3. Lock lid; close pressure-release valve. Adjust to Pressure Cook on high for 3 minutes. Quick-release pressure. A thermometer inserted in pork should read at least 145°F (63°C). Press Cancel. Remove pork to serving plate and keep warm. 4. In a small bowl, mix remaining ¼ cup flour and ¼ cup broth until smooth; stir into pressure cooker. Select Sauté setting and adjust for low heat. Simmer, stirring constantly, until thickened, 1 to 2 minutes. Serve with pork.

Spiced Short Ribs

Prep time: 5 minutes | Cook time: 55 minutes | Serves 4 to 6

1 cup beef broth
¾ cup dry red wine
½ cup hoisin sauce
3 cloves garlic, minced or pressed
1 teaspoon ground allspice
1 teaspoon cinnamon
1 teaspoon Chinese five spice powder (optional)
5 to 6 pounds (2.3 to 2.7 kg) bone-in short ribs
Kosher salt and black pepper, for seasoning
1 large Spanish or yellow onion, quartered
¼ cup cornstarch
½ cup honey

1. Create the sauce by whisking together the beef broth, red wine, hoisin sauce, garlic, allspice, cinnamon, and five spice powder (if using). Set aside. 2. Lightly rub the short ribs all over with kosher salt and black pepper. 3. Hit Sauté and Adjust so it's on the More or High setting. After 2 minutes of heating, working in batches, sear the short ribs for 1 minute on each side and set aside. 4. Add about ½ cup of the sauce to the pot and stir, scraping up any browned bits from the bottom. Once the bottom is clear, hit Keep Warm/Cancel to turn the pot off. 5. Add the onion wedges, rounded side down, then rest all the short ribs on top of the onion and pour the remaining sauce on top. 6. Secure the lid, move the valve to the sealing position, hit Keep Warm/Cancel, and then hit Manual or Pressure Cook on High Pressure for 45 minutes. Allow a 15-minute natural release when done, followed by a quick release. 7. Meanwhile, combine the cornstarch with ¼ cup cold water to form a slurry and set aside. 8. Carefully remove the ribs from the pot (they will be tender and prone to falling apart) and place in a serving dish. Hit Keep Warm/Cancel followed by Sauté and Adjust so it's on the High or More setting and bring the sauce to a bubble. Add the honey and the cornstarch slurry, stirring immediately. Let simmer for 30 seconds before hitting Keep Warm/Cancel to turn the pot off. Let stand 5 minutes. 9. Pour the sauce over the short ribs and serve with some bread to sop up the extra sauce.

Easy Boneless Beef Short Ribs

Prep time: 15 minutes | Cook time: 1 hour | Serves 4 to 6

2 teaspoons olive oil
2 pounds (907 g) boneless beef short ribs
1 medium onion, chopped
1 medium carrot, diced
3 cloves garlic, minced
4 sprigs thyme
½ cup red wine
2 tablespoons balsamic vinegar
2 tablespoons cold salted butter
Coarse salt
Freshly ground black pepper

1. Press Sauté to preheat the Instant Pot. Once hot, add the olive oil. When the oil is shimmering, add the short ribs and brown on all sides, about 10 minutes. Remove the ribs and set them aside. 2. Add the onion and carrot to the pot. Cook until the onion is starting to soften, about 5 minutes. Add the garlic and sauté for about another minute, stirring frequently. Add the thyme sprigs, wine and vinegar, stirring well to scrape up any browned bits from the bottom. Cook until the wine is reduced by half, about 5 minutes. Press Cancel to turn off the Instant Pot. 3. Return the ribs to the pot. Secure the lid with the steam vent in the sealed position. Press Manual and immediately adjust the timer to 40 minutes. Check that the display light is beneath high pressure. 4. When the timer sounds, quick release the pressure and carefully remove the lid. Remove the ribs and place on a serving platter. 5. Stir the butter into the liquid left in the pot and season to taste with salt and pepper. Pour the sauce over the ribs and serve.

Easy Beef Biryani

Prep time: 20 minutes | Cook time: 26 minutes | Serves 6

1 tablespoon ghee or unsalted butter
1 medium yellow onion, peeled and sliced
1 pound (454 g) top round, cut into ½-inch strips
¼ cup golden raisins
1 tablespoon minced fresh ginger
2 cloves garlic, peeled and minced
½ teaspoon ground cloves
½ teaspoon ground cardamom
½ teaspoon ground coriander
½ teaspoon ground black pepper
½ teaspoon cinnamon
½ teaspoon ground cumin
1 teaspoon salt
1 cup plain full-fat yogurt
1 (28-ounce / 794-g) can whole stewed tomatoes, including juice
2 cups cooked basmati rice
¼ cup chopped fresh mint leaves

1. Press the Sauté button on the Instant Pot and heat ghee 30 seconds. Add onion to pot and sauté 5 minutes until onions are browned and starting to caramelize. Add all remaining ingredients except rice and mint to pot. Lock lid. 2. Press the Manual or Pressure Cook button and adjust cook time to 10 minutes. When timer beeps, quick-release pressure until float valve drops and then unlock lid. Simmer mixture uncovered for 10 minutes until most of liquid has evaporated. 3. Transfer into six bowls over cooked basmati rice. Garnish with mint leaves and serve warm.

Pork and Beans

Prep time: 10 minutes | Cook time: 57 minutes | Serves 6 to 8

- 1½ tablespoons vegetable oil
- 3 pounds (1.4 kg) pork shoulder, cut into 1½-inch pieces
- 1 large yellow onion, sliced
- 2 cups dried white beans
- 6 cups water or chicken broth
- 1½ cups tomatoes, chopped
- 2 teaspoons chili powder
- 2 teaspoons garlic, minced
- ½ cup light brown sugar
- 1 sprig fresh thyme
- 2 tablespoons Creole mustard
- ½ teaspoon ground black pepper
- 1 bay leaf
- 1 teaspoon kosher salt
- Spices:
- 2½ tablespoons paprika
- 1 tablespoon onion powder
- 1 tablespoon dried thyme
- 1 tablespoon dried leaf oregano
- 1 tablespoon black pepper
- 1 tablespoon cayenne pepper
- 2 tablespoons garlic powder
- 2 teaspoons salt

1. In a small bowl, combine all spices. 2. Sprinkle the pork pieces with spice mix and rub them all over until coated. 3. Set your Instant Pot on Sauté mode, add the oil and heat it up. 4. Add the pork and cook, stirring occasionally, for 4 to 5 minutes until the meat has turned light brown. You may have to do it in two batches. 5. Transfer the meat to a bowl. 6. Add the onion to the pot and sauté for 2 minutes. 7. Add the beans and pour in the water or broth, mix well. Deglaze the pot by scraping the bottom to remove all of the brown bits. 8. Close and lock the lid. Select Manual and cook at High pressure for 20 minutes. 9. When the timer beeps, use a natural release for 15 minutes. Uncover the pot. 10. Add the tomatoes, chili powder, garlic, light brown sugar, thyme, mustard, black pepper, bay leaf and return pork to the pot. Stir. 11. Close and lock the lid. Select Manual and cook at High pressure for 20 minutes. 12. When the timer beeps, use a natural release for 15 minutes. Uncover the pot. 13. Select Sauté, bring to a simmer and season with salt. Simmer for 10 minutes. 14. Serve.

Braised Pork with Ginger and Star Anise

Prep time: 15 minutes | Cook time: 35 minutes | Serves 4

- 2 tablespoons grapeseed or other neutral oil
- 4 medium shallots, halved and thinly sliced
- Ground white pepper
- 1 (3-inch) piece fresh ginger, peeled, cut into 3 pieces and smashed
- 1 teaspoon grated ginger
- 8 medium garlic cloves, smashed and peeled
- 3 star anise pods
- 3 tablespoons packed brown sugar
- ⅓ cup low-sodium soy sauce
- 3 pounds (1.4 kg) boneless pork shoulder, trimmed and cut into 1-inch chunks
- 1 tablespoon cornstarch
- Roughly chopped fresh cilantro, to serve

1. On a 6-quart Instant Pot, select Normal/Medium Sauté. Add the oil and heat until shimmering. Add the shallots and ½ teaspoon white pepper, then cook, stirring occasionally, until the shallots are golden brown, about 5 minutes. 2. Add the smashed ginger, garlic, star anise and sugar, then cook, stirring, until fragrant, about 30 seconds. Pour in the soy sauce and ⅓ cup water, scraping up any browned bits. Add the pork; stir to combine, then distribute in an even layer. Fast: 3. Press Cancel, lock the lid in place and move the pressure valve to Sealing. Select Pressure Cook or Manual; make sure the pressure level is set to High. Set the cooking time for 25 minutes. When pressure cooking is complete, allow the pressure to reduce naturally for 15 minutes, then release the remaining steam by moving the pressure valve to Venting. Press Cancel, then carefully open the pot. Slow: Select More/High Sauté and bring the mixture to a boil. Press Cancel, lock the lid in place and move the pressure valve to Venting. Select Slow Cook and set the temperature to More/High. Set the cooking time for 5 to 6 hours; the braise is done when a skewer inserted into a chunk of pork meets no resistance. Press Cancel, then carefully open the pot. 4. Using a large spoon, skim off and discard the fat from the surface, then remove and discard the star anise and ginger. 5. In a small bowl, whisk the cornstarch with ¼ cup of the cooking liquid until combined, then stir into the pot. 6. Select Normal/Medium Sauté and bring the mixture to a simmer, stirring constantly, then cook, stirring, until lightly thickened, about 1 minute. 7. Press Cancel to turn off the pot, then stir in the grated ginger. Taste and season with white pepper. Serve sprinkled with cilantro.

Smoky Shredded Beef Tacos

Prep time: 20 minutes | Cook time: 53 minutes | Serves 4

- 1 tablespoon olive oil
- 2¼ pounds (1 kg) beef chuck roast, cut into 6 large pieces
- Salt and freshly ground black pepper
- ⅓ cup store-bought beef broth, or homemade
- 1 (10-ounce / 283-g) can Ro-Tel tomatoes, with juice
- 3 medium garlic cloves, chopped
- 1 chipotle pepper in adobo, chopped
- 1 tablespoon ground cumin
- 8 (6-inch) flour tortillas, warmed
- Optional Garnishes:
- Guacamole
- Shredded Cheddar cheese
- Shredded romaine lettuce

1. Select Sauté, adjust to More/High heat, and add the oil. Season the beef liberally with salt and pepper. When the pot is hot, add the meat and cook until browned all over, about 8 minutes. (Don't overcrowd the meat; you may want to do this in batches.) Transfer to a plate. Press Cancel. 2. Add the broth and cook, scraping up any browned bits on the bottom of the pot. Add the tomatoes, garlic, chipotle pepper, and cumin and stir to combine. Return the meat and any accumulated juices to the pot and turn the meat in the tomato mixture to coat. Lock on the lid, select the Pressure Cook function, and adjust to High for 35 minutes. Make sure the steam valve is in the Sealing position. 3. When the cooking time is up, let the pressure come down naturally for 20 minutes and then quick-release the remaining pressure. Transfer the meat to a cutting board and shred or chop it, discarding the fat and connective tissue. Put the beef in a large serving bowl. Use a slotted spoon to retrieve the tomatoes and garlic from the cooking liquid; add them to the beef. Cover. 4. If you'd like to serve the beef with the cooking liquid, select Sauté and adjust to More/High. Simmer the cooking liquid until it is reduced by about half, about 10 minutes. Liquid fat will pool around the edges of the pot while it's simmering; use a ladle to skim this off and discard it. Press Cancel. If you don't want to take this extra step, just spoon a few tablespoons of the liquid over the beef to moisten it and discard the remaining liquid. Serve the beef with the tortillas and optional garnishes.

Streamlined Bollito Misto

Prep time: 20 minutes | Cook time: 1½ hours | Serves 8

3½ to 4 pounds (1.6 to 1.8 kg) beef bottom round roast	1 cup plus 1 tablespoon white wine vinegar
1 medium yellow onion, peeled and halved	Water as needed
	1 cup fresh bread crumbs
2 medium carrots, halved widthwise	4 cups loosely packed fresh parsley leaves and stems
2 medium celery stalks, halved widthwise	4 jarred anchovy fillets
	3 medium garlic cloves, peeled and minced
1 (6-inch) rosemary sprig	
6 large fresh sage leaves	2 teaspoons drained and rinsed capers
2 teaspoons kosher salt	
1 teaspoon ground black pepper	½ cup olive oil
2 bay leaves	

1. Set the beef in a 6- or 8-quart cooker. Put the onion, carrots, celery, rosemary, sage, salt, pepper, and bay leaves around the beef. Drizzle 1 tablespoon vinegar over everything, then add enough water to a depth of about three-quarters of the way up the meat. (The liquid level must not go above the max fill line. Set the meat in the pot so that it's as flat as possible.) Secure the lid with the steam vent in the sealed position. 2. Select Meat/Stew, Pressure Cook or Manual, and set on High for 1 hour 30 minutes with the Keep Warm setting off. 3. Meanwhile, mix the bread crumbs and the remaining 1 cup vinegar in a large bowl and set aside for 20 minutes. 4. When the machine has finished cooking, turn it off and let its pressure return to normal naturally, about 40 minutes. 5. Unlatch the lid and open the cooker. Use a large, metal spatula and a big cooking spoon (mostly for balance) to transfer the beef to a nearby cutting board. Use a slotted spoon to find and discard everything else in the pot. Tent the meat with aluminum foil while you make the parsley sauce. 6. Squeeze the bread crumbs dry by handfuls over the sink, then add them to a food processor. Add the parsley, anchovies, capers, and ¼ cup olive oil. Cover and pulse to create a coarse sauce, stopping the machine to scrape down the inside occasionally and adding more olive oil through the feed tube to get a saucy consistency. 7. Carve the beef into ½-inch-thick slices and serve with lots of the parsley sauce on top. The leftover sauce can stay in a covered container in the fridge for up to 3 days, so long as you smooth it out in a container and pour a thin layer of olive oil on top of it to prevent oxidation (aka browning).

Spoon Lamb

Prep time: 20 minutes | Cook time: 1¾ hours | Serves 6 to 8

2 tablespoons olive oil	and halved
1 (3- to 4-pound / 1.4- to 1.8-kg) boneless lamb leg	4 whole cloves
	3 medium Roma or plum tomatoes, chopped
1 teaspoon table salt	
½ teaspoon ground black pepper	2 large carrots, cut into 2-inch sections
1 cup dry, light red wine	
½ cup chicken broth	6 large garlic cloves, peeled
1 medium yellow onion, peeled	2 teaspoon dried thyme

1. Press the Sauté button, and set on Medium or Normal for 15 minutes. 2. Warm the oil in a 6- or 8-quart cooker for a minute or two. Season the lamb with the salt and pepper, then set it in the pot and brown well on all sides, even the ends, turning occasionally, about 12 minutes. Transfer the leg of lamb to a nearby bowl. 3. Pour in the wine and broth, then scrape up any browned bits on the pot's bottom. Turn off the Sauté function. Stud the onion pieces with the whole cloves; add these to the pot along with the tomatoes, carrots, garlic, and thyme. Return the lamb to the cooker and lock the lid onto the pot. 4. Select Meat/Stew, Pressure Cook or Manual, and cook on high for 1 hour 30 minutes with the Keep Warm Setting off. 5. When the machine has finished cooking, turn it off and let its pressure return to normal naturally, about 25 minutes. 6. Unlatch and open the lid. Transfer the leg of lamb to a clean cutting board. 7. Fish out and discard the onions, carrots, and the cloves that have slipped off the onions. Use an immersion blender right in the cooker to blend the remaining ingredients in the pot into a sauce—or pour the contents of the insert into a blender, cover, remove the center knob, cover the hole with a clean kitchen towel, and blend until smooth. To serve, carve the meat into 1-inch slices and/or chunks, then serve them with the sauce ladled on top.

Carnitas with Pickled Red Onions

Prep time: 10 minutes | Cook time: 45 minutes | Serves 4 to 6

2 tablespoons grapeseed or other neutral oil	1-inch chunks
	2 tablespoons ground cumin
1 large yellow onion, halved and thinly sliced	2 tablespoons ground coriander
	2 teaspoons dried oregano
10 medium garlic cloves, smashed and peeled	½ teaspoon dried thyme
	1 teaspoon red pepper flakes
3 pounds (1.4 kg) untrimmed, boneless pork butt, cut into	Kosher salt and ground black pepper

1. On a 6-quart Instant Pot, select More/High Sauté. Add the oil and heat until shimmering. Add the onion and cook, stirring occasionally, until softened, about 3 minutes. 2. Stir in the garlic and cook until fragrant, about 30 seconds. Add the pork, cumin, coriander, oregano, thyme, pepper flakes and 1 teaspoon salt and 1 cup water; stir to combine, then distribute in an even layer. Fast: 3. Press Cancel, lock the lid in place and move the pressure valve to Sealing. Select Pressure Cook or Manual; make sure the pressure level is set to High. Set the cooking time for 25 minutes. When pressure cooking is complete, allow the pressure to reduce naturally for 15 minutes, then release the remaining steam by moving the pressure valve to Venting. Press Cancel, then carefully open the pot. Slow: With the pot still on More/High Sauté, bring the mixture to a boil. Press Cancel, lock the lid in place and move the pressure valve to Venting. Select Slow Cook and set the temperature to More/High. Set the cooking time for 5 to 6 hours; the meat is done when a skewer inserted into a chunk meets no resistance. Press Cancel, then carefully open the pot. 4. Using a slotted spoon, transfer the meat to a large bowl and cool for 5 minutes. Using two forks, shred the meat into bite-size pieces. Using a large spoon, skim off the fat from the surface of the cooking liquid. 5. Select More/High Sauté. Bring the liquid to a boil and cook, stirring occasionally, until reduced to about 1 cup (or ½-inch depth in the pot), 10 to 15 minutes. 6. Press Cancel to turn off the pot. Add the pork and stir until heated through, about 2 minutes. Taste and season with salt and pepper.

Beef Pot Roast and Potatoes

Prep time: 20 minutes | Cook time: 1 hour | Serves 2

1 tablespoon oil
1½ pounds (680 g) lean beef shoulder roast, trimmed
Kosher salt
Freshly ground black pepper
1 medium onion, chopped
3 garlic cloves, crushed

2 large carrots, peeled and chopped
12 ounces (340 g) fingerling potatoes
2 cups beef stock
1 tablespoon Worcestershire sauce
1 tablespoon cornstarch
Fresh thyme, for garnish

1. Preheat the pressure cooker on Sauté mode. When the display reads hot, add the oil. Season the roast with salt and pepper and use tongs to lower it into the pot. Sear on all sides, 3 to 4 minutes each side. Press Cancel. 2. Arrange the onion, garlic, carrots, and potatoes around the roast. Pour in the stock and add the Worcestershire sauce. 3. Secure the lid and cook on High pressure for 60 minutes, then allow the pressure to naturally release, about 10 minutes. Open the vent at the top and remove the lid. Press Cancel. 4. Transfer the roast and vegetables to a serving platter. Let rest while you make the gravy. Strain the beef stock into a bowl, discarding the fat solids. Return all but 2 tablespoons of the stock to the pot and select Sauté. Whisk the cornstarch into the reserved stock in the bowl, then stir the slurry into the pot and bring to a simmer, stirring often, for 5 minutes, or until thickened. Taste and season with more salt, pepper, or Worcestershire sauce if desired. Pour the gravy into a gravy boat. 5. Serve the pot roast and veggies with the gravy and garnish with fresh thyme.

Pork Chili Verde

Prep time: 25 minutes | Cook time: 30 minutes | Serves 8

3 tablespoons canola oil
1 (3 pounds / 1.4 kg) boneless pork sirloin roast, cut into 1-inch cubes
4 medium carrot, sliced
1 medium onion, thinly sliced
4 garlic cloves, minced

1 (28-ounce / 794-g) can green enchilada sauce
¼ cup cold water
2 jalapeño pepper, seeded and chopped
1 cup minced fresh cilantro
Hot cooked rice
Flour tortillas (8 inch)

1. Select Sauté setting on a 6-quart electric pressure cooker and adjust for high heat; add oil. In batches, sauté the pork, carrots, onion and garlic until browned. Return all items to the pressure cooker. 2. Add enchilada sauce, water, jalapeños and cilantro. Lock lid; make sure vent is closed. Select Manual; adjust pressure to High and set time for 30 minutes. When finished cooking, allow pressure to naturally release for 10 minutes and then quick-release any remaining pressure according to the manufacturer's instructions. Serve with rice and tortillas.

Corned Beef and Cabbage

Prep time: 10 minutes | Cook time: 1½ hours | Serves 4

1 cup beef stock
3 pounds (1.4 kg) corned beef
1 pound (454 g) baby potatoes, quartered

1 pound (454 g) baby carrots
1 head cabbage, thickly sliced, core removed

1. In the Instant Pot, combine the beef stock and the corned beef along with the contents of its seasoning packet. 2. Secure the lid with the steam vent in the sealed position. Press Manual and immediately adjust the timer to 80 minutes. Check that the display light is beneath high pressure. 3. When the timer sounds, quick release the pressure and carefully remove the lid. Remove the corned beef and place on a serving platter. Tent with foil to keep warm and prevent the beef from drying out. 4. Add the potatoes, carrots and cabbage to the pot. Secure the lid with the steam vent in the sealed position. Press Manual and immediately adjust the timer to 4 minutes. Check that the display light is beneath high pressure. 5. When the timer sounds, quick release the pressure and carefully remove the lid. Transfer the potatoes, carrots and cabbage to the serving platter, then drizzle some of the juice from the pot over everything. Serve immediately.

Chapter 4 Poultry

Chapter 4 Poultry

Chicken Chile Verde

Prep time: 5 minutes | Cook time: 15 minutes | Serves 4

3 pounds (1.4 kg) bone-in, skin-on chicken drumsticks and/or thighs
1 (15-ounce / 425-g) jar salsa verde (green chile salsa)
1 (27-ounce / 765-g) can roasted poblano peppers, drained
1 (7-ounce / 198-g) jar chopped green chiles, drained
1 tablespoon chopped jalapeño (optional)
1 onion, chopped
4 teaspoons minced garlic
1 tablespoon ground cumin
1 teaspoon fine sea salt

1. Combine the chicken, salsa verde, poblano peppers, green chiles, jalapeño (if using), onion, garlic, cumin, and salt in the inner cooking pot. Stir to mix well. 2. Lock the lid into place and turn the valve to Sealing. Select Manual or Pressure Cook and adjust the pressure to High. Set the time for 15 minutes. When cooking ends, carefully turn the valve to Venting to quick release the pressure. 3. Unlock and remove the lid. Use tongs to transfer the chicken to a plate. When the chicken is cool enough to handle, remove and discard the bones and skin. Shred the chicken with two forks or cut it into bite-size pieces. Return the chicken to the sauce and stir.

Chicken Penne Puttanesca

Prep time: 10 minutes | Cook time: 10 minutes | Serves 4

2 small (6- to 7-ounce / 170- to 198-g) boneless, skinless chicken breasts
Salt and freshly ground black pepper
2 tablespoons olive oil
12 ounces (340 g) dry penne pasta
2½ cups store-bought chicken or vegetable broth, or homemade
1 (14½-ounce / 411-g) can diced tomatoes with Italian herbs, with juices
½ cup oil-cured black or Kalamata olives
4 oil-packed rolled anchovies with capers, plus 1 tablespoon oil from the jar
Pinch of red pepper flakes

1. Pat the chicken dry with paper towels. Season the chicken all over with salt and several grinds of pepper. Put the oil in the pot, select Sauté, and adjust to Normal/Medium heat. When the oil is hot, add the chicken and cook until golden brown on one side, 3 minutes. Press Cancel. 2. Add the penne, broth, tomatoes, olives, anchovies and oil, red pepper flakes, and several grinds of pepper. Stir everything together and place the chicken breasts on top of the pasta mixture. Lock on the lid, select the Pressure Cook function, and adjust to Low pressure for 6 minutes. Make sure the steam valve is in the Sealing position. 3. When the cooking time is up, quick-release the pressure. Transfer the chicken to a cutting board and chop it into bite-size pieces. Return the chicken to the pot and stir to combine. Loosely cover the pot with the lid and let stand for 5 minutes; the liquid will thicken upon standing.

Chicken Potato Casserole

Prep time: 10 minutes | Cook time: 15 minutes | Serves 4

3 medium russet potatoes, peeled and chopped
1 pound (454 g) boneless, skinless chicken thighs
4 tablespoons unsalted butter
4 tablespoons all-purpose flour
½ teaspoon salt
¼ teaspoon black pepper
1 cup heavy whipping cream
1 cup shredded Cheddar cheese
1 cup water

1. Place potatoes and chicken in a 6-cup metal bowl. Mix. 2. Press Sauté button and place butter into Instant Pot. 3. Once butter is melted, whisk in flour. Continue to whisk until fully combined and flour is browned, 2 minutes. 4. Season with salt and pepper and mix an additional 30 seconds. 5. Slowly whisk in cream. Continue to whisk 2 minutes until sauce is thickened and no longer lumpy. 6. Pour sauce over chicken and potatoes. Top with Cheddar cheese. Spray a piece of foil with cooking spray and tightly cover top of bowl with foil. 7. Clean inner pot and place back inside Instant Pot and pour in water. Place trivet inside Instant Pot. Create a foil sling and carefully lower bowl into Instant Pot. 8. Close lid and set pressure release to Sealing. 9. Press Manual or Pressure Cook button and adjust time to 10 minutes. 10. When the timer beeps, allow pressure to release naturally and then unlock lid and remove it. Remove pan from Instant Pot using foil sling and then remove foil from top of bowl. Serve.

Cornish Hens with Ginger-Cherry Glaze

Prep time: 5 minutes | Cook time: 15 minutes | Serves 2

2 (1½-pound / 680-g) Cornish hens
¼ cup cherry preserves
1 tablespoon tamari
2 teaspoons ground ginger
1 tablespoon orange zest
1 orange, quartered
1½ cups water

1. Pat down Cornish hens with a paper towel. Set aside. 2. In a small bowl, combine preserves, tamari, ground ginger, and orange zest. Reserve 2 tablespoons of mixture. Rub remaining mixture over Cornish hens. Insert orange quarters into the cavities of the hens. 3. Add water to the Instant Pot. Insert steamer basket and place hens in basket. Lock lid. 4. Press the Meat button and adjust cook time to 10 minutes. When timer beeps, let pressure release naturally for 5 minutes. Quick-release any additional pressure until float valve drops and then unlock lid. Check hens using a meat thermometer to ensure the internal temperature is at least 165ºF (74ºC). 5. Preheat oven to broiler for 500ºF (260ºC). 6. Transfer hens to a baking sheet and brush remaining cherry preserve mixture on hens. Remove and discard orange from cavities of hens. Broil 5 minutes. 7. Transfer hens to a serving dish. Serve warm.

Easy Pesto Chicken and Red Potatoes

Prep time: 5 minutes | Cook time: 10 minutes | Serves 8

3 pounds (1.4 kg) boneless chicken thighs
¾ cup pesto
2 pounds (907 g, 8 medium) red potatoes, quartered
1 large sweet onion, peeled and chopped
1 cup chicken broth

1. Place chicken in a bowl or plastic bag. Add pesto. Toss or shake chicken to distribute the pesto evenly over the thighs. Set aside in the refrigerator. 2. Layer potatoes and onions in the Instant Pot. Pour in the chicken broth. Place chicken on top. Lock lid. 3. Press the Manual button and adjust time to 10 minutes. When timer beeps, let pressure release naturally for 10 minutes. Quick-release any additional pressure until float valve drops and then unlock lid. Check the chicken using a meat thermometer to ensure the internal temperature is at least 165ºF (74ºC). 4. Using a slotted spoon, remove chicken and potatoes and transfer to a platter. Discard liquid. Serve warm.

Salsa Chicken Tacos

Prep time: 5 minutes | Cook time: 10 minutes | Serves 4

2 cups chunky salsa
1 cup chicken broth
1 (1-ounce / 28-g) packet taco seasoning
1 pound (454 g) boneless, skinless chicken breasts
8 crunchy taco shells
2 cups shredded romaine lettuce
1 cup grated Mexican-blend cheese

1. In a medium bowl, combine chunky salsa, broth, and taco seasoning. Whisk to combine. Pour salsa mixture into Instant Pot. 2. Add chicken breast to Instant Pot and stir. 3. Close lid and set pressure release to Sealing. 4. Press Manual or Pressure Cook button and adjust time to 10 minutes. 5. When the timer beeps, allow pressure to release naturally for 10 minutes and then quick release remaining pressure. Unlock lid and remove it. 6. Use two forks to shred chicken. 7. Serve chicken in taco shells topped with shredded lettuce and cheese.

Creamy Southwest Chicken

Prep time: 15 minutes | Cook time: 10 minutes | Serves 6

1 tablespoon chili powder
2 teaspoons paprika
1 teaspoon ground cumin
1 teaspoon ground coriander
1 teaspoon garlic powder
1 teaspoon sea salt, plus more to taste
½ teaspoon cayenne pepper
2 pounds (907 g) boneless chicken thighs or breasts
2 tablespoons avocado oil or extra-virgin olive oil
1 cup chicken stock
¼ cup fresh lime juice, plus more to taste
2 red bell peppers, seeded and sliced
½ cup full-fat canned coconut milk or half-and-half
1 tablespoon water
1 tablespoon arrowroot starch, plus more if needed
Fresh cilantro, for garnish
Cooked rice, cauliflower rice, vegetable noodles or pasta, for serving

1. In a small bowl, mix together the chili powder, paprika, cumin, coriander, garlic powder, salt and cayenne. Rub the chicken with the spice mixture. Reserve any leftover spice mixture. 2. Select Sauté on the Instant Pot, and once hot, coat the bottom of the pot with the oil. Add the chicken to the pot and cook on each side for about a minute or two to seal in the spices. Select Cancel. 3. Place the chicken stock, lime juice, leftover spices and bell peppers on top of the chicken. 4. Secure the lid with the steam vent in the sealed position. Select Manual or Pressure Cook, and cook on high for 7 minutes. 5. Use a quick release. Open the lid and pour in the coconut milk. 6. In a small bowl, mix together the water and arrowroot starch and add to thicken the sauce. If you want an even thicker sauce, add another tablespoon of arrowroot. 7. Add more salt to taste, and additional lime juice for more flavor. Garnish with fresh cilantro and serve over rice, cauliflower rice, vegetable noodles or pasta.

Autumn Apple Chicken

Prep time: 25 minutes | Cook time: 20 minutes | Serves 4

4 bone-in chicken thighs, skin removed
¼ teaspoon salt
¼ teaspoon pepper
1 tablespoon canola oil
½ cup apple cider or juice
1 medium onion, chopped
⅓ cup barbecue sauce
1 tablespoon honey
1 garlic clove, minced
2 medium Fuji or Gala apples, coarsely chopped

1. Sprinkle chicken with salt and pepper. Select Sauté setting on a 6-quart electric pressure cooker. Adjust for medium heat; add oil. When oil is hot, brown chicken; remove and keep warm. 2. Add apple cider, stirring to loosen browned bits from pan. Stir in the onion, barbecue sauce, honey, garlic and chicken. Press Cancel. Lock lid; close pressure-release valve. Adjust to Pressure Cook on high for 10 minutes. Let pressure release naturally for 5 minutes; quick-release any remaining pressure. Press Cancel. A thermometer inserted in chicken should read at least 170ºF (77ºC). 3. Remove chicken; keep warm. Select Sauté setting and adjust for low heat. Add apples; simmer, stirring constantly, until apples are tender, about 10 minutes. Serve with chicken.

Spicy Lime Chicken

Prep time: 10 minutes | Cook time: 6 minutes | Serves 6

4 (6-ounce / 170-g) boneless skinless chicken breast halves
2 cups chicken broth
3 tablespoons lime juice
1 tablespoon chili powder
1 teaspoon grated lime zest
Fresh cilantro leaves (optional)

1. Place chicken in a 6-quart electric pressure cooker. Combine broth, lime juice and chili powder; pour over chicken. Lock lid; close pressure-release valve. Adjust to Pressure Cook on high for 6 minutes. 2. Quick-release pressure. A thermometer inserted in chicken should read at least 165ºF (74ºC). 3. Remove the chicken. When cool enough to handle, shred meat with 2 forks; return to pressure cooker. Stir in lime zest. If desired, serve with cilantro.

Turkey Sausage and Cabbage

Prep time: 10 minutes | Cook time: 12 minutes | Serves 2

½ pound (227 g) turkey sausage, sliced
1 tablespoon olive oil
½ yellow onion, chopped
2 cloves garlic, minced
½ cabbage head, shredded
¼ cup water or chicken broth
1 teaspoon mustard
1 teaspoon balsamic vinegar
1 teaspoon sugar
½ teaspoon kosher salt
¼ teaspoon ground black pepper

1. Select the Sauté setting on the Instant Pot and heat the oil. 2. Add the onion and garlic and cook for 2 minutes. 3. Add the turkey sausage and sauté for another 5 minutes. 4. Add the cabbage, water, mustard, vinegar, sugar, salt and pepper, stir well. 5. Close and lock the lid. Select the Manual setting and set the cooking time for 5 minutes at High pressure. 6. Once cooking is complete, use a natural release for 5 minutes, then release any remaining pressure manually. Open the lid. 7. Serve.

Black Bean Chicken Nachos

Prep time: 10 minutes | Cook time: 8 minutes | Serves 8

1½ pounds (680 g) boneless skinless chicken breasts
2 (16-ounce / 454-g) jars black bean and corn salsa
1 medium green pepper, chopped
1 medium sweet red pepper, chopped
1 (12-ounce / 340-g) package tortilla chips
2 cups shredded Mexican cheese blend
Optional toppings: minced fresh cilantro, pickled jalapeño slices and sour cream

1. Place chicken, salsa and peppers in a 6-quart electric pressure cooker. Lock lid; make sure vent is closed. Select Manual setting; adjust pressure to High and set time for 8 minutes. When finished cooking, allow pressure to naturally release for 7 minutes and then quick-release any remaining pressure according to manufacturer's instructions. 2. Remove chicken; shred with two forks. Return to pressure cooker. Using a slotted spoon, serve chicken over chips; sprinkle with cheese and, if desired, cilantro. Serve with the toppings as desired.

Chicken Scarpariello

Prep time: 5 minutes | Cook time: 20 minutes | Serves 4 to 6

¼ cup extra-virgin olive oil
3 pounds (1.4 kg) boneless or bone-in, skinless chicken thighs
4 tablespoons (½ stick) salted butter
1 large Vidalia (sweet) onion, diced
1 pound (454 g) baby bella mushrooms, sliced
6 cloves garlic, minced
1 pound (454 g) sweet or hot Italian sausage, with casings, sliced into ½-inch-thick pieces
¾ cup dry Marsala wine
¼ cup chicken broth
1 teaspoon dried rosemary
1 teaspoon dried thyme
1 teaspoon Italian seasoning
1 teaspoon seasoned salt
2½ tablespoons cornstarch
¼ cup heavy cream or half-and-half
1 (12-ounce / 340-g) jar roasted red peppers, drained and sliced into ¼-inch strips
½ cup grated Parmesan cheese

1. On the Instant Pot, hit Sauté and Adjust so it's on the High or More setting. Pour in the olive oil and heat about 3 minutes. In batches, add the chicken and sauté for 30 seconds on each side until lightly seared but not cooked, constantly moving the thighs around so they don't stick to the pot too much (it's fine if some do). When done, transfer the chicken to a plate to rest. 2. Add the butter and onion, and as the butter melts, scrape the bottom of the pot of most chicken bits. Add the mushrooms and garlic and sauté for 3 minutes, until just softened. 3. Add the sausage and sauté for 2 minutes. 4. Pour in the Marsala wine and bring to a simmer, once more scraping the bottom of the pot to free it of most browned bits. Stir in the broth, rosemary, thyme, Italian seasoning, and seasoned salt. Place the chicken back in the pot, resting on top of everything. 5. Secure the lid, move the valve to the sealing position, and hit Keep Warm/Cancel followed by Manual or Pressure Cook on High Pressure for 6 minutes. Quick release when done. Use tongs to remove the chicken to a serving dish to rest. 6. Make a cornstarch slurry by mixing the cornstarch with 2½ tablespoons cold water. Set aside. 7. Stir in the cream and roasted red peppers. Hit Keep Warm/Cancel and then Sauté and Adjust so it's on the High or More setting. Once it begins to bubble, immediately stir in the cornstarch slurry and Parmesan. Let simmer for 30 seconds, turn off the pot, and let stand for 5 minutes to let the sauce thicken before draping over the chicken.

Chicken Tikka Masala

Prep time: 20 minutes | Cook time: 20 minutes | Serves 8

2 tablespoons olive oil
½ large onion, finely chopped
4½ teaspoons minced fresh gingerroot
4 garlic cloves, minced
1 tablespoon garam masala
2½ teaspoons salt
1½ teaspoons ground cumin
1 teaspoon paprika
¾ teaspoon pepper
½ teaspoon cayenne pepper
¼ teaspoon ground cinnamon
2½ pounds (1.1 kg) boneless skinless chicken breasts, cut into 1½-inch cubes
1 (29-ounce / 822-g) can tomato purée
⅓ cup water
1 jalapeño pepper, halved and seeded
1 bay leaf
1 tablespoon cornstarch
1½ cups (12 ounces / 340 g) plain yogurt
Hot cooked basmati rice
Chopped fresh cilantro, optional

1. Select Sauté setting on a 6-quart electric pressure cooker and adjust for medium heat; add oil. Cook onion until tender. Add gingerroot and garlic; cook 1 minute. Stir in seasonings and cook 30 seconds. Add chicken, tomato purée, water, jalapeño and bay leaf. 2. Lock lid; make sure vent is closed. Select Manual setting; adjust pressure to High and set time for 10 minutes. When finished cooking, quick-release the pressure according to manufacturer's directions. Discard bay leaf. 3. Select Sauté setting and adjust for medium heat; bring mixture to a boil. In a small bowl, mix cornstarch and yogurt until smooth; gradually stir into sauce. Cook and stir until sauce is thickened, about 3 minutes. Serve with rice. If desired, sprinkle with cilantro.

Thanksgiving Turkey and Gravy

Prep time: 25 minutes | Cook time: 15 minutes | Serves 4

1 (4½- to 5-pound / 2.0- to 2.3-kg) bone-in turkey breast
4 teaspoons poultry seasoning
¾ teaspoon fine sea salt
1 cup low-sodium chicken broth
2 tablespoons unsalted butter, melted
2 tablespoons all-purpose flour
2 tablespoons heavy cream (optional)

1. Pat the turkey breast dry. Mix together the poultry seasoning and salt. Rub about half of the mixture on the skin and in the cavity on the underside of the breast; reserve the rest. 2. Pour the chicken broth into the inner cooking pot. Place a trivet in the pot. Place the turkey breast, skin-side up if possible, on the trivet. Lock the lid into place and turn the valve to Sealing. Select Pressure Cook or Manual and adjust the pressure to High. Set the time to 15 minutes. 3. When cooking ends, let the pressure release naturally for 8 minutes, then turn the valve to Venting to quick release the remaining pressure. Unlock and remove the lid. 4. While the turkey pressure cooks, preheat the oven to 400ºF (205ºC). Mix the remaining seasoning mixture with the butter. When the turkey is ready, remove it from the pot and place it, skin-side up, on a rack set over a rimmed baking sheet. 5. Brush the turkey skin with the seasoned butter. Roast the turkey for 10 to 15 minutes, until the skin is browned and the interior temperature reaches at least 155ºF (68ºC). 6. While the turkey roasts, remove the trivet from the inner cooking pot. Remove about ½ cup of the cooking liquid and leave the rest in the pot. Select Sauté and adjust the heat to Medium. 7. In a small bowl, stir together the flour and the ½ cup cooking liquid. When the liquid in the pot is simmering, gradually stir in the flour mixture. Cook for 3 to 5 minutes, until the gravy comes to a boil and is thickened. For a creamier gravy, stir in the optional cream. 8. When the turkey is done, remove it from the oven and let it rest for about 10 minutes before slicing.

Apricot Chicken

Prep time: 10 minutes | Cook time: 17 minutes | Serves 4 to 6

2½ pounds (1.1 kg) skinless chicken thighs
1 tablespoon vegetable oil
1 teaspoon kosher salt
1 teaspoon ground black pepper
3 cloves garlic, minced
1 large onion, chopped
⅛ teaspoon allspice powder
½ cup chicken broth
8 ounces (227 g) canned apricots
1 pound (454 g) canned tomatoes, diced
1 tablespoon fresh ginger, grated
½ teaspoon ground cinnamon
Fresh parsley, chopped (optional)

1. Set your Instant Pot on Sauté mode, add the oil and heat it up. 2. Season the chicken thighs with salt and pepper. 3. Add the chicken, garlic, and onion to the Instant Pot. 4. Sprinkle with the allspice powder and cook for 5 minutes or until nicely browned. 5. Pour the broth. Add the apricots, tomatoes, fresh ginger, and cinnamon to the pot. Stir well. Close and lock the lid. 6. Press the Cancel button to reset the cooking program. Select the Manual setting and set the cooking time for 12 minutes at High pressure. 7. When the timer beeps, use a quick release. Carefully unlock the lid. 8. Transfer the dish to a serving bowl, top with parsley and serve.

Huli Huli Chicken Thighs

Prep time: 5 minutes | Cook time: 10 minutes | Serves 8

1 cup crushed pineapple, drained
¾ cup ketchup
⅓ cup reduced-sodium soy sauce
3 tablespoons packed brown sugar
3 tablespoons lime juice
1 garlic clove, minced
8 boneless skinless chicken thighs (about 2 pounds / 907 g)
Hot cooked rice
Green onions, thinly sliced, optional

1. Mix first six ingredients. Place chicken in a 6-quart electric pressure cooker; top with pineapple mixture. Lock lid; make sure vent is closed. Select Manual setting; adjust pressure to High and set time for 10 minutes. When finished cooking, allow pressure to naturally release for 5 minutes and then quick-release any remaining pressure according to manufacturer's instructions. Serve with rice. If desired, top with green onions.

Lemon Chicken with Basil

Prep time: 10 minutes | Cook time: 6 minutes | Serves 4

4 (6-ounce / 170-g) boneless skinless chicken breast halves
2 medium lemons
1 bunch fresh basil leaves
2 cups chicken stock

1. Place the chicken in a 6-quart electric pressure cooker. Finely grate enough zest from lemons to measure 4 teaspoons Cut lemons in half; squeeze juice. Add zest and juice to pressure cooker. 2. Tear fresh basil leaves directly into pressure cooker; add chicken stock. Lock lid; close pressure-release valve. Adjust to Pressure Cook on high for 6 minutes. Quick-release pressure. A thermometer inserted in chicken should read at least 165ºF (74ºC). 3. When cool enough to handle, shred meat with 2 forks; return to pressure cooker. If desired, stir in additional lemon zest and chopped basil. Serve with a slotted spoon.

Orange Chicken

Prep time: 2 minutes | Cook time: 20 minutes | Serves 4

4 chicken breasts
¼ cup water
¾ cup orange juice
¾ cup barbecue sauce
2 tablespoons soy sauce
1 tablespoon cornstarch plus 2 tablespoons water
2 tablespoons green onions, chopped

1. Add the chicken breasts, ¼ cup of water, orange juice, barbecue sauce, and soy sauce to the Instant Pot. Stir well. 2. Close and lock the lid. Select the Poultry setting and set the cooking time for 15 minutes. 3. Once pressure cooking is complete, use a quick release. Unlock and carefully open the lid. 4. In a cup, combine the cornstarch and 2 tablespoons of water. 5. Select the Sauté setting and add the cornstarch slurry to the pot. 6. Simmer for 5 minutes or until the sauce has thickened. 7. Add green onions and serve.

Sicilian-Style Braised Bone-in Chicken Breasts

Prep time: 20 minutes | Cook time: 31 minutes | Serves 4

2 tablespoons olive oil
4 (10- to 12-ounce / 283- to 340-g) bone-in skin-on chicken breasts
1 medium yellow onion, chopped
1 medium red bell pepper, stemmed, cored, and cut into thin strips
1 medium green bell pepper, stemmed, cored, and cut into thin strips
1 medium yellow bell pepper, stemmed, cored, and cut into thin strips
3 medium garlic cloves, peeled and minced
1 tablespoon packed fresh rosemary leaves, minced
1 tablespoon packed fresh oregano leaves, minced
1 to 2 jarred anchovy fillets, finely chopped
¼ teaspoon table salt
2 tablespoons balsamic vinegar
1¼ cups chicken broth

1. Press the Sauté button, and set on Medium or Normal for 15 minutes. 2. Warm the oil for a minute or two in a 6- or 8-quart cooker. Add two of the chicken breasts skin side down and brown well without turning, about 5 minutes. Transfer the breasts to a bowl and brown the other two in the same way before transferring them to the bowl. 3. Add the onion and all the bell pepper strips. Cook, stirring occasionally, until softened, about 4 minutes. Stir in the garlic, rosemary, oregano, anchovies (if using), and salt until aromatic, just a few seconds. 4. Pour in the vinegar and scrape up any browned bits on the pot's bottom. Turn off the Sauté function. Pour in the broth and stir well. Nestle the chicken breasts skin side up in the sauce; drizzle any juice from their bowl over them. Secure the lid with the steam vent in the sealed position. 5. Select Meat/Stew, Pressure Cook or Manual, and cook on high for 16 minutes with the Keep Warm setting off. 6. Use the quick-release method to bring the pressure back to normal. Unlatch the lid and open the pot. Transfer the chicken breasts to serving plates or a serving platter. Spoon some of the sauce over them before serving.

Sticky Sesame Chicken

Prep time: 5 minutes | Cook time: 15 minutes | Serves 4 to 6

6 boneless chicken thigh fillets
5 tablespoons sweet chili sauce
5 tablespoons hoisin sauce
1 chunk peeled and grated fresh ginger
4 peeled and crushed cloves garlic
1 tablespoon rice vinegar
1½ tablespoons sesame seeds
1 tablespoon soy sauce
½ cup chicken stock

1. In a medium bowl, whisk together the chili sauce, hoisin sauce, ginger, garlic, vinegar, sesame seeds, soy sauce, and chicken stock until combined. 2. Add the chicken thigh fillets to the Instant Pot and pour over the sauce mixture. 3. Close and lock the lid. Select Manual and cook at High pressure for 15 minutes. 4. Once cooking is complete, let the pressure release naturally for 10 minutes. Release any remaining steam manually. Open the lid. 5. Serve with cooked rice, mashed potato or any other garnish.

Chipotle Chicken Fajita Lettuce Cups

Prep time: 15 minutes | Cook time: 6 to 10 minutes | Serves 2

1 tablespoon oil
¼ red onion, sliced
½ green bell pepper, sliced
2 skinless, boneless chicken breasts
½ cup water
2 canned chipotle chiles in adobo sauce, seeded and minced
Kosher salt
¼ red onion, sliced
¼ cup sour cream
3 tablespoons mayonnaise
½ tablespoon freshly squeezed lime juice
Freshly ground black pepper

1. Preheat the pressure cooker on Sauté mode. When the display reads hot, add the oil. Add the onion and bell pepper and sauté for 3 to 4 minutes, or until softened. Transfer to a bowl and set aside to cool. 2. Put the chicken, water, and a few teaspoons of the adobo sauce (to taste) in the pot and season with salt. Secure the lid and cook on the Poultry setting for 6 minutes. (If using frozen chicken, cook on the Poultry setting for 10 minutes.) 3. Allow the cooker to release naturally for 5 minutes, then do a quick release. Transfer the chicken to a cutting board and let rest for 5 to 10 minutes. Cut the chicken into cubes. 4. In a medium bowl, combine the chicken, cooked onion and bell pepper, sour cream, mayonnaise, chipotle chiles, and lime juice. Season with salt and pepper and stir to evenly combine. 5. Serve the fajita filling in Bibb or romaine lettuce leaves, sprinkled with queso fresco and cilantro.

Curried Chicken Couscous Casserole

Prep time: 15 minutes | Cook time: 17 minutes | Serves 4 to 6

2 tablespoons butter or ghee
1 medium yellow onion, chopped
1½ pounds (680 g) boneless skinless chicken breasts, cut into 1-inch chunks
2 teaspoons yellow curry powder
½ teaspoon ground cinnamon
½ teaspoon ground cumin
½ teaspoon table salt
¼ teaspoon ground cloves
1 quart chicken broth
½ cup raisins
¼ cup shelled unsalted pistachios
2⅔ cups quick-cooking or instant couscous

1. Press the Sauté button, and set on Medium or Normal for 10 minutes. 2. Melt the butter or ghee in a 6- or 8-quart cooker. Add the onion and cook, stirring often, until softened, about 4 minutes. Add the chicken and cook, stirring frequently, just until it loses its raw, pink color, about 2 minutes. 3. Stir in the curry powder, cinnamon, cumin, salt, and cloves to coat the chicken. Pour in the broth and scrape up any browned bits on the pot's bottom. Turn off the Sauté function, then stir in the raisins and pistachios. Secure the lid with the steam vent in the sealed position. 4. Select Pressure Cook or Manual, and set on High for 7 minutes with the Keep Warm setting off. 5. Use the quick-release method to bring the pressure back to normal. Unlatch the lid and open the pot. Stir in the couscous until uniform. Remove the insert from the pot and set the lid askew over the insert for 10 minutes so that the couscous can absorb the liquid and get tender. Stir again before serving.

One-Pot Turkey Bolognese with "Spaghetti"

Prep time: 5 minutes | Cook time: 23 minutes | Serves 4

1 tablespoon extra-virgin olive oil
1 yellow onion, chopped
2 cloves garlic, minced
1 pound (454 g) ground turkey
Fine sea salt
1 (28-ounce / 794-g) can diced tomatoes
2 celery stalks, diced
2 carrots, diced
1 tablespoon aged balsamic vinegar
1 teaspoon pure maple syrup
½ teaspoon dried oregano
1 teaspoon dried basil
1 (3-pound / 1.4-kg) spaghetti squash
¼ cup full-fat coconut milk (optional)
Freshly ground black pepper
Fresh basil, for garnish (optional)

1. Press Sauté and add the olive oil, onion, garlic, turkey, and 1 teaspoon salt to the Instant Pot. Sauté until the turkey is browned and cooked through, breaking it up with a wooden spoon as you stir, about 8 minutes. While the meat is cooking, pour the diced tomatoes with their juices into a blender and blend until smooth. Set aside until the meat is browned. 2. Press Cancel to stop the cooking cycle. Add the blended tomatoes, the celery, carrots, vinegar, maple syrup, oregano, basil, and ½ teaspoon salt and stir well. 3. Wash the spaghetti squash and carefully pierce the skin once with a sharp knife to vent. Place the whole squash directly into the sauce, pierced side up. Secure the lid and move the steam release valve to Sealing. Select Manual or Pressure Cook to cook on High pressure for 15 minutes. 4. When the cooking cycle is complete, let the pressure naturally release for 10 minutes, then move the steam release valve to Venting to release any remaining pressure. When the floating valve drops, remove the lid. Use oven mitts to lift the spaghetti squash out of the pot. Transfer it to a cutting board to cool slightly. Stir the coconut milk into the sauce and season with salt and pepper, to taste. 5. Cut the cooked squash in half crosswise and use a spoon to remove the seeds from the center. Use a fork to scrape out "noodles" from the squash and place them on plates. Spoon the Bolognese sauce on top of the noodles and serve. Store leftovers in an airtight container in the fridge for 3 or 4 days.

Chicken-Bacon Stew

Prep time: 25 minutes | Cook time: 15 minutes | Serves 2

1 tablespoon oil
1 pound (454 g) skin-on, bone-in chicken thighs and/or drumsticks
Kosher salt
Freshly ground black pepper
5 to 6 slices thick-cut bacon, chopped into ½-inch pieces
1 small onion, diced
2 medium carrots, peeled and chopped
1 tablespoon tomato paste
½ teaspoon dried thyme
1 dried bay leaf
3 garlic cloves, chopped
¼ cup white wine (or stock)
1 cup chicken stock
1 large potato, cut into 1-inch cubes
2 teaspoons sherry vinegar

1. Preheat the pressure cooker on Sauté mode. When the display reads hot, add the oil. Pat the chicken pieces dry with paper towels and season with salt and pepper. 2. In the pot, brown the chicken on all sides, 4 minutes per side. Transfer to a plate and set aside. 3. Add the bacon and cook until it begins to crisp, 2 to 3 minutes. Add the onion, carrots, tomato paste, thyme, and bay leaf and sauté until softened, 3 to 4 minutes. Add the garlic and cook, stirring, for 1 minute. 4. Pour in the wine and deglaze the pot, scraping up the browned bits from the bottom and stirring them into the liquid. Cook for 2 minutes, or until the wine is reduced by half. 5. Add the stock and potato and stir well. Return the browned chicken to the pot. 6. Secure the lid and cook on High pressure for 15 minutes, then allow the pressure to naturally release for about 10 minutes. Open the vent at the top and remove the lid. 7. Remove the bay leaf and discard, then carefully transfer the chicken to a bowl. Remove and discard the skin and bones and shred the meat. 8. Return the chicken meat to the pot to reheat and stir well. Stir in the sherry vinegar. Taste and season with more salt and pepper as needed.

Southern-Style Braised Bone-in Chicken Thighs

Prep time: 20 minutes | Cook time: 51 minutes | Serves 4

4 ounces (113 g) thin strips of bacon, chopped
4 (10- to 12-ounce / 283- to 340-g) bone-in skinless chicken thighs
1 medium yellow onion, chopped
1 medium green bell pepper, stemmed, cored, and chopped
1 medium red bell pepper, stemmed, cored, and chopped
1 teaspoon Dijon mustard
½ teaspoon dried thyme
½ teaspoon caraway seeds
½ teaspoon celery seeds
½ teaspoon table salt
½ teaspoon ground black pepper
½ cup dry white wine or unsweetened apple cider
½ cup chicken broth
3 medium sweet potatoes, peeled and quartered lengthwise into wedges

1. Press the Sauté button, and set on Medium or Normal for 25 minutes. 2. Cook the bacon in a 6-quart cooker until crisp, stirring occasionally, about 4 minutes. Use a slotted spoon to transfer the bacon pieces to a nearby bowl. Add two of the thighs and brown well on both sides, turning a couple of times, about 6 minutes. Transfer these thighs to a bowl, add the other two, and brown them in the same way before transferring them to that bowl. 3. Add the onion and both bell peppers. Cook, stirring occasionally, until softened, about 4 minutes. Stir in the mustard, thyme, caraway seeds, celery seeds, salt, and pepper until aromatic, just a few seconds. Pour in the wine and scrape up any browned bits on the pot's bottom. 4. Turn off the Sauté function. Pour in the broth and stir well. Return the chicken thighs and any juices in their bowl to the pot. Scatter the sweet potatoes pieces on top of everything. Lock the lid onto the cooker. 5. Select Meat/Stew, Pressure Cook or Manual, and cook on high for 16 minutes with the Keep Warm setting off. 6. When the machine has finished cooking, when the pot has finished cooking, use the quick-release method to bring its pressure back to normal. 7. Unlatch the lid and open the cooker. Use kitchen tongs to transfer the thighs and sweet potato pieces to serving plates or a serving platter. Use a flatware tablespoon to skim any excess surface fat from the sauce. 8. Press the Sauté button, and set on High or More for 10 minutes. 9. Bring the sauce to a boil and cook, stirring quite often, until reduced to about half its volume, 2 to 4 minutes. Turn off the Sauté function. Spoon this sauce over the chicken and sweet potatoes before serving.

Shredded Chicken with Marinara

Prep time: 2 minutes | Cook time: 25 minutes | Serves 4 to 6

4 pounds (1.8 kg) chicken breasts
½ cup chicken broth
½ teaspoon black pepper
1 teaspoon salt
2 cups marinara sauce

1. Add the chicken breasts, broth, pepper, and salt to the Instant Pot, stir well. 2. Close and lock the lid. Select Manual and cook at High pressure for 20 minutes. 3. Once pressure cooking is complete, use a quick release. Unlock and carefully open the lid. 4. Shred the chicken in the pot. 5. Select the Sauté setting. Add the marinara sauce and simmer for 5 minutes. 6. Serve with cooked rice, potato, peas or green salad.

Caprese Chicken Bowl

Prep time: 10 minutes | Cook time: 5 minutes | Serves 4

1½ pounds (680 g) boneless, skinless chicken breasts, cut into 1-inch cubes
1 (28-ounce / 794-g) can diced tomatoes, including juice
1 (8-ounce / 227-g) ball fresh mozzarella, cubed
1 tablespoon olive oil
½ teaspoon salt
½ teaspoon ground black pepper
½ cup julienned fresh basil leaves

1. Add chicken and tomatoes with juice to the Instant Pot. Lock lid. 2. Press the Manual or Pressure Cook button and adjust cook time to 5 minutes. When timer beeps, let pressure release naturally for 10 minutes. Quick-release any additional pressure until float valve drops and then unlock lid. Check chicken using a meat thermometer to ensure the internal temperature is at least 165ºF (74ºC). 3. Using a slotted spoon, transfer chicken and tomatoes to four bowls. Garnish chicken with mozzarella cubes. Drizzle with olive oil. Season with salt, pepper, and basil, and serve.

Pulled Chicken with Chipotle Chilies

Prep time: 15 minutes | Cook time: 25 minutes | Serves 4

3 or 4 chipotle chilies in adobo sauce, minced, plus 2 tablespoons adobo sauce
Kosher salt and ground black pepper
2½ pounds (1.1 kg) boneless, skinless chicken thighs, patted dry and halved crosswise
1 tablespoon extra-virgin olive oil
1 large white onion, halved and thinly sliced
6 medium garlic cloves, finely chopped
1 tablespoon ground cumin
2 (6-inch) corn tortillas, torn into rough 2-inch pieces
1 (28-ounce / 794-g) can crushed tomatoes
½ cup finely chopped fresh cilantro

1. In a large bowl, combine the adobo sauce and 1 teaspoon salt, then add the chicken and stir to coat. On a 6-quart Instant Pot, select More/High Sauté. Add the oil and heat until shimmering. Add the onion and cook, stirring occasionally, until softened, about 5 minutes. 2. Stir in the garlic, cumin and chipotle chilies, then cook, stirring, until fragrant, about 1 minute. Add ½ cup water, scraping up any browned bits. Add the chicken, stir to combine, then distribute in an even layer. 3. Scatter the tortilla pieces evenly over the chicken. Pour the tomatoes over the top but do not stir. Fast: 4. Press Cancel, lock the lid in place and move the pressure valve to Sealing. Select Pressure Cook or Manual; make sure the pressure level is set to High. Set the cooking time for 8 minutes. When pressure cooking is complete, allow the pressure to reduce naturally for 15 minutes, then release the remaining steam by moving the pressure valve to Venting. Press Cancel, then carefully open the pot. Slow: With the pot still on More/High Sauté, bring the mixture to a boil. Press Cancel, lock the lid in place and move the pressure valve to Venting. Select Slow Cook and set the temperature to Less/Low. Set the cooking time for 4 to 5 hours; the chicken is done when a skewer inserted into the largest piece meets no resistance. Press Cancel, then carefully open the pot. 5. Using a slotted spoon, transfer the chicken to a large bowl and let cool for about 5 minutes. Using two forks, shred the meat. Select More/High Sauté and bring the sauce to a simmer. Cook, stirring often and scraping the bottom of the pot, until slightly thickened, 5 to 8 minutes. 6. Press Cancel to turn off the pot. Return the chicken to the pot, add the cilantro and stir to combine. Taste and season with salt and pepper.

Sweet and Tangy Thai Bash Orange Chicken

Prep time: 10 minutes | Cook time: 19 minutes | Serves 4

2 tablespoons grass-fed butter, ghee or avocado oil
1 large shallot, thinly sliced
5 cloves garlic, finely chopped
1 (1-inch) chunk fresh ginger, peeled and finely minced or grated
¾ teaspoon sea salt
¼ teaspoon red pepper flakes (optional)
¼ cup honey
¾ cup freshly squeezed orange juice
¼ cup cider vinegar
2 tablespoons coconut aminos
2 teaspoons Asian fish sauce
2 pounds (907 g) boneless, skinless chicken breast
1 cup fresh Thai basil leaves, plus more for garnish
¼ cup finely chopped fresh mint

1. Place your healthy fat of choice in the Instant Pot and press Sauté. Once the fat has melted, add the shallot and sauté, stirring occasionally, for 3 minutes, or until fragrant. Add the garlic and ginger and sauté for 2 minutes, stirring occasionally. Press Keep Warm/Cancel. 2. Add the salt, red pepper flakes (if using), honey, orange juice, vinegar, coconut aminos, fish sauce and chicken and give the mixture a stir, making sure the chicken is submerged in the liquid. 3. Secure the lid with the steam vent in the sealed position. Press Manual and set on High Pressure for 9 minutes. 4. Once the timer sounds, press Keep Warm/Cancel. Using an oven mitt, do a quick release. When the steam venting stops and the silver dial drops, carefully open the lid. 5. With tongs or a large slotted spoon, transfer the chicken to a plate or cutting board. Cut the chicken into bite-size chunks, then set aside. 6. Press Sauté and allow the liquid to come to a simmer, then simmer for about 5 minutes, or until the liquid slightly thickens. Press Keep Warm/Cancel. Add the shredded chicken, Thai basil and mint, stir a few times until the fresh herbs have wilted into the sauce, then allow the mixture to rest for 10 minutes. 7. Serve immediately garnished with fresh Thai basil leaves.

Smothered Chicken with Mushrooms

Prep time: 15 minutes | Cook time: 32 minutes | Serves 4

¼ cup all-purpose flour
4 bone-in, skinless chicken thighs or breasts
1 teaspoon fine sea salt
1 teaspoon ground black pepper
4 tablespoons olive oil, divided
2 bacon slices, cut into 1-inch pieces (optional)
8 ounces (227 g) mushrooms, sliced
1 small onion, chopped
2 garlic cloves, minced
1 cup low-sodium chicken broth
1 cup tomato sauce
1 (10-ounce / 283-g) can condensed cream of mushroom soup

1. Put the flour in a wide, shallow bowl. Season the chicken with the salt and pepper. Use 2 tablespoons of oil to coat each piece of chicken, then roll it in the flour to coat. 2. Select Sauté and adjust the heat to Medium. Add the remaining 2 tablespoons of oil to the pot. When the oil is hot, add the chicken and cook until browned, about 3 minutes on each side. 3. Add the bacon (if using), mushrooms, onion, and garlic and sauté for 5 minutes. Add the broth and stir to loosen any ingredients that may have stuck to the bottom of the pot. Add the tomato sauce and cook, stirring, for 1 minute. 4. Lock the lid into place and turn the valve to Sealing. Select Manual or Pressure Cook and adjust the pressure to High. Set the time for 20 minutes. When cooking ends, let the pressure release naturally for 5 minutes, then turn the valve to Venting to quick release the remaining pressure. 5. Unlock and remove the lid and stir in the cream of mushroom soup until heated through.

Greek Chicken

Prep time: 20 minutes | Cook time: 12 minutes | Serves 5 to 6

½ teaspoon salt, plus more for serving
¼ teaspoon freshly ground black pepper or lemon pepper, plus more for serving
2 pounds (907 g) boneless, skinless chicken thighs
2 tablespoons olive or avocado oil
3 cloves garlic, crushed
1 (8-ounce / 227-g) jar marinated artichoke hearts, drained
1 (12-ounce / 340-g) jar marinated roasted red peppers, drained and diced
1 cup Kalamata olives
½ medium red onion, sliced
⅔ cup chicken stock
¼ cup red wine vinegar
Juice of ½ lemon
1 teaspoon dried oregano
1 teaspoon dried thyme
1 to 2 tablespoons arrowroot starch
Cooked potatoes, rice or cauliflower rice (optional)
3 tablespoons chopped fresh basil, for garnish
½ cup crumbled feta (optional)

1. Select Sauté on the Instant Pot. While the pot is heating, sprinkle the salt and black pepper on each side of the chicken thighs. Add the oil to the hot pot, then the garlic. Cook for 1 minute, then add the chicken. Sear the chicken on each side for about 2 minutes (no need to cook all the way through). 2. Arrange the artichoke hearts, roasted red peppers and olives around the chicken, filling in the gaps on the bottom of the Instant Pot (if there are any). It's okay to let some of those veggies sit on top of the chicken. Top with the sliced red onion. 3. In a bowl, stir together the chicken stock, vinegar, lemon juice, oregano and thyme. Pour on top of the chicken mixture. 4. Secure the lid with the steam vent in the sealed position. Select Manual or Pressure Cook. Use the plus and minus buttons to adjust the time until the display reads 7 minutes. 5. Use a quick release. Remove the lid. 6. Spoon out some of the pan juices into a small bowl once the cooking is complete. Whisk the arrowroot starch into the juices and pour back into the Instant Pot. 7. Allow the sauce to thicken for a few minutes before serving. 8. Serve over cooked potatoes, rice or cauliflower rice (if using). Garnish with the basil and sprinkle with additional salt, black pepper and feta (if using).

Chicken Nachos

Prep time: 2 minutes | Cook time: 15 minutes | Serves 6

2 pounds (907 g) boneless, skinless chicken thighs
1 tablespoon olive oil
1 (1-ounce / 28-g) package taco seasoning mix
⅔ cup mild red salsa
⅓ cup mild Herdez salsa verde

1. Select the Sauté setting on the Instant Pot and heat the oil. 2. Add the chicken thighs and brown the meat nicely for a few minutes on each side. 3. In a medium bowl, combine the taco seasoning and salsa. 4. Pour the mixture in the pot and stir well. Close and lock the lid. 5. Press the Cancel button to reset the cooking program, then select the Manual setting and set the cooking time for 15 minutes at High pressure. 6. Once cooking is complete, use a natural release for 10 minutes, then release any remaining pressure manually. Uncover the pot. 7. Shred the meat. Serve with tortilla chips.

Forgotten Jambalaya

Prep time: 35 minutes | Cook time: 15 minutes | Serves 11

1 (14½-ounce / 411-g) can diced tomatoes, undrained
1 (14½-ounce / 411-g) can beef broth or chicken broth
1 (6-ounce / 170-g) can tomato paste
3 celery ribs, chopped
2 medium green peppers, chopped
1 medium onion, chopped
5 garlic cloves, minced
3 teaspoons dried parsley flakes
2 teaspoons dried basil
1½ teaspoons dried oregano
1¼ teaspoons salt
½ teaspoon cayenne pepper
½ teaspoon hot pepper sauce
1 pound (454 g) boneless skinless chicken breasts, cut into 1-inch cubes
1 pound (454 g) smoked sausage, halved and cut into ¼-inch slices
½ pound (227 g) uncooked shrimp (41 to 50 per pound), peeled and deveined
Hot cooked rice

1. In a 6-quart electric pressure cooker, combine tomatoes, broth and tomato paste. Stir in the celery, green peppers, onion, garlic and seasonings. Stir in chicken and sausage. 2. Lock lid; make sure vent is closed. Select Manual setting; adjust pressure to High and set time for 8 minutes. When finished cooking, quick release pressure according to manufacturer's instructions. 3. Select Sauté setting and adjust for high heat. Stir in the shrimp. Cook 5 minutes longer or until shrimp turn pink. Serve with rice.

Spicy Sichuan Steamed Chicken

Prep time: 15 minutes | Cook time: 15 minutes | Serves 4

¼ cup chili oil
1 (1-inch) piece fresh ginger, peeled and thinly sliced
1 bunch cilantro, stems minced, leaves chopped, reserved separately
2 teaspoons Sichuan peppercorns
3 tablespoons soy sauce
2 tablespoons unseasoned rice vinegar
2 teaspoons white sugar
3 bone-in, skin-on chicken breasts, skin removed and discarded
1 tablespoon cornstarch
¼ cup roasted peanuts, chopped

1. On a 6-quart Instant Pot, select Normal/Medium Sauté. Add the chili oil, ginger, cilantro stems and Sichuan peppercorns. Cook, stirring, until sizzling and fragrant, 2 to 3 minutes. 2. Press Cancel and let the mixture cool until the sizzling stops, about 5 minutes. Whisk in the soy sauce, vinegar, sugar and ¼ cup water. Place the chicken breasts flesh side down in the liquid. 3. Lock the lid in place and move the pressure valve to Sealing. Select Pressure Cook or Manual; adjust the pressure level to Low. Set the cooking time for 8 minutes. 4. When pressure cooking is complete, allow the pressure to reduce naturally, then release any remaining steam by moving the pressure valve to Venting. Press Cancel, then carefully open the pot. 5. Transfer the chicken to a deep serving platter. Set a fine mesh strainer over a medium bowl. Using potholders, carefully remove the insert from the housing and pour the cooking liquid through the strainer; return the insert to the housing. 6. Press on the solids in the strainer to remove as much liquid as possible; discard the solids. Add the cornstarch to the strained liquid and whisk to combine. Return the liquid to the insert and add the peanuts, then select Normal/Medium Sauté. Bring to a simmer, stirring constantly, until lightly thickened, 2 to 3 minutes. 7. Press Cancel to turn off the pot. Carve the chicken off the bones, slicing the breasts crosswise into ¼-inch slices, and return to the platter. Sprinkle with the cilantro leaves, then pour the sauce over. Let stand for about 10 minutes before serving.

Carolina-Style Vinegar BBQ Chicken

Prep time: 5 minutes | Cook time: 5 minutes | Serves 6

2 cups water
1 cup white vinegar
¼ cup sugar
1 tablespoon reduced-sodium chicken base
1 teaspoon crushed red pepper flakes
¾ teaspoon salt
1½ pounds (680 g) boneless skinless chicken breasts
6 whole wheat hamburger buns, split, optional

1. In a 6-quart electric pressure cooker, mix the first six ingredients; add chicken. Lock lid; make sure vent is closed. Select Manual setting; adjust pressure to High and set time for 5 minutes. 2. When finished cooking, allow pressure to naturally release for 8 minutes, then quick-release any remaining pressure according to manufacturer's directions. 3. Remove chicken; cool slightly. Reserve 1 cup of cooking juices; discard remaining juices. Shred chicken with two forks. Combine with reserved juices. If desired, serve chicken mixture on buns.

French Cider and Mustard-Braised Chicken

Prep time: 15 minutes | Cook time: 35 minutes | Serves 4

2 slices thick-cut bacon, chopped
8 bone-in chicken thighs, skin removed and fat trimmed
Salt and freshly ground black pepper
4 cups quartered cremini mushrooms (8 ounces / 227 g)
2 large shallots, thinly sliced (¾ cup)
1½ cups bottled hard apple cider (12 ounces / 340 g)
2 tablespoons grainy mustard

1. Select Sauté and adjust to Normal/Medium heat. Add the bacon and cook, stirring occasionally, until the bacon is browned, 3 to 4 minutes. Transfer to a bowl with a slotted spoon; leave the drippings in the pot. Season the chicken all over with salt and pepper. Add half the chicken to the pot and cook until browned on one side, 3 minutes. Transfer to a plate. (This step adds flavor to the sauce. Do not brown the other chicken.) 2. Add the mushrooms and shallots to the pot and sauté until the shallots are tender, 3 minutes. Add the cider and mustard and bring to a simmer, scraping up any browned bits on the bottom of the pot. Press Cancel. 3. Add all the chicken, any accumulated juices, and the bacon to the pot. Lock on the lid, select the Pressure Cook function, and adjust to High pressure for 20 minutes. Make sure the steam valve is in the Sealing position. 4. When the cooking time is up, quick-release the pressure. Remove the lid and transfer the chicken and vegetables to a serving dish with a slotted spoon. Cover with foil and set aside. 5. Select Sauté, adjust to More/High heat, and bring to a simmer. Using a ladle, skim any liquid fat that pools on top of the sauce and discard. Cook until the sauce is reduced by half, 5 minutes. Press Cancel. Pour the sauce over the chicken and serve.

Italian Duck

Prep time: 10 minutes | Cook time: 15 minutes | Serves 4

2 pounds (907 g) duck breasts, halved
2 tablespoons olive oil
½ tablespoon Italian seasoning
½ teaspoon ground black pepper
¼ teaspoon salt
2 cloves garlic, minced
½ cup chicken stock
¾ cup heavy cream
½ cup sun-dried tomatoes, chopped
1 cup spinach, chopped
½ cup Parmesan cheese, grated

1. In a bowl, combine the oil, Italian seasoning, pepper, salt, and garlic. Stir well. 2. Rub all sides of the duck breasts with the spice mix. 3. Preheat the Instant Pot by selecting Sauté. 4. Add the duck to the pot. Cook on both sides until the breasts have turned golden brown. 5. Press the Cancel button to reset the cooking program. 6. Add the chicken stock. Close and lock the lid. 7. Select the Manual setting and set the cooking time for 4 minutes at High pressure. 8. Once pressure cooking is complete, use a quick release. Unlock and carefully open the lid. 9. Add the heavy cream, tomatoes, spinach, and cheese, stir. 10. Close and lock the lid. Select Manual and cook at High pressure for 5 minutes. 11. When the timer beeps, use a quick release. Carefully unlock the lid. 12. Serve.

DIY Turkey Lunchmeat

Prep time: 10 minutes | Cook time: 20 minutes | Serves 6

- 1 tablespoon smoked paprika
- 1 teaspoon coarse salt
- 1 teaspoon freshly ground black pepper
- 3 pounds (1.4 kg) turkey breast
- 1 cup water or chicken stock

1. In a small bowl, mix together the paprika, salt and pepper and rub the mixture all over the outside of the turkey breast. 2. Pour the water or chicken stock into the Instant Pot and insert the steam trivet. Place the turkey breast on the trivet. 3. Secure the lid with the steam vent in the sealed position. Press Manual and immediately adjust the timer to 20 minutes. Check that the display light is beneath high pressure. 4. When the timer sounds, quick release the pressure and carefully remove the lid. Remove the turkey breast and place on a carving board. Once cooled enough to handle, thinly slice the turkey and place in an airtight container or resealable plastic bag and store in the refrigerator.

Faux-Tisserie Roasted Chicken Dinner

Prep time: 15 minutes | Cook time: 40 minutes | Serves 4 to 6

- 1 (4-pound / 1.8-kg) whole roasting chicken, neck and giblets in cavity removed and reserved
- 1 pound (454 g) red potatoes, cut into 1¼-inch chunks
- 2 large carrots, peeled and cut into 1-inch pieces
- 2 tablespoons olive oil
- 4 teaspoons lemon pepper seasoning (not salt-free)
- Optional Gravy:
- 1½ tablespoons all-purpose flour
- 1½ tablespoons butter, at room temperature
- Salt and freshly ground black pepper

1. Place a trivet with handles in the pot and add 1 cup water. Place the neck and giblets, if you have them, in the water. Toss the vegetables with 1 tablespoon of the oil and 1 teaspoon of the lemon pepper seasoning. Stuff about half the potatoes and carrots into the chicken cavity; do not pack them in or they will not cook evenly. Tuck the wings behind the chicken's back and tie the drumsticks together with butcher's twine. Season the outside of the chicken with the remaining lemon pepper seasoning. 2. Place the chicken breast-side up on the trivet. Place the remaining carrots and potatoes around the chicken. Drizzle with the remaining 1 tablespoon oil. Lock on the lid, select the Pressure Cook function, and adjust to High pressure for 28 minutes. Make sure the steam valve is in the Sealing position and that the Keep Warm button is off. 3. When the cooking time is up, quick-release the pressure. An instant-read thermometer should read 160ºF (71ºC) when inserted into the breast. If the chicken is not done, cover with a regular pot lid, select Sauté, and adjust to Normal/Medium for 5 minutes. Press Cancel. 4. For crispy skin, preheat the broiler and adjust the oven rack so that it is 8 inches below the broiler element. Transfer the chicken on the trivet to a foil-lined baking sheet. Place the loose vegetables in a serving bowl and cover with foil. Broil the chicken, rotating the pan once, until the skin on top is browned, about 6 minutes. Carve the chicken and serve with the vegetables and a little of the cooking liquid. 5. If you'd like to make gravy, with the cooking liquid still in the pot, select Sauté and adjust to More/High heat. Liquid fat will pool around the edges of the pot as the liquid comes to a simmer. Use a ladle to skim off the fat; discard. In a small bowl, stir the butter and flour together until smooth. Whisk the flour mixture into the cooking liquid and simmer until thickened, 2 minutes. Press Cancel. Serve with the chicken.

Sweet and Sour Chicken

Prep time: 10 minutes | Cook time: 7 minutes | Serves 6

- 1 cup apple cider vinegar
- 1 cup granulated sugar
- ½ cup ketchup
- 2 tablespoons soy sauce
- 1½ teaspoons garlic powder
- 1 teaspoon salt
- 1 cup cornstarch
- 2 pounds (907 g) boneless, skinless chicken breasts, cut into 1-inch chunks
- ½ teaspoon salt
- ¼ teaspoon black pepper
- ¼ cup vegetable oil
- 3 large eggs, beaten

1. In a small bowl, whisk together vinegar, sugar, ketchup, soy sauce, garlic powder, and salt. Set aside. 2. Pour cornstarch into a gallon-sized zip-top bag. 3. Season chicken with salt and pepper and place inside the bag of cornstarch. Close bag and shake until chicken is coated evenly. 4. Press Sauté button on Instant Pot. Pour in oil and let heat 1 minute. 5. Working in batches, remove chicken pieces from bag and dip into beaten eggs. 6. Shake to remove any excess egg, then layer chicken evenly in hot oil on the bottom of pot. Let cook, unmoved, for 30 seconds. 7. Flip and cook another 30 seconds. 8. Remove from pot and continue with remaining chicken. 9. Once chicken is cooked and removed from Instant Pot, pour sauce into pot and deglaze the pot. 10. Add chicken and turn to coat with sauce. 11. Close lid and set pressure release to Sealing. 12. Press Manual or Pressure Cook button and adjust time to 3 minutes. 13. When the timer beeps, allow pressure to release naturally and then unlock lid and remove it. Serve warm.

Persian Chicken

Prep time: 10 minutes | Cook time: 7 minutes | Serves 6

- 1 tablespoon honey
- 1 tablespoon olive oil
- 1 teaspoon lime zest
- 3 cloves garlic, peeled and quartered
- 1 teaspoon turmeric
- 1 teaspoon ground cinnamon
- ½ teaspoon ground cumin
- ⅛ teaspoon ground nutmeg
- ⅛ teaspoon allspice
- ½ teaspoon salt
- ¼ teaspoon ground black pepper
- 3 pounds (1.4 kg) boneless, skinless chicken thighs
- 1 cup water
- 1 lime, quartered

1. In a medium bowl, combine honey, olive oil, lime zest, garlic, turmeric, cinnamon, cumin, nutmeg, allspice, salt, and pepper. Add chicken thighs and toss. Refrigerate covered at least 1 hour or up to overnight. 2. Add water to the Instant Pot and insert steamer basket. Arrange thighs evenly in steamer basket. Lock lid. 3. Press the Manual or Pressure Cook button and adjust cook time to 7 minutes. When timer beeps, quick-release pressure until float valve drops and then unlock lid. Check chicken using a meat thermometer to ensure the internal temperature is at least 165ºF (74ºC). 4. Transfer chicken thighs to serving dish and garnish with lime. Serve warm.

Lemon Mustard Chicken with Potatoes

Prep time: 10 minutes | Cook time: 18 minutes | Serves 6 to 8

2 pounds (907 g) chicken thighs
2 tablespoons olive oil
3 pounds (1.4 kg) red potatoes, peeled and quartered
2 tablespoons Italian seasoning
3 tablespoons Dijon mustard
¾ cup chicken broth
¼ cup lemon juice
1 teaspoon salt
1 teaspoon ground black pepper

1. Select the Sauté setting on the Instant Pot and heat the oil. 2. Add the chicken thighs to the pot and sauté for 2 to 3 minutes, until starting to brown. 3. Add the potatoes, Italian seasoning, and Dijon mustard. Cook, stir occasionally, for 2 minutes. 4. Pour the broth and lemon juice into the pot, stir. 5. Season with salt and pepper. Close and lock the lid. 6. Press the Cancel button to reset the cooking program. Select the Poultry setting and set the cooking time for 15 minutes. 7. When the timer beeps, let the pressure release naturally for 10 minutes, then release any remaining steam manually. Carefully unlock the lid. 8. Serve.

Buffalo Chicken

Prep time: 10 minutes | Cook time: 15 minutes | Serves 4

¾ cup mild hot sauce
3 tablespoons butter, melted
1 tablespoon Worcestershire sauce
½ tablespoon red wine vinegar
½ teaspoon cornstarch
1 pound (454 g) boneless, skinless chicken breasts

1. In the Instant Pot, whisk together hot sauce, butter, Worcestershire, vinegar, and cornstarch. 2. Place chicken in Instant Pot and turn to coat in sauce. 3. Close lid and set pressure release to Sealing. 4. Press Manual or Pressure Cook button and adjust time to 15 minutes. 5. When the timer beeps, allow pressure to release naturally and then unlock lid and remove it. 6. Serve.

Thai Green Curry Chicken and Cauliflower

Prep time: 5 minutes | Cook time: 25 minutes | Serves 2

½ tablespoon oil
3 shallots, thinly sliced
1 large garlic clove, crushed
1 (¼-inch) piece peeled fresh ginger, minced
1 cup coconut milk, solids and liquid separated
2 tablespoons green curry paste
2 skinless, boneless chicken breasts, cut into strips
1 teaspoon kosher salt
3 red chiles, stemmed, seeded, and cut into strips
½ cup chicken stock or water
1 tablespoon fish sauce
1 tablespoon soy sauce, plus more for seasoning (optional)
½ tablespoon packed brown sugar, plus more for seasoning (optional)
Juice of ½ lime
2 cups cauliflower florets

1. Preheat the pressure cooker on Sauté mode. When the display reads hot, add the oil in the pot until shimmering. Stir in the shallots, garlic, and ginger and cook until the shallots start to soften, 2 to 3 minutes. 2. Stir in the coconut milk solids and curry paste. Cook for 3 to 4 minutes, stirring often, until the curry paste darkens. Add the coconut milk liquid. Stir well. 3. Season the chicken with the salt, add to the pot, and stir to coat with the curry paste. Stir in the red chiles, stock, fish sauce, 1 tablespoon of soy sauce, and ½ tablespoon of brown sugar. 4. Secure the lid and cook on High pressure for 10 minutes, then quick release the pressure in the pot and remove the lid. 5. Select Sauté mode. Stir in the lime juice and cauliflower, then simmer for 5 to 6 minutes to let the cauliflower soften and absorb the flavors. 6. Taste the curry for seasoning, adding more soy sauce or brown sugar as desired. 7. Ladle the curry into bowls over cooked rice and garnish with cilantro and basil. Serve with lime wedges and roti.

Senegalese Braised Chicken with Onions and Lime

Prep time: 10 minutes | Cook time: 35 minutes | Serves 4

2 tablespoons grated lime zest, plus ¼ cup lime juice
1 habanero chili, stemmed, seeded and minced
3 tablespoons grapeseed or other neutral oil, divided
Kosher salt and ground black pepper
2 medium yellow onions, halved and thinly sliced
3 pounds (1.4 kg) bone-in, skin on chicken thighs, skin removed and discarded
1 tablespoon cornstarch
Chopped fresh chives, to serve

1. In a small bowl, mix together the lime zest, habanero, 1 tablespoon oil, 1 tablespoon salt and 1 teaspoon pepper. Measure out 1 tablespoon of the mixture into another small bowl and set aside. 2. On a 6-quart Instant Pot, select Medium/Normal Sauté. Heat the remaining 2 tablespoons oil until shimmering. Add the onions and cook without stirring until golden brown on the bottom, about 7 minutes. 3. Stir and continue to cook, stirring only occasionally, until the onions are evenly golden brown, another 7 to 10 minutes. Press Cancel. Add the lime juice, 2 tablespoons water and remaining zest-habanero mixture, scraping up any browned bits. 4. Nestle the chicken in an even layer, skin side down, slightly overlapping the pieces if needed. Fast: 5. Lock the lid in place and move the pressure release valve to Sealing. Select Pressure Cook or Manual; make sure the pressure level is set to High. Set the cooking time for 10 minutes. When pressure cooking is complete, allow the pressure to release naturally for 15 minutes, then release any remaining steam by moving the pressure valve to Venting. Press Cancel, then carefully open the pot. Slow: Select More/High Sauté and bring the mixture to a boil. Press Cancel, lock the lid in place and move the pressure valve to Venting. Select Slow Cook and set the temperature to Less/Low. Set the cooking time for 4 to 5 hours; the chicken is done when a skewer inserted into the largest thigh meets no resistance. Press Cancel, then carefully open the pot. 6. Using tongs, transfer the chicken to a serving dish and tent with foil. In a small bowl, whisk together the cornstarch and ¼ cup of the cooking liquid until combined, then stir into the pot. 7. Select Normal/Medium Sauté and bring to a simmer, stirring constantly, then cook until lightly thickened, about 1 minute. Stir in the reserved zest-habanero mixture, then taste and season with salt and pepper. 8. Using potholders, carefully remove the insert from the housing and pour the sauce over the chicken, then sprinkle with chives.

Thai-Inspired Pulled Chicken Breasts

Prep time: 10 minutes | Cook time: 25 minutes | Serves 6

½ cup chicken broth
½ cup regular coconut milk
2 medium shallots, thinly sliced and separated into rings
4 medium garlic cloves, peeled and slivered
2 tablespoons thinly sliced thin lemongrass
2 tablespoons hot red pepper sauce
2 tablespoons light brown sugar
½ teaspoon ground dried turmeric
½ teaspoon table salt
2½ pounds (1.1 kg) boneless skinless chicken breasts

1. Mix the broth, coconut milk, shallots, garlic, lemongrass, pepper sauce, brown sugar, turmeric, and salt in a 6-quart cooker until the brown sugar dissolves. Set the chicken breasts into this sauce, turning the pieces to coat them on all sides. Secure the lid with the steam vent in the sealed position. 2. Select Meat/Stew, Pressure Cook or Manual, and set on High for 25 minutes with the Keep Warm setting off. 3. When the machine has finished cooking, turn it off and let the pressure return to normal naturally, about 15 minutes. 4. Unlatch the lid and open the pot. Use two forks to shred the chicken right in the pot. Stir well, then set the lid askew over the pot and set aside for 5 to 10 minutes to blend the flavors and allow the meat to absorb some of the sauce.

Korean Gochujang Chicken Legs

Prep time: 10 minutes | Cook time: 15 minutes | Serves 4

¼ cup gluten-free gochujang sauce
2 tablespoons rice vinegar
2 tablespoons honey
1 tablespoon tamari
2 cloves garlic, peeled and quartered
1 (1-inch) piece knob fresh ginger, scrubbed and sliced
2 pounds (907 g) chicken legs
1 cup water
2 tablespoons toasted sesame seeds
¼ cup chopped fresh cilantro

1. In a large bowl, combine gochujang, rice vinegar, honey, tamari, garlic, and ginger. Set aside ¼ cup of mixture. Add chicken legs to the bowl and toss. Cover and refrigerate at least 30 minutes or up to overnight. 2. Add water to the Instant Pot and insert steam rack. Press the Adjust button and change temperature to Less. Arrange chicken standing up, meaty side down, on the steam rack. Lock lid. 3. Press the Poultry button and cook for the default time of 15 minutes. When timer beeps, quick-release pressure until float valve drops and then unlock lid. Check chicken using a meat thermometer to ensure the internal temperature is at least 165°F (74°C). 4. Transfer chicken to a serving dish. Brush with reserved sauce and garnish with sesame seeds and cilantro. Serve warm.

Lemon and Ginger Pulled Turkey

Prep time: 10 minutes | Cook time: 25 minutes | Serves 6

1 tablespoon lemon pepper seasoning blend
2½ pounds (1.1 kg) boneless turkey tenderloins
⅔ cup chicken broth
¼ cup ginger jam
2 tablespoons fresh lemon juice
2 tablespoons red wine vinegar
2 tablespoons packed fresh oregano leaves, minced
½ teaspoon red pepper flakes

1. Pat and massage the lemon pepper seasoning into the turkey tenderloins or pieces. Mix the broth, jam, lemon juice, vinegar, oregano, and red pepper flakes in a 6-quart cooker until the jam dissolves into the sauce. Set the turkey into this sauce (without turning the meat over). Secure the lid with the steam vent in the sealed position. 2. Select Meat/Stew, Pressure Cook or Manual, and set on High for 25 minutes with the Keep Warm setting off. 3. When the machine has finished cooking, turn it off and let its pressure return to normal naturally, about 20 minutes. Unlatch the lid and open the pot. Shred the meat with two forks in the pot, then stir well to coat with sauce. Set the lid askew over the pot for 5 to 10 minutes to blend the flavors and allow the meat to continue to absorb the sauce.

Chicken alla Diavola

Prep time: 10 minutes | Cook time: 20 minutes | Serves 4

1 teaspoon sea salt
2 cloves garlic, minced
2 tablespoons apple cider vinegar
4 tablespoons olive oil, divided
1 teaspoon sriracha
1 teaspoon chili powder
¼ teaspoon cayenne pepper
1 pound (454 g) boneless, skinless chicken breast, cut into 1-inch cubes
2 cups water

1. In a medium bowl, whisk together salt, garlic, vinegar, 2 tablespoons oil, sriracha, chili powder, and cayenne pepper. Toss chicken into mixture and coat evenly. Cover and refrigerate for 1 hour. 2. Press the Sauté button on the Instant Pot. Heat remaining 2 tablespoons oil and add the chicken pieces. Stir-fry for about 4 minutes or until browned on all sides. Remove chicken and set aside. 3. Insert trivet into Instant Pot. Add water. Transfer chicken to a large square (about 10 × 10-inch) of aluminum foil. Set the foil onto the trivet. Lock lid. 4. Press the Poultry button and cook for the default time of 15 minutes. When timer beeps, let pressure release naturally for 10 minutes. Quick-release any additional pressure until float valve drops and then unlock lid. Check the chicken using a meat thermometer to ensure the internal temperature is at least 165°F (74°C). Serve warm.

Chicken Oreganata

Prep time: 5 minutes | Cook time: 25 minutes | Serves 4 to 6

2 pounds (907 g) boneless, skinless chicken breasts, sliced into ¼ inch thick
½ cup all-purpose flour
¼ cup extra-virgin olive oil
4 tablespoons (½ stick) salted butter, divided
2 large shallots, diced
3 cloves garlic, minced or pressed
½ cup dry white wine
Juice of 1 lemon
¾ cup garlic broth or chicken broth
2 teaspoons dried oregano, plus more for topping
½ teaspoon kosher salt
½ teaspoon black pepper
1 tablespoon cornstarch
1 (14-ounce / 397-g) can artichoke hearts, drained and quartered
¼ cup Italian or garlic-and-herb bread crumbs
¼ cup grated Parmesan cheese

1. Dredge the chicken on both sides in the flour mixture and set aside. 2. Pour the olive oil and 2 tablespoons of the butter in the Instant Pot and hit Sauté and Adjust so it's on the More or High setting, and heat about 3 minutes, until the butter's melted. 3. Working in batches, sear the chicken for 1 minute on each side until very lightly browned, remove the chicken with tongs, and set aside on a plate. Leave any excess oil in the pot for more flavor. 4. Add the remaining 2 tablespoons of butter and scrape up any browned bits from the bottom of the pot. Add the shallots and sauté for about 2 minutes, until beginning to brown, then add the garlic and sauté for 1 more minute. Add the wine and lemon juice and bring to a simmer. 5. Add the broth, oregano, kosher salt, and pepper and stir well, giving the bottom of the pot one last scrape for good measure. Return the chicken to the pot. 6. Secure the lid, move the valve to the sealing position, and hit Keep Warm/Cancel and then Manual or Pressure Cook on High Pressure for 5 minutes. Quick release when done and preheat the oven to broil. 7. Mix the cornstarch with 1 tablespoon water to form a slurry. Set aside. 8. When the pot is done cooking, remove the lid and transfer the chicken to a casserole dish. Hit Keep Warm/Cancel and then hit Sauté and Adjust so it's on the More or High setting. 9. Once the sauce bubbles, immediately add the cornstarch slurry and stir for 30 seconds, as the sauce thickens. Then hit Keep Warm/Cancel, and once the bubbles die down, the sauce will have thickened beautifully. Stir in the artichokes and then pour the sauce over the chicken in the casserole dish. 10. Once the broiler is heated, mix the bread crumbs and Parmesan, sprinkle evenly over the chicken and top with a few more shakes of oregano. Place the casserole dish on the top rack of the oven and broil for 2 to 3 minutes (keep an eye on it, as oven temperatures vary and we don't want the bread crumbs to burn). 11. Remove and serve immediately over rice or angel-hair pasta (cooked separately), if you wish. And of course, get some Italian or French bread to dip in that remarkable sauce.

Chapter 5 Fish and Seafood

Chapter 5 Fish and Seafood

Umami Calamari

Prep time: 15 minutes | Cook time: 20 minutes | Serves 4

1 tablespoon olive oil	basil, divided
1 small onion, peeled and diced	1 teaspoon sea salt
2 cloves garlic, minced	½ teaspoon ground black pepper
¼ cup dry red wine	2 teaspoons anchovy paste
1 (14½-ounce / 411-g) can diced tomatoes, including juice	1 bay leaf
1 cup chicken broth	1 pound (454 g) calamari tubes, cut into ¼-inch rings
¼ cup chopped fresh parsley	¼ cup grated Parmesan cheese
6 tablespoons chopped fresh	

1. Press the Sauté button on Instant Pot. Add olive oil and heat. Add onion and sauté for 3 to 5 minutes until onions are translucent. Add garlic and sauté for an additional minute. Add red wine, press Adjust button to change temperature to Less, and simmer unlidded for 5 minutes. 2. Add remaining ingredients except 2 tablespoons basil and Parmesan cheese. Lock lid. 3. Press the Manual button and adjust time to 10 minutes. When timer beeps, let pressure release naturally for 10 minutes. Quick-release any additional pressure until the float valve drops and then unlock lid. 4. Remove bay leaf. Use a slotted spoon to transfer pot ingredients to four bowls. Garnish each bowl with equal amounts Parmesan cheese and ½ tablespoon basil.

Tuna Noodle Casserole

Prep time: 25 minutes | Cook time: 15 minutes | Serves 10

¼ cup butter, cubed	broth
½ pound (227 g) sliced fresh mushrooms	2 cups half-and-half cream
1 medium onion, chopped	4 cups (8 ounces / 227 g) uncooked egg noodles
1 medium sweet pepper, chopped	3 (5-ounce / 142-g) cans light tuna in water
1 teaspoon salt, divided	2 tablespoons lemon juice
1 teaspoon pepper, divided	2 cups shredded Monterey Jack cheese
2 garlic cloves, minced	
¼ cup all-purpose flour	2 cups frozen peas, thawed
2 cups reduced-sodium chicken	2 cups crushed potato chips

1. Select Sauté setting on a 6-quart electric pressure cooker and adjust for high heat. Add butter. When melted, add mushrooms, onion, sweet pepper, ½ teaspoon salt and ½ teaspoon pepper; cook and stir until vegetables are tender, 6 to 8 minutes. Add garlic; cook 1 minute longer. Stir in flour until blended. Gradually whisk in broth. Bring to a boil, stirring constantly; cook and stir until thickened, 1 to 2 minutes. Stir in cream and noodles. Lock lid; make sure vent is closed. Select Manual setting; adjust pressure to High and set time for 3 minutes. When finished cooking, allow pressure to naturally release for 3 minutes, then quick-release any remaining pressure according to manufacturer's directions. 2. Meanwhile, in a small bowl, combine tuna, lemon juice and the remaining salt and pepper. Select Sauté setting and adjust for low heat. Stir cheese, tuna mixture and peas into noodle mixture. Cook until heated through. Just before serving, sprinkle with potato chips.

Seasoned Steamed Shrimp

Prep time: 10 minutes | Cook time: 0 minutes | Serves 4

2 pounds (907 g) large uncooked shrimp, peeled and deveined	2 tablespoons Old Bay Seasoning
1 lemon, quartered	1 cup water

1. Place shrimp in a bowl. Squeeze lemon quarters over shrimp. Toss squeezed lemons in bowl with shrimp. Sprinkle Old Bay Seasoning over shrimp and toss until evenly coated. 2. Add water to the Instant Pot and insert steamer basket. Place shrimp in basket. Lock lid. 3. Press the Steam button and adjust time to 0 minutes. When timer beeps, quick-release pressure until float valve drops and then unlock lid. Discard lemons. 4. Transfer shrimp to serving dish and serve warm or cold.

Shrimp Linguini with Spinach Pesto

Prep time: 10 minutes | Cook time: 10 minutes | Serves 4

12 ounces (340 g) linguini, broken in half	1¼ pounds (567 g) large (16/20 count) frozen peeled and deveined shrimp
⅓ cup olive oil	
4 medium garlic cloves	3 cups baby spinach or fresh basil leaves
1½ cups store-bought vegetable or chicken broth, or homemade	
Salt and freshly ground black pepper	⅓ cup pine nuts, toasted
	Finely grated zest and juice of ½ lemon

1. Put the linguini, 1 tablespoon of the oil, and 1 tablespoon of the garlic in the pot and toss to coat the pasta (this will keep the pasta from clumping). Add the broth, 1¼ cups hot water, ½ teaspoon salt, and several grinds of pepper and stir to combine, making sure most of the pasta is submerged. Place the frozen shrimp on top of the pasta mixture, but don't stir. Lock on the lid, select the Pressure Cook function, and adjust to Low pressure for 5 minutes. Make sure the steam valve is in the Sealing position. 2. While the pasta is cooking, make the pesto. In a food processor or blender, blend the spinach or basil, the remaining olive oil, remaining garlic, 2 tablespoons of the pine nuts, the lemon zest, lemon juice, ½ teaspoon salt, and ¼ teaspoon pepper until combined. 3. When the cooking time is up, quick-release the pressure. Remove the lid and add the pesto. Stir with tongs, cover with the lid set to the Venting position, and allow the pasta to stand in the pot for 5 minutes. Don't skip this step—the pasta will finish cooking and absorb more of the sauce as it stands. Season with salt and pepper and serve garnished with the remaining pine nuts.

Tiger Prawns Paella

Prep time: 10 minutes | Cook time: 13 minutes | Serves 2 to 4

1 cup tiger prawns, peeled and deveined
1 tablespoon olive oil
1 small red onion, roughly chopped
1 red bell pepper, chopped
2 chorizo sausage slices
¾ cup risotto rice or paella rice
2 cups vegetable stock (or chicken stock)
¾ cup green peas, frozen
1 cup sweet corn
1 tablespoon fresh parsley, finely chopped
1 teaspoon salt
A pinch of saffron threads
1 whole lemon, quartered

1. Preheat the Instant Pot by selecting Sauté. Add and heat the oil. 2. Add the onion and chorizo slices. Stir and sauté for 3 minute. 3. Add the tiger prawns and cook for 2 to 3 minutes more, stirring occasionally. 4. Add the rice and stock. Stir well. 5. Add the peas, sweet corn, and parsley. Season with salt and saffron. 6. Close and lock the lid. Select Manual and cook at High pressure for 7 minutes. 7. Once pressure cooking is complete, use a quick release. Unlock and carefully open the lid. 8. Place the lemon on top. Close the lid and let sit for 10 minutes. Serve.

Cajun Fish Cakes

Prep time: 15 minutes | Cook time: 15 minutes | Serves 4

1 pound (454 g) cooked cod, shredded
1½ cups bread crumbs, divided
2 large eggs, lightly beaten
2 tablespoons full-fat sour cream
2 teaspoons lemon juice
1 tablespoon Cajun seasoning
4 tablespoons olive oil

1. In a large bowl, combine cod, bread crumbs, eggs, sour cream, lemon juice, and Cajun seasoning. Mix together with clean hands until combined. 2. Press Sauté button on Instant Pot and add oil. 3. Take golf ball-sized clumps of cod mixture. Roll into balls and then flatten to form a cake. Place fish cakes in an even layer in Instant Pot. 4. Let cook 2 minutes until golden brown. Flip and cook an additional 2 minutes. 5. Repeat with remaining cod mixture. 6. Store Cajun fish cakes under foil until ready to serve.

Almond Tilapia

Prep time: 2 minutes | Cook time: 5 minutes | Serves 4

4 tilapia fillets
1 cup water
1 teaspoon olive oil
¼ teaspoon lemon pepper
2 tablespoons Dijon mustard
⅔ cup sliced almonds

1. Add the water to the Instant Pot and place the trivet on top. 2. In a bowl, combine the oil, lemon pepper, and Dijon mustard, mix well. 3. Brush the fish fillets with the mixture. 4. Transfer the fillets to the almond to coat both sides. 5. Place on the trivet. Close and lock the lid. 6. Select Manual and cook at High pressure for 5 minutes. 7. When the timer goes off, use a quick release. Carefully open the lid. 8. Serve.

Fast Salmon with Broccoli

Prep time: 2 minutes | Cook time: 5 minutes | Serves 2

8 ounces (227 g) salmon fillets
1 cup water
8 ounces (227 g) broccoli
Salt and ground black pepper, to taste

1. Add the water to the Instant Pot and place a trivet on top. 2. Cut the broccoli into florets. 3. Season the salmon fillets and broccoli with salt and pepper to taste. Place them on the trivet. 4. Close and lock the lid. Select Steam and cook for 5 minutes. 5. Once cooking is complete, use a natural release for 10 minutes, then release any remaining pressure manually. Open the lid. 6. Serve.

Tilapia Fish Cakes

Prep time: 15 minutes | Cook time: 15 minutes | Serves 4

½ pound (227 g) cooked tilapia fillets, shredded
1½ cups bread crumbs, divided
1 cup peeled and shredded russet potato
2 large eggs, lightly beaten
2 tablespoons full-fat sour cream
2 teaspoons lemon juice
1 teaspoon salt
½ teaspoon chili powder
¼ teaspoon black pepper
⅛ teaspoon cayenne pepper
4 tablespoons olive oil

1. In a large bowl, combine tilapia, bread crumbs, potato, eggs, sour cream, lemon juice, salt, chili powder, black pepper, and cayenne pepper. Mix together with clean hands until combined. 2. Press Sauté button on Instant Pot and add oil. 3. Take golf ball-sized clumps of tilapia mixture. Roll into balls and then flatten to form a cake. Place tilapia cakes in an even layer in Instant Pot. 4. Cook 2 minutes until golden brown. Flip and cook an additional 2 minutes. 5. Repeat with remaining tilapia mixture. 6. Store tilapia cakes under foil until ready to serve.

Honey Garlic Salmon

Prep time: 10 minutes | Cook time: 0 minutes | Serves 4

1 cup water
1 pound (454 g) salmon fillets
½ teaspoon salt
¼ teaspoon black pepper
½ cup honey
4 tablespoons soy sauce
2 tablespoons rice vinegar
4 cloves garlic, minced
1 teaspoon sesame seeds

1. Pour water into Instant Pot and add trivet. 2. Season salmon with salt and pepper and place on trivet. 3. Close lid and set pressure release to Sealing. 4. Press Manual or Pressure Cook button and adjust time to 0 minutes. 5. Once the timer beeps, allow pressure to release naturally for 10 minutes and then quick release remaining pressure. Unlock lid and remove it. 6. In a small bowl, whisk together honey, soy sauce, vinegar, garlic, and sesame seeds. 7. Pour sauce over salmon and serve.

Cheddar Haddock

Prep time: 2 minutes | Cook time: 11 minutes | Serves 2

1 pound (454 g) fresh or frozen haddock fillets
1 tablespoon butter
1 tablespoon flour
¼ teaspoon salt
Ground black pepper, to taste
½ cup milk
1 cup Parmesan cheese, grated
1 cup water

1. To preheat the Instant Pot, select Sauté. Add the butter and melt it. 2. Add the flour, salt and pepper, stir well. Sauté for 1 minute. 3. Gradually pour the milk, cook for 3 to 5 minutes, stirring occasionally, until the sauce is smooth and thick. 4. Add the cheese to the pot and stir. 5. Press the Cancel button to stop the Sauté function. 6. In a pan, combine the fish fillets with sauce. Cover tightly with foil. 7. Clean the inner pot with water. 8. Pour a cup of water into the pot and set a trivet in it. 9. Place the pan on the trivet. 10. Select Manual and cook at High pressure for 5 minutes. 11. Once pressure cooking is complete, use a quick release. Unlock and carefully open the lid. 12. Serve.

Seafood Paella

Prep time: 10 minutes | Cook time: 12 minutes | Serves 6

2 cups chopped white fish and scallops
2 cups mussels and shrimp
4 tablespoons olive oil
1 onion, diced
1 red bell pepper, diced
1 green bell pepper, diced
2 cups rice
A few saffron threads
2 cups fish stock
Salt and ground black pepper, to taste

1. Set your Instant Pot on Sauté mode, add the oil and heat it up. 2. Add the onion and bell peppers and sauté for 4 minutes. 3. Add the fish, rice, and saffron, stir. Cook for 2 minutes more. 4. Pour in the fish stock and season with salt and pepper, stir. 5. Place the shellfish on top. 6. Press the Cancel button to stop the Sauté function. 7. Close and lock the lid. Select Manual and cook at High pressure for 6 minutes. 8. Once cooking is complete, select Cancel and let naturally release for 10 minutes. Release any remaining steam manually. Uncover the pot. 9. Stir the dish and let sit for 5 minutes. Serve.

Curried Cod with Tomatoes and Okra

Prep time: 15 minutes | Cook time: 25 minutes | Serves 6

2 tablespoons vegetable, corn, or canola oil
1 medium red onion, chopped
2 medium garlic cloves, peeled and minced
2 tablespoons minced peeled fresh ginger
1 tablespoon yellow curry powder
2 teaspoons mild smoked paprika
½ teaspoon table salt
1 (28-ounce / 794-g) can diced tomatoes with chiles
1 pound (454 g) frozen sliced okra
½ cup water
1½ pounds (680 g) skinless cod fillets, cut into 10 to 12 pieces

1. Press the Sauté button, and set on Medium or Normal for 10 minutes. 2. Warm the oil in a 6- or 8-quart cooker for a minute or two. Add the onion and cook, stirring often, until softened, about 5 minutes. Add the garlic and ginger; cook until aromatic, stirring all the while, maybe half a minute. Stir in the curry powder, smoked paprika, and salt until fragrant, just a few seconds. 3. Pour in the tomatoes and scrape up any browned bits on the pot's bottom. Turn off the Sauté function and stir in the okra and water. Secure the lid with the steam vent in the sealed position. 4. Select Pressure Cook or Manual, and set on High for 5 minutes with the Keep Warm setting off. 5. Use the quick-release method to bring the pressure back to normal. Unlatch the lid and open the cooker. Nestle the cod pieces into the sauce. Set the lid askew over the pot. 6. Press the Sauté button, and set on Low or Less for 10 minutes. 7. Simmer the cod in the sauce until cooked through, about 10 minutes. Turn off the Sauté function and remove the hot insert from the pot to stop the cooking. Serve warm.

Red Clam Sauce

Prep time: 20 minutes | Cook time: 5 minutes | Serves 4

1 tablespoon canola oil
1 medium onion, chopped
2 garlic cloves, minced
2 (6½-ounce / 184-g) cans chopped clams, undrained
1 (14½-ounce / 411-g) can diced tomatoes, undrained
1 (6-ounce / 170-g) can tomato paste
¼ cup minced fresh parsley
1 bay leaf
1 teaspoon sugar
1 teaspoon dried basil
½ teaspoon dried thyme
6 ounces (170 g) hot cooked linguine, drained

1. Select Sauté setting on a 6-quart electric pressure cooker and adjust for high heat. Add oil. When hot, add onion; sauté until tender. Add garlic; cook 1 minute longer. 2. Stir in next eight ingredients. Lock lid; make sure vent is closed. Select Manual setting; adjust pressure to High and set time for 3 minutes. When finished cooking, allow pressure to naturally release for 5 minutes, then quick-release any remaining pressure according to manufacturer's directions. Discard bay leaf. Serve with linguine.

Sea Scallops with Cherry Sauce

Prep time: 5 minutes | Cook time: 2 minutes | Serves 2

¼ cup cherry preserves
1 teaspoon lemon juice
1 teaspoon tamari
1 tablespoon unsalted butter
1 pound (454 g) fresh sea scallops
½ teaspoon salt
1 cup water

1. In a small bowl, whisk together preserves, lemon juice, and tamari. Set aside. 2. Press the Sauté button on the Instant Pot. Add butter to pot and heat 30 seconds. Season scallops with salt, add to pot, and sear 30 seconds per side. Transfer to steamer basket. Top scallops with preserve mixture. 3. Add water to the Instant Pot. Insert steamer basket. Lock lid. 4. Press the Manual or Pressure Cook button and adjust cook time to 0 minutes. When timer beeps, quick-release pressure until float valve drops and then unlock lid. 5. Transfer scallops to two plates. Serve warm.

Dilly Ranch Salmon

Prep time: 10 minutes | Cook time: 12 minutes | Serves 2 to 4

½ teaspoon salt
¼ teaspoon garlic powder
¼ teaspoon onion powder
¼ teaspoon dried chives
¼ teaspoon freshly ground black pepper
2 (12-ounce / 340-g) salmon fillets
1 tablespoon olive oil
1 tablespoon unsalted butter
Juice of ½ lemon
1 tablespoon white wine
1½ teaspoons chopped fresh dill
1½ teaspoons chopped fresh parsley

1. In a small bowl, mix together the salt, garlic powder, onion powder, chives and pepper. Season each salmon fillet liberally with the mixture. 2. Press Sauté on the Instant Pot. Make sure the display light is beneath normal. Once hot, add the oil and butter. 3. Add the salmon fillets, skin side down. Sauté for 7 to 9 minutes, or until the skin is nice and crispy. 4. Press Cancel and carefully remove the salmon with a fish spatula. Some parts of the skin might stick; work carefully so as to not break the fish. Transfer the fish to a large plate. 5. Deglaze the pot with the lemon juice and white wine. Scrape up any browned bits from the bottom of the pot. 6. Insert the steam trivet into the pot. Place the fillets on the trivet. Secure the lid with the steam vent in the sealed position. Press Steam and then use the plus and minus buttons to adjust the time until the display reads 3 minutes. 7. When the timer sounds, quick release the pressure. Remove the lid and carefully transfer each fillet to a serving plate. Spoon some of the sauce from the pot over each fish, then top with fresh dill and parsley.

Teriyaki Salmon Salad

Prep time: 10 minutes | Cook time: 3 to 4 minutes | Serves 2

¼ cup sesame oil
¼ cup soy sauce
¼ cup lime juice
2 tablespoons honey
2 tablespoons fish sauce
1 tablespoon sesame seeds
1 teaspoon grated peeled fresh ginger
1 teaspoon minced garlic
Grated zest of 1 lime
1 scallion, chopped, plus more for serving
2 (4- to 6-ounce / 113- to 170-g) skinless or skin-on salmon fillets
2 teaspoons cornstarch

1. In a gallon-size zip-top bag, combine the sesame oil, soy sauce, lime juice, honey, fish sauce, sesame seeds, ginger, garlic, lime zest, scallion, and salmon. Seal the bag and shake gently. Let the fish marinate in the refrigerator for 1 to 2 hours. 2. Preheat the pressure cooker on Sauté mode. Remove the salmon from the marinade and transfer to a plate. When the display reads hot, pour the marinade from the bag into the pot and bring to a simmer. Press Cancel. 3. Add the salmon to the pot (skin-side up, if using skin-on fillets). Spoon the marinade over the fish. 4. Secure the lid and cook on High pressure for 4 minutes, then quick release the pressure in the pot and remove the lid. Press Cancel. 5. Use a spatula to gently transfer the fish to a clean plate. Remove the skin if necessary. Transfer 2 teaspoons of the warm teriyaki liquid from the pot to a small bowl. Whisk in the cornstarch, then pour it back into the pot. Select Sauté and let the liquid simmer, stirring frequently, for 8 to 10 minutes, or until reduced to a glaze-like consistency. 6. To serve, toss salad greens with shredded cabbage and carrots, sliced bell pepper, edamame, mandarin orange sections, and slivered almonds and divide between two plates. Top each with a salmon fillet. 7. Brush or spoon the teriyaki sauce over the fish and salad.

Mussels Fra Diavolo with Linguine

Prep time: 15 minutes | Cook time: 3 minutes | Serves 2

6 ounces (170 g) linguine
1 tablespoon oil, plus more for the pasta
½ large onion, chopped
3 garlic cloves, minced
2 tablespoons red pepper flakes
½ cup dry white wine
1 (14-ounce / 397-g) can fire-roasted crushed tomatoes with their juices
4 ounces (113 g) canned clam juice
Kosher salt
Freshly ground black pepper
1 pound (454 g) fresh mussels, rinsed, scrubbed, and debearded
⅓ cup fresh chopped basil

1. Cook the pasta according to package directions. Drain and toss with some oil. 2. Sort through the mussels and discard any that aren't fully closed or have broken shells. 3. Preheat the pressure cooker on Sauté mode. When the display reads hot, add 1 tablespoon of oil. Add the onion and sauté until softened, 2 minutes. Add the garlic and red pepper flakes and sauté until fragrant, about 1 minute. 4. Pour in the wine and deglaze the pot, scraping up the browned bits from the bottom. Cook for 1 to 2 minutes, or until the wine is reduced by half. 5. Add the tomatoes and their juices and the clam juice and stir well. Season with salt and pepper. Let the mixture simmer briefly, then stir in the mussels. 6. Secure the lid and cook on High pressure for 3 minutes, then quick release the pressure in the pot and remove the lid. Press Cancel. 7. Stir in the chopped basil. Season with more salt and pepper as desired. 8. Portion the pasta into bowls and immediately ladle the mussels and sauce on top. Serve with lime wedges and crusty bread.

Coconut Curry Sea Bass

Prep time: 5 minutes | Cook time: 3 minutes | Serves 3

1 (14½-ounce / 411-g) can coconut milk
Juice of 1 lime
1 tablespoon red curry paste
1 teaspoon fish sauce
1 teaspoon coconut aminos
1 teaspoon honey
2 teaspoons sriracha
2 cloves garlic, minced
1 teaspoon ground turmeric
1 teaspoon ground ginger
½ teaspoon sea salt
½ teaspoon white pepper
1 pound (454 g) sea bass, cut into 1-inch cubes
¼ cup chopped fresh cilantro
3 lime wedges

1. In a large bowl, whisk together coconut milk, lime juice, red curry paste, fish sauce, coconut aminos, honey, sriracha, garlic, turmeric, ginger, sea salt, and white pepper. 2. Place sea bass in the bottom of Instant Pot. Pour coconut milk mixture over the fish. Lock lid. 3. Press the Manual button and adjust time to 3 minutes. When timer beeps, quick-release pressure until float valve drops and then unlock lid. 4. Transfer fish and broth into three bowls. Garnish each with equal amounts of chopped cilantro and a lime wedge. Serve.

Perfect Lobster Tails with Lemon-Butter Sauce

Prep time: 5 minutes | Cook time: 3 minutes | Serves 2

1 cup chicken stock or water
1 teaspoon Old Bay seasoning
2 (about 1-pound / 454-g) fresh Maine lobster tails
Juice of 1 lemon, divided
½ cup butter, melted
½ tablespoon minced garlic
½ lemon, cut into wedges

1. Add the stock and Old Bay to your pressure cooker and place the trivet in the bottom. Place each lobster tail shell-side down, meat-side up on the trivet. Drizzle half of the lemon juice over the lobster. 2. Secure the cooker lid and cook on High pressure for 3 minutes. Quick release the pressure in the pot, then remove the lid. 3. While the pressure releases, fill a large bowl with ice water. Using tongs, immediately transfer the lobster tails to the ice bath to avoid overcooking. Let chill for 1 to 2 minutes. 4. In a small bowl, whisk together the butter, the remaining lemon juice, and the garlic. 5. Transfer the lobster tails to a dish towel-covered cutting board. Butterfly the lobster tail using kitchen shears or a large knife: with the meat side of the tail up, cut the underside of the tail down the center. 6. Serve with the lemon wedges and the lemon-butter sauce for dipping.

Steamed Fish

Prep time: 10 minutes | Cook time: 10 minutes | Serves 4

4 white fish fillets
1 cup water
1 pound (454 g) cherry tomatoes, cut into halves
1 cup olives, pitted and chopped
1 tablespoon olive oil
1 clove garlic, minced
½ teaspoon dried thyme
Salt and ground black pepper, to taste

1. Prepare the Instant Pot by adding the water to the pot and placing the steamer basket in it. 2. Place the fish fillets in the basket. 3. Place the tomatoes and olives on top. Add the olive oil, garlic, thyme, salt and pepper. 4. Close and lock the lid. Select Manual and cook at Low pressure for 10 minutes. 5. Once cooking is complete, select Cancel and use a natural release for 10 minutes. Open the lid. 6. Serve the fish with tomatoes mix.

Oysters-in-the-Shell

Prep time: 5 minutes | Cook time: 3 minutes | Serves 6

36 in-shell oysters
1 cup water
Salt and ground black pepper, to taste
6 tablespoons butter, melted

1. Clean the oysters well. 2. Add the water, oysters, salt and pepper to the Instant Pot. 3. Close and lock the lid. Select the Manual setting and set the cooking time for 3 minutes at High pressure. 4. When the timer beeps, use a quick release. Carefully unlock the lid. 5. Serve with melted butter.

Teriyaki Salmon

Prep time: 5 minutes | Cook time: 0 minutes | Serves 4

1 pound (454 g) salmon fillets
½ cup soy sauce
½ cup rice vinegar
½ cup packed light brown sugar
1 tablespoon cornstarch
1 teaspoon minced ginger
¼ teaspoon garlic powder

1. Place salmon in Instant Pot. 2. In a small bowl, mix together soy sauce, rice vinegar, brown sugar, cornstarch, ginger, and garlic power. Pour over salmon, turning to coat. 3. Close lid and set pressure release to Sealing. 4. Press Manual or Pressure Cook button and adjust time to 0 minutes. 5. When the timer beeps, allow pressure to release naturally for 10 minutes and then quick release remaining pressure. Unlock lid and remove it. 6. Serve hot.

Mediterranean Squid

Prep time: 10 minutes | Cook time: 4 minutes | Serves 2 to 4

2 pounds (907 g) squid, chopped
2 tablespoons olive oil
Salt and ground black pepper, to taste
1 cup red wine
3 stalks of celery, chopped
1 (28-ounce / 794-g) can crushed tomatoes
1 red onion, sliced
3 cloves garlic, chopped
3 sprigs fresh rosemary
½ cup Italian parsley, chopped

1. In a bowl, combine the olive oil, squid, salt and pepper. 2. Add the wine, tomatoes, onion, garlic, rosemary, and celery to the pot. 3. Set a steamer basket in the pot. 4. Place the squid in the steamer basket. 5. Close and lock the lid. Select Manual and cook at High pressure for 4 minutes. 6. Once timer goes off, let the pressure release naturally for 10 minutes, then release any remaining steam manually. Open the lid. 7. Top with fresh parsley and serve.

Lemon Pepper Tilapia "Bake"

Prep time: 10 minutes | Cook time: 11 minutes | Serves 4

1 cup water
½ pound (227 g) tilapia fillets, cut into 2-inch chunks
1 medium yellow squash, sliced and halved
1 medium zucchini, sliced and halved
¼ cup grated Parmesan cheese
2 tablespoons olive oil
1 tablespoon lemon pepper
¾ teaspoon salt

1. Pour water into Instant Pot and add trivet. 2. Combine tilapia, squash, zucchini, Parmesan, oil, lemon pepper, and salt in a 7-inch cake pan. Mix well. Cover pan tightly with foil. 3. Create a foil sling and carefully lower cake pan into Instant Pot. 4. Close lid and set pressure release to Sealing. 5. Press Manual or Pressure Cook button and adjust time to 11 minutes. 6. When the timer beeps, quick release pressure and then unlock lid and remove it. 7. Remove cake pan using foil sling. Serve hot.

Dijon Salmon

Prep time: 2 minutes | Cook time: 5 minutes | Serves 2

2 fish fillets or steaks, such as salmon, cod, or halibut (1-inch-thick)
1 cup water
Salt and ground black pepper, to taste
2 teaspoons Dijon mustard

1. Pour the water into the Instant Pot and insert a trivet. 2. Sprinkle the fish with salt and pepper. 3. Place the fillets on the trivet skin-side down and spread the Dijon mustard on top of each fillets or steaks. 4. Close and lock the lid. Select Manual and cook at High pressure for 5 minutes. 5. When the timer goes off, use a quick release. Carefully open the lid.

Steamed Crab Legs

Prep time: 5 minutes | Cook time: 3 minutes | Serves 2

1 cup water
4 cloves garlic, quartered
1 small onion, peeled and diced large
1 tablespoon Old Bay Seasoning
2 sprigs fresh thyme
2 pounds (907 g) crab legs

1. Add water, garlic, onion, Old Bay Seasoning, and thyme to the Instant Pot; stir to combine. 2. Insert trivet. Add crab legs. Lock lid. 3. Press the Steam button and adjust time to 3 minutes. When the timer beeps, quick-release the pressure until float valve drops and then unlock lid. 4. Transfer crab legs to a serving platter.

Crawfish Étouffée

Prep time: 15 minutes | Cook time: 16 minutes | Serves 4

6 tablespoons unsalted butter
¼ cup gluten-free all-purpose flour
1 medium sweet onion, peeled and diced
2 stalks celery, diced
1 medium green bell pepper, seeded and diced
4 cloves garlic, peeled and minced
1 (14½-ounce / 411-g) can diced tomatoes, including juice
¼ cup chicken broth
1 pound (454 g) crawfish tails, peeled
1 tablespoon Creole seasoning
½ teaspoon salt
½ teaspoon ground black pepper
⅛ teaspoon hot sauce
1 tablespoon cooking sherry
4 cups cooked long-grain white rice
¼ cup sliced green onions
¼ cup chopped fresh parsley

1. Press the Sauté button on the Instant Pot. Add butter to pot and heat 30 seconds. Slowly whisk in flour and cook 5 minutes until browned. Add onion, celery, green pepper, and garlic to pot and heat while stirring for an additional 2 minutes. 2. Add diced tomatoes with juice and stir, scraping any bits on the bottom and sides of pot. Add broth, crawfish, Creole seasoning, salt, pepper, hot sauce, and cooking sherry. Lock lid. 3. Press the Manual or Pressure Cook button and adjust cook time to 8 minutes. When timer beeps, quick-release pressure until float valve drops and then unlock lid. 4. Ladle étouffée into four bowls. Garnish each bowl with 1 cup rice, green onions, and parsley. Serve warm.

Steamed Mussels with Peppers

Prep time: 30 minutes | Cook time: 5 minutes | Serves 4

2 pounds (907 g) fresh mussels, scrubbed and beards removed
2 tablespoons olive oil
1 jalapeño pepper, seeded and chopped
3 garlic cloves, minced
1 (8-ounce / 227-g) bottle clam juice
½ cup white wine or additional clam juice
⅓ cup chopped sweet red pepper
3 green onions, sliced
½ teaspoon dried oregano
1 bay leaf
2 tablespoons minced fresh parsley
¼ teaspoon salt
¼ teaspoon pepper
French bread baguette, sliced (optional)

1. Tap mussels; discard any that do not close. Set aside. Select Sauté setting on a 6-quart electric pressure cooker. Adjust for medium heat; add oil. When oil is hot, cook and stir chopped jalapeño until crisp-tender, 2 to 3 minutes. 2. Add garlic; cook for 1 minute longer. Press Cancel. Stir in mussels, clam juice, wine, red pepper, green onions, oregano and bay leaf. Lock lid; close pressure-release valve. Adjust to Pressure Cook on high 2 minutes. Quick-release pressure. Discard bay leaf and any unopened mussels. Sprinkle with parsley, salt and pepper. If desired, serve with baguette slices.

Coconut-Lime Shrimp

Prep time: 10 minutes | Cook time: 4 to 7 minutes | Serves 4

1 cup full-fat coconut milk
2 tablespoons freshly squeezed lime juice
1 tablespoon Sriracha
1 red bell pepper, seeded and chopped
½ teaspoon fine sea salt
Freshly ground black pepper
1 small head cauliflower, cut into florets (about 8 ounces / 227 g)
1 pound (454 g) fresh or frozen raw shrimp, peeled and deveined
8 ounces (227 g) sugar snap peas
½ cup lightly packed chopped fresh cilantro
Lime wedges, for serving

1. Combine the coconut milk, lime juice, Sriracha, bell pepper, salt, and several grinds of pepper in the Instant Pot. 2. Arrange a steamer basket over the sauce in the bottom of the pot and place the cauliflower in the basket. Secure the lid and move the steam release valve to Sealing. Select Manual or Pressure Cook to cook on High pressure for 1 minute. 3. When the cooking cycle is complete, quickly release the pressure by moving the steam release valve to Venting. When the floating valve drops, remove the lid and press Cancel to stop the cooking cycle. 4. Use oven mitts to lift the steamer basket of cauliflower out of the pot. Press Sauté and add the shrimp and snap peas to the pot. Stir well, simmering the shrimp in the sauce until they are cooked through with a pink exterior, about 3 minutes for fresh and 5 to 6 minutes for frozen. 5. Transfer the cooked cauliflower to a large bowl and use a potato masher to break up the florets into rice-like pieces. 6. Add the cilantro to the pot, then ladle the shrimp and vegetables over the cauliflower "rice". Serve with lime wedges on the side.

Ginger-Glazed Mahi-Mahi

Prep time: 5 minutes | Cook time: 5 minutes | Serves 2

2 tablespoons tamari
2 tablespoons rice wine vinegar
2 teaspoons sesame oil
2 tablespoons honey
1 teaspoon peeled and grated ginger
1/8 teaspoon cayenne pepper
2 (6-ounce / 170-g) mahi-mahi fillets
1 cup water

1. Whisk together tamari, rice wine vinegar, sesame oil, honey, ginger, and cayenne pepper. Brush half of glaze on mahi-mahi fillets. 2. Add water to the Instant Pot. Insert steamer basket. Add fillets to basket. Lock lid. 3. Press the Manual or Pressure Cook button and adjust cook time to 5 minutes. When timer beeps, let pressure release naturally for 5 minutes. Quick-release any additional pressure until float valve drops and then unlock lid. 4. Transfer fish to two plates and brush with remaining glaze. Serve warm.

Salmon with Pecan Coating

Prep time: 5 minutes | Cook time: 10 minutes | Serves 2 to 4

2 salmon fillets
½ cup olive oil
½ teaspoon salt
¼ cup flour
1 egg, beaten
¼ cup pecans, finely chopped
1 cup water

1. Preheat the Instant Pot by selecting Sauté. Add and heat the oil. 2. Season the fillets with salt. 3. Dip the fillets in the flour, then in whisked egg, then in pecans. 4. Add to the pot and brown the fish on both sides. 5. Press the Cancel button to stop the Sauté function. 6. Remove the salmon from the pot and place the trivet in it. Pour in the water. 7. Place the fillets on the trivet. Close and lock the lid. 8. Select the Manual setting and set the cooking time for 4 minutes at High pressure. 9. When the timer beeps, use a natural release for 10 minutes. Uncover the pot. 10. Serve.

Quick Shrimp Scampi

Prep time: 10 minutes | Cook time: 10 minutes | Serves 2

6 ounces (170 g) linguine
1 tablespoon oil
1 tablespoon butter
1 shallot, chopped
1 tablespoon minced garlic
Pinch red pepper flakes, plus more for seasoning (optional)
¼ cup white wine
¼ cup chicken stock
1 tablespoon freshly squeezed lemon juice
¾ pound (340 g) thawed frozen raw jumbo shrimp, tails removed, peeled and deveined
Kosher salt
Freshly ground black pepper

1. Cook the pasta according to package directions while you cook everything else in the pressure cooker. Drain the pasta but do not rinse, transfer to a serving bowl, cover, and set aside. 2. Preheat the pressure cooker on Sauté mode. When the display reads hot, add the oil and butter and stir to melt. Add the shallot, garlic, and red pepper flakes and sauté for 2 minutes. 3. Pour in the wine and deglaze the pot, scraping up the browned bits from the bottom using a wooden spoon and stirring them into the liquid. Let cook for 1 minute to reduce by half. Press Cancel. 4. Add the stock, lemon juice, and shrimp. Secure the lid. Set the cooker timer for 0 minutes, which will cause the cooker to come to pressure, then immediately depressurize. Quick release the pressure in the pot, then remove the lid. Press Cancel. 5. Season with salt, pepper, and additional red pepper flakes (if desired) and stir in the parsley. Pour into the serving bowl with the pasta and toss. Serve with slices of crusty bread.

Mini Tuna Casseroles

Prep time: 15 minutes | Cook time: 15 minutes | Serves 6

1 cup water
1 (12-ounce / 340-g) can tuna, drained and flaked
1 (10½-ounce / 298-g) can cream of mushroom soup
½ pound (227 g) small shell pasta, cooked
1 cup shredded Cheddar cheese, divided
¾ cup frozen peas, thawed
¾ teaspoon salt
½ teaspoon garlic powder
½ teaspoon black pepper
24 potato chips

1. Pour water into Instant Pot and add trivet. 2. In a large bowl, combine tuna, cream of mushroom soup, pasta, ½ cup Cheddar, peas, salt, garlic powder, and pepper. Mix. 3. Spray six ramekins with cooking spray. 4. Evenly divide tuna mixture into each ramekin and top with remaining cheese. Cover each ramekin tightly with foil and place on top of trivet, stacked two by two. 5. Close lid and set pressure release to Sealing. 6. Press Manual or Pressure Cook button and adjust time to 15 minutes. 7. When the timer beeps, quick release pressure and then unlock lid and remove it. 8. Carefully remove ramekins from Instant Pot and remove foil. 9. Sprinkle four crushed-up potato chips over each casserole before serving.

Shrimp Creole

Prep time: 10 minutes | Cook time: 7 minutes | Serves 2 to 4

1 pound (454 g) frozen jumbo shrimp, peeled and deveined
2 teaspoons olive oil
2 cloves garlic, minced
1 medium onion, chopped
2 stalks celery, diced
1 bell pepper, diced
1 tablespoon tomato paste
1 (28-ounce / 794-g) can crushed tomatoes
1 bay leaf
1 teaspoon thyme
1 teaspoon kosher salt
½ teaspoon pepper
¼ teaspoon cayenne pepper

1. Select the Sauté setting on the Instant Pot and heat the oil. 2. Add the garlic, onion, celery, and bell pepper. Sauté the veggies for 3 to 4 minutes. 3. Add the tomato paste and cook for 1 minute more, stirring occasionally. 4. Add the shrimp, tomatoes, bay leaf, thyme, salt, pepper, and cayenne pepper, stir well. Close and lock the lid. 5. Press the Cancel button to stop the Sauté function. 6. Select Manual and cook at High pressure for 2 minutes. 7. When the timer beeps, use a quick release. Carefully unlock the lid. 8. Serve with cooked rice.

Tasty Squid

Prep time: 5 minutes | Cook time: 15 minutes | Serves 2 to 4

- 1 pound (454 g) squid
- 1 teaspoon onion powder
- 2 tablespoons starch
- 1 tablespoon garlic, minced
- 1 tablespoon chives
- ¼ teaspoon chili pepper, chopped
- 1 teaspoon salt
- 1 teaspoon white pepper
- 1 tablespoon lemon juice
- 3 tablespoons fish sauce
- 2 tablespoons butter

1. Slice the squid. 2. In a large bowl, combine the onion powder, starch, garlic, chives, chili pepper, salt, and white pepper. Mix well. 3. Add the squid to the spice mix. Stir gently. 4. Season the mixture with the lemon juice and fish sauce, stir. Set aside the mixture for 10 minutes. 5. Preheat the Instant Pot by selecting Sauté. Once hot, add the butter and melt it. 6. Add the squid mixture to the pot and secure the lid. 7. Select the Meat/Stew setting and cook for 13 minutes. 8. Once cooking is complete, uncover the pot and serve.

Coconut Poached Halibut

Prep time: 10 minutes | Cook time: 3 minutes | Serves 2

- 1 (13½-ounce / 383-g) can coconut milk
- Juice of 1 lime
- Zest of 1 lime
- 2 teaspoons red curry paste
- 2 teaspoons honey
- ⅛ teaspoon red pepper flakes
- 1 pound (454 g) halibut fillets, cubed
- ½ cup julienned fresh basil leaves, divided

1. Whisk together milk, lime juice, lime zest, red curry paste, honey, and pepper flakes in the Instant Pot. Add halibut and ¼ cup basil. Lock lid. 2. Press the Manual or Pressure Cook button and adjust cook time to 3 minutes. When timer beeps, quick-release pressure until float valve drops and then unlock lid. 3. Ladle mixture into two bowls and garnish with remaining basil. Serve warm.

Poached Salmon with Horseradish Sauce

Prep time: 20 minutes | Cook time: 4 minutes | Serves 6

- 5 cups vegetable broth
- 1 cup dry white wine
- 1 small lemon, scrubbed to remove any waxy coating, thinly sliced and seeded
- 4 or 5 fresh dill fronds
- 1 teaspoon black peppercorns
- 1 bay leaf
- 1 (2-pound / 907-g) skin-on salmon fillet
- ½ cup regular or low-fat mayonnaise
- ½ cup regular or low-fat sour cream
- 2 tablespoons fresh lemon juice
- 2 tablespoons minced dill fronds
- 2 tablespoons jarred prepared white horseradish
- 1 tablespoon minced chives or scallion (green part only)
- ½ teaspoon ground black pepper

1. Mix the broth, wine, lemon, dill, peppercorns, and bay leaf in a 6- or 8-quart cooker. Set the salmon skin side down in the broth mixture. Secure the lid with the steam vent in the sealed position. 2. Select Pressure Cook or Manual, and cook on low for 4 minutes with the Keep Warm setting off. 3. Use the quick-release method to bring the pressure back to normal. Unlatch the lid and open the cooker. Remove the hot insert from the cooker and set aside at room temperature for 10 minutes, then set the insert (with the salmon inside) on a towel on a shelf in the refrigerator and cool for 1 hour. 4. Meanwhile, whisk the mayonnaise, sour cream, lemon juice, dill, horseradish, chives, and pepper in a small bowl until smooth. Cover and refrigerate until you're ready to serve. 5. After an hour, transfer the salmon from the insert to a platter. Discard the liquid and solids in the insert. Slice the fish and serve at once—or cover and refrigerate for up to 2 days, offering the horseradish sauce on the side.

Salmon with Lemon Sauce

Prep time: 5 minutes | Cook time: 5 minutes | Serves 2 to 4

- 1 pound (454 g) salmon fillets
- ¼ cup olive oil
- 1 tablespoon red wine vinegar
- 1 clove garlic, minced
- 1 tablespoon lemon juice
- ¼ teaspoon dried oregano
- Salt and ground black pepper, to taste
- 1 tablespoon feta cheese, crumbled
- 1 cup water
- 2 slices lemon
- 2 sprigs fresh rosemary

1. In a bowl, combine the olive oil, vinegar, garlic, lemon juice, oregano, salt, pepper, and cheese. Mix well. 2. Pour the water into the Instant Pot and set a trivet in the pot. 3. Place the salmon on the trivet. 4. Pour the mixture over the salmon fillets. Top with the lemon slices and rosemary. 5. Close and lock the lid. Select Manual and cook at High pressure for 5 minutes. 6. Once pressure cooking is complete, use a quick release. Unlock and carefully open the lid. 7. Serve the salmon with the sauce.

Mussels in White Wine Sauce

Prep time: 5 minutes | Cook time: 8 minutes | Serves 4 to 6

- 6 tablespoons (¾ stick) salted butter
- 4 shallots, minced
- 9 cloves garlic, minced or pressed
- ¾ cup dry white wine
- 3 tablespoons parsley flakes
- 3 to 5 pounds (1.4 to 2.3 kg) fresh mussels, rinsed and debearded
- 1½ cups chicken broth or garlic broth
- Juice of 3 lemons
- A fresh, crusty baguette, for serving

1. Place the butter in the Instant Pot, then hit Sauté and Adjust so it's on the More or High setting. Once the butter's melted, add the shallots and cook for about 2 minutes until beginning to brown, then add the garlic and sauté for 1 minute more. 2. Add the wine and stir, scraping up any browned bits from the bottom of the pot. Let simmer 1 to 2 minutes, until slightly thickened. 3. Stir in the parsley and add the mussels (you can fill the pot to the brim so long as there's room for the lid) and pour the broth and lemon juice over everything. 4. Secure the lid, move the valve to the sealing position, hit Keep Warm/Cancel and then hit Manual or Pressure Cook on High Pressure for 3 minutes. Quick release when done. 5. Serve immediately, sopping up any juices with the crusty baguette.

Steamed Mussels in White Wine

Prep time: 10 minutes | Cook time: 8 minutes | Serves 4

2 tablespoons ghee	1 teaspoon cayenne pepper
1 medium onion, peeled and diced	1 teaspoon sea salt
	Juice of 1 lemon
3 cloves garlic, minced	2 pounds (907 g) fresh mussels, cleaned and debearded
½ cup dry white wine	
1 (14½-ounce / 411-g) can diced tomatoes, including juice	4 tablespoons chopped fresh parsley

1. Press the Sauté button on Instant Pot. Add the ghee and melt. Add onion and sauté for 3 to 5 minutes until translucent. Add garlic and cook for an additional minute. Stir in white wine and let cook 2 minutes. Add tomatoes, cayenne pepper, salt, and lemon juice. 2. Insert steamer basket. Place mussels on top. Lock lid. 3. Press the Manual button and adjust time to 0 minutes. When timer beeps, quick-release pressure until float valve drops and then unlock lid. 4. Remove mussels and discard any that haven't opened. Transfer mussels to four bowls and pour liquid from Instant Pot equally among bowls. Garnish each bowl with 1 tablespoon parsley. Serve immediately.

Shrimp Curry

Prep time: 10 minutes | Cook time: 4 minutes | Serves 2 to 4

1 pound (454 g) shrimp, peeled and deveined	1 tablespoon garlic, minced
	1 teaspoon curry powder
2 cups water	Salt and ground black pepper, to taste
8 ounces (227 g) unsweetened coconut milk	

1. Add the water to the Instant Pot and insert a trivet. 2. In a large bowl, combine the shrimp, coconut milk, garlic, and curry powder. Season with salt and pepper. 3. Pour the mixture into the pan and place on the trivet, uncovered. 4. Close and lock the lid. Select the Manual setting and set the cooking time for 4 minutes at Low pressure. 5. When the timer beeps, use a quick release. Carefully unlock the lid. 6. Stir the curry and serve.

Spicy Buttery Shrimp

Prep time: 20 minutes | Cook time: 12 minutes | Serves 6 to 8

3 cups chicken broth	1 teaspoon dried oregano
1 cup beer, preferably an amber ale	1 teaspoon fennel seeds
	1 teaspoon red pepper flakes
½ cup (1 stick) butter, cut into chunks	½ teaspoon table salt
	½ teaspoon celery seeds (optional)
⅓ cup tomato paste	
6 medium garlic cloves, peeled and minced	3 pounds (1.4 kg) large shrimp, peeled and deveined
2 teaspoons dried thyme	Crunchy bread, for serving

1. Stir the broth, beer, butter, tomato paste, garlic, thyme, oregano, fennel seeds, red pepper flakes, salt, and celery seed (if using) in a 6- or 8-quart cooker. Secure the lid with the steam vent in the sealed position. 2. Select Meat/Stew, Pressure Cook or Manual, and cook on high for 7 minutes with the Keep Warm setting off. 3. Use the quick-release method to bring the pressure back to normal. Unlatch the lid and open the pot. 4. Press the Sauté button, and set on Medium or Normal for 5 minutes. 5. Stir the sauce as it comes to a simmer. Add the shrimp, stir well, and set the lid askew over the pot. Cook until the shrimp are pink and firm, about 2 minutes. Turn off the Sauté function and remove the hot insert from the machine to stop the cooking. Pour the contents of the insert into a large serving bowl and serve with the crunchy bread to sop up the sauce.

Catfish Bites with Creamy Slaw

Prep time: 10 minutes | Cook time: 3 minutes | Serves 4

Creamy Slaw:	2 teaspoons Dijon mustard
1 (14-ounce / 397-g) bag coleslaw mix (shredded cabbage and carrots)	½ teaspoon salt
	¼ teaspoon ground black pepper
	Catfish:
½ cup mayonnaise	1 cup water
⅓ cup sour cream	2 pounds (907 g) catfish fillets, rinsed and cut into 1-inch pieces
2 teaspoons granulated sugar	
2 teaspoons dill pickle juice, from the jar	1 teaspoon salt
	¼ teaspoon ground black pepper

1. In a small bowl, combine slaw ingredients and refrigerate covered until ready to serve. 2. Add water to the Instant Pot. Season catfish with salt and pepper. Place fish in steamer basket and insert into pot. Lock lid. 3. Press the Manual or Pressure Cook button and adjust cook time to 3 minutes. When timer beeps, quick-release pressure until float valve drops and then unlock lid. 4. Transfer catfish to four plates. Serve warm with chilled slaw.

Louisiana Grouper

Prep time: 10 minutes | Cook time: 20 minutes | Serves 4

2 tablespoons olive oil	1 tablespoon tomato paste
1 small onion, peeled and diced	1 teaspoon honey
1 stalk celery, diced	Pinch of dried basil
1 small green bell pepper, seeded and diced	2 teaspoons Creole seasoning
	4 grouper fillets, rinsed and cut into bite-sized pieces
1 (15-ounce / 425-g) can diced tomatoes	
	½ teaspoon sea salt
¼ cup water	¼ teaspoon ground black pepper

1. Press Sauté button on Instant Pot. Heat oil and add onion, celery, and bell pepper. Sauté for 3 to 5 minutes until onions are translucent and peppers are tender. 2. Stir in undrained tomatoes, water, tomato paste, honey, basil, and Creole seasoning. 3. Sprinkle fish with salt and pepper. Gently toss the fish pieces into the sauce in the Instant Pot. Lock lid. 4. Press the Manual button and adjust time to 5 minutes. When timer beeps, quick-release the pressure until float valve drops and then unlock lid. 5. Transfer fish to a serving platter. Press Sauté button on Instant Pot, press Adjust button to change the temperature to Less, and simmer juices unlidded for 10 minutes. Transfer tomatoes and preferred amount of sauce over fish. Serve immediately.

Shrimp Boil

Prep time: 15 minutes | Cook time: 10 minutes | Serves 4

2 pounds (907 g) shell-on small shrimp, deveined
1½ pounds (680 g) small red-skinned potatoes, halved
2 tablespoons olive oil
2 tablespoons Old Bay seasoning or other fish boil seasoning
2 cups water
1 cup red chile sauce, such as Heinz chili sauce
2 tablespoons fresh lemon juice
1 tablespoon prepared jarred white horseradish
1 tablespoon minced fresh dill fronds
Several dashes hot red pepper sauce

1. Mix the shrimp, potatoes, olive oil, and seasoning blend in a large bowl until the shrimp and potatoes are evenly and thoroughly coated. 2. Pour the water into a 6- or 8-quart cooker. Set a heat- and pressure-safe collapsible steaming basket in the pot. Open it out as much you can. Pile the shrimp and potatoes into the basket. Secure the lid with the steam vent in the sealed position. 3. Select Steam, Pressure Cook or Manual, and cook on high for 10 minutes with the Keep Warm setting off. 4. Meanwhile, make the cocktail sauce. Whisk the chile sauce, lemon juice, horseradish, dill, and hot red pepper sauce in a small serving bowl. Set aside. 5. Use the quick-release method to bring the pressure back to normal. Unlatch the lid and open the pot. Lift the hot steamer out of the pot and pour the shrimp and potatoes onto a serving plate. Serve with the cocktail sauce on the side.

Salmon with Citrus Horseradish-Mustard Aioli

Prep time: 10 minutes | Cook time: 5 minutes | Serves 2

Aioli:
¼ cup mayonnaise
1 tablespoon lemon juice
1 teaspoon lemon zest
2 teaspoons Dijon mustard
2 teaspoons prepared horseradish
1 clove garlic, peeled and minced
Salmon:
2 (5-ounce / 142-g) salmon fillets
½ teaspoon salt
1 cup water
1 tablespoon chopped fresh dill

1. In a small bowl, combine aioli ingredients. Refrigerate covered until ready to serve. 2. Pat salmon fillets dry with a paper towel and place in steamer basket. Season fillets with salt. 3. Add water to the Instant Pot. Insert steam rack. Place steamer basket on top of steam rack. Lock lid. 4. Press the Manual or Pressure Cook button and adjust cook time to 5 minutes. When timer beeps, quick-release pressure until float valve drops and then unlock lid. 5. Transfer fish to two plates and drizzle sauce over each fillet. Garnish with dill and serve immediately.

Chipotle-Lime Salmon

Prep time: 10 minutes | Cook time: 4 minutes | Serves 3 to 4

1 cup water
¾ teaspoon sea salt, divided
½ teaspoon chipotle chili powder
1 teaspoon ground cumin
3 to 4 (5-ounce / 142-g) salmon fillets with skin, about 1-inch thick
Juice of 2 limes
1 tablespoon white vinegar
½ cup avocado oil or olive oil
1 chipotle pepper in adobo sauce
1 tablespoon adobo sauce
¼ cup chopped fresh cilantro
Cooked rice or cauliflower rice, for serving

1. Pour the water into the Instant Pot and insert the steam trivet. 2. In a small bowl, combine ¼ teaspoon of the salt and the chipotle chili powder and cumin. Season the salmon with the spice mixture, rubbing it onto the fillets. Place the salmon, skin side down, on the steam trivet. 3. Secure the lid with the steam vent in the sealed position. Select Steam or Manual and use the plus and minus buttons to adjust the time until the display reads 4 minutes. If the salmon is thicker than 1 inch, add an additional 1 minute per ½ inch. 4. Meanwhile, make the chipotle-lime vinaigrette: In a blender or food processor, combine the lime juice, vinegar, oil, chipotle pepper, adobo sauce, cilantro and remaining ½ teaspoon of salt and blend until smooth. Set aside. 5. When the salmon is finished cooking, use a quick release. Serve the salmon over a bed of rice or cauliflower rice and pour the vinaigrette on top.

Carolina Shrimp and Cheddar Grits

Prep time: 15 minutes | Cook time: 20 minutes | Serves 6

4 cups water
1 large garlic cloves, minced
½ teaspoon salt
¼ teaspoon pepper
1 cup uncooked stone-ground grits
2 cups shredded Cheddar cheese
¼ cup butter, cubed
1 pound (454 g) peeled and deveined cooked shrimp (31 to 40 per pound)
2 medium tomatoes, seeded and finely chopped
4 green onions, finely chopped
2 tablespoons minced fresh parsley
4 teaspoons lemon juice
2 to 3 teaspoons Cajun seasoning

1. Select Sauté setting on a 6-quart electric pressure cooker and adjust for high heat. Add the first four ingredients and stir to combine; bring to a boil. Slowly add the grits, stirring constantly to avoid lumps. Select Sauté setting, reduce heat to low and cook about 15 minutes, stirring occasionally. Stir in cheese and butter until melted. Stir in the remaining ingredients. Cook for 3 to 4 minutes or until heated through.

Blue Cheese Pancetta Mussels

Prep time: 10 minutes | Cook time: 9 minutes | Serves 4

2 tablespoons unsalted butter
4 ounces (113 g) pancetta or thick-sliced bacon, diced
1 medium red onion, peeled and diced
4 cloves garlic, peeled and minced
2 cans gluten-free beer

2 pounds (907 g) fresh mussels, cleaned and debearded
1 teaspoon salt
1 teaspoon smoked paprika
½ cup crumbled blue cheese
¼ cup chopped fresh basil leaves

1. Press the Sauté button on the Instant Pot. Add butter to pot and heat 30 seconds. Add pancetta and onion and cook 5 minutes until onions are translucent. Add garlic and cook for an additional minute. Stir in beer and cook 2 minutes. 2. Insert steamer basket into pot. Place mussels in basket. Sprinkle mussels with salt and smoked paprika. Lock lid. 3. Press the Manual or Pressure Cook button and adjust cook time to 0 minutes. When timer beeps, quick-release pressure until float valve drops and then unlock lid. 4. Remove mussels and discard any that haven't opened. Transfer mussels to four bowls and distribute liquid, veggies, and pancetta from pot equally among bowls. Garnish each bowl with blue cheese and basil. Serve immediately.

Chapter 6 Vegetables and Sides

Chapter 6 Vegetables and Sides

Sweet Potato Curry Pot

Prep time: 10 minutes | Cook time: 17 minutes | Serves 4

1 tablespoon coconut oil
1 cup sweet onion, sliced
3 cloves garlic, crushed and minced
1 tablespoon fresh grated ginger
1 Thai green chili pepper
2 cups tomatoes, chopped
1 tablespoon curry powder
1 teaspoon coriander
½ teaspoon cinnamon
½ teaspoon salt
1 teaspoon coarse ground black pepper
3 cups sweet potatoes, peeled and cubed
2 cups canned chickpeas, rinsed and drained
2 cups vegetable broth
1 cup coconut milk
2 tablespoons natural peanut butter
2 cups fresh spinach, chopped
1 tablespoon fresh lemongrass
½ cup chopped peanuts

1. Place the coconut oil in the Instant Pot and select the Sauté setting. 2. Once the oil is hot, add in the onions, garlic, ginger, and thai green chili pepper. Sauté the mixture for 5 minutes. 3. Next, add in the tomatoes, curry powder, coriander, cinnamon, salt and black pepper. Stir while cooking for 1 to 2 minutes. 4. Next, add in the sweet potatoes and chickpeas. 5. Quickly whisk together the vegetable broth, coconut milk and peanut butter. Pour the sauce into the cooker. 6. Seal the lid of the cooker. Using the Pressure Cook option, cook on high for 10 minutes. 7. Use the quick release option to release the steam from the cooker. 8. Carefully open the lid and stir in the fresh spinach. Let sit for 10 minutes before serving. 9. Garnish each portion with fresh lemongrass and chopped peanuts before serving.

Cheesy Cauliflower Au Gratin

Prep time: 15 minutes | Cook time: 13 minutes | Serves 4 to 6

Grass-fed butter, ghee or avocado oil, for casserole dish
½ cup softened cream cheese
¼ cup milk or heavy cream
¾ cup shredded Gruyère cheese, divided
½ cup shredded Parmesan cheese, divided
¼ cup shredded Swiss cheese, divided
1 teaspoon sea salt
½ teaspoon garlic granules or garlic powder
½ teaspoon dried thyme
2 tablespoons chopped fresh flat-leaf parsley, plus more for garnish (optional)
1 large head cauliflower, chopped into bite-size florets
1½ cups water

1. Use your healthy fat of choice to grease a 1½-quart casserole dish that fits in the Instant Pot. Set aside. 2. In a very large bowl, combine the cream cheese and milk and give it a stir. Add three-quarters of the cheeses (reserving the rest) and the salt, garlic, thyme, parsley and cauliflower florets and gently toss until everything is combined. 3. Transfer to the prepared casserole dish and sprinkle with the remaining quarter of the cheeses. Cover the casserole dish with its glass lid. 4. Pour the water into the Instant Pot and insert the steam trivet. Carefully set the covered casserole dish on the trivet. 5. Secure the lid with the steam vent in the sealed position. Press Manual and set on High Pressure for 10 minutes. 6. Once the timer sounds, press Keep Warm/Cancel. Allow the Instant Pot to release pressure naturally for 15 minutes. Using an oven mitt, do a quick release. If there is any steam left over, allow it to release until the silver dial drops, then carefully open the lid. 7. Carefully remove the casserole dish from the Instant Pot and remove the lid. Place the casserole dish on a baking sheet and place in the oven under a preheated broiler for 2 to 3 minutes, just until the cheese becomes light golden brown, then remove from the broiler and allow to rest for 15 minutes before serving. 8. Serve as is or garnished with chopped fresh flat-leaf parsley.

Easiest Rosemary Potatoes

Prep time: 10 minutes | Cook time: 10 minutes | Serves 4

4 cups red potatoes, cubed
1 cup water
1 tablespoon olive oil
1 tablespoon fresh rosemary
1 teaspoon granulated garlic
½ teaspoon salt
1 teaspoon coarse ground black pepper

1. Add the water into the bottom of the Instant Pot. Next, place the steamer rack into the cooker. 2. Place the cubed potatoes onto the steamer rack. 3. Seal the cooker and, using the steam option, cook for 8 minutes. 4. Use the quick release option to release the steam from the cooker. 5. While the potatoes are steaming, preheat the broiler of your oven and line a baking sheet with aluminum foil. 6. Carefully open the lid to the cooker and remove the potatoes. 7. Spread the steamed potatoes out on the baking sheet. 8. Drizzle the potatoes with the olive oil and season them with the fresh rosemary, granulated garlic, salt and coarse ground black pepper. Toss gently, taking care to smash the steamed potatoes. 9. Place the baking sheet under the broiler for 2 minutes. 10. Remove and serve immediately.

Better Syracuse Potatoes

Prep time: 5 minutes | Cook time: 2 minutes | Serves 6

6 cups water
1 cup kosher salt
1 cup distilled white vinegar
3 pounds (1.4 kg) small red-skinned potatoes, each 1 to 1½ inches in diameter

1. Mix the water, salt, and vinegar in a 6- or 8-quart cooker until the salt dissolves. Add the potatoes and stir well. Lock the lid onto the cooker. 2. Select Pressure Cook or Manual, and cook on high for 2 minutes with the Keep Warm setting off. 3. When the machine has finished cooking, turn it off and let its pressure return to normal naturally for 15 minutes. Then use the quick-release method to get rid of any residual pressure in the pot. Unlatch the lid and open the cooker. Drain the potatoes in a large colander set in the sink. Serve warm.

Seitan-Stuffed Acorn Squash

Prep time: 5 minutes | Cook time: 20 minutes | Serves 2

1 acorn squash
Pinch of sea salt
1 teaspoon extra-virgin olive oil
¼ cup chopped onion
¼ cup chopped celery
1 cup crumbled seitan
1 cup diced shiitake mushrooms
½ teaspoon dried sage
¼ teaspoon dried thyme
¼ teaspoon ground black pepper
1 teaspoon Sriracha or your favorite hot sauce

1. Cut the squash in half and scoop out the seeds. Cut or scoop out enough squash flesh to make room for ½ cup of the seitan filling in each cavity—you'll end up with about ¼ cup squash flesh: chop and set aside. Sprinkle a little salt over the squash halves and set aside. 2. In a skillet, heat the olive oil over medium-high heat. Add the onion and celery and sauté until the onion is translucent, 2 to 3 minutes. Add the chopped squash, seitan, mushrooms, sage, thyme, pepper, and Sriracha and stir to combine. Sauté for about 5 minutes, until the seitan is lightly browned. Spoon the sautéed seitan mixture into the 2 squash halves. 3. Place a trivet in the pressure cooker, place a steamer basket on top of the trivet, and add enough water to come up to, but not in, the basket. Bring the water to a boil. Place the squash in the steamer basket. If the squash halves do not fit in the basket, turn the basket upside down for a flat surface. Place foil loosely over the top of the squash. 4. Cover and bring to pressure. Cook at pressure for 10 minutes. Use a quick release. 5. Remove the pressure cooker lid, remove the foil, and let the squash sit for 3 to 5 minutes in the uncovered pressure cooker. Remove the squash from the pressure cooker with tongs (handle gently) and serve.

Lemony Asparagus with Gremolata

Prep time: 10 minutes | Cook time: 2 minutes | Serves 2 to 4

Gremolata:
1 cup loosely packed fresh Italian flat-leaf parsley leaves
3 garlic cloves, peeled
2 small or 1 extra-large organic lemon
Asparagus:
1½ pounds (680 g) asparagus, trimmed
Lemony Vinaigrette:
1½ tablespoons fresh lemon juice
1 teaspoon pure maple syrup
1 teaspoon Dijon mustard
2 tablespoons extra-virgin olive oil
Kosher salt or sea salt and freshly cracked black pepper
Optional Garnish:
2 to 3 tablespoons slivered almonds, to taste (not nut-free)

1. Make the gremolata: Finely chop the parsley. Using a Microplane, grate the garlic directly over the parsley and then zest the lemon(s) on top. Mix the garlic and lemon into the parsley and chop the parsley until finely minced. 2. Cook the asparagus: Pour 1 cup water into the inner pot of the Instant Pot. Arrange the asparagus in a steamer basket or place them on top of the steamer rack. Lower the steamer basket or steamer rack (handles facing up) into the Instant Pot. 3. Secure the lid and set the Pressure Release to Sealing. Select the Steam setting at low pressure and set the cook time to 2 minutes. 4. Meanwhile, prepare the lemony vinaigrette: In a bowl, combine the lemon juice, maple syrup, and mustard and whisk to combine. Slowly drizzle in the olive oil and continue to whisk. Season generously with salt and pepper to taste. 5. Once the 2-minute timer has completed and beeps, perform a quick pressure release by carefully switching the Pressure Release knob from Sealing to Venting. 6. Open the pot and, using oven mitts, carefully remove the steamer basket or steamer rack from the Instant Pot. 7. Transfer the asparagus to a serving platter, drizzle with the vinaigrette, and sprinkle on the gremolata. Taste for seasonings and add more salt or pepper as needed. If desired, finish the asparagus with slivered almonds.

"Baked" Potatoes

Prep time: 5 minutes | Cook time: 20 minutes | Serves 4

1 cup water
½ teaspoon salt
4 medium russet potatoes

1. Pour water and salt into Instant Pot and add trivet. 2. Pierce potatoes with a fork on both sides, top and bottom. Place potatoes on top of the trivet. 3. Close lid and set pressure release to Sealing. 4. Press Manual or Pressure Cook button and adjust time to 20 minutes. 5. When the timer beeps, quick release pressure and then unlock lid and remove it. 6. Serve potatoes.

Carrot Purée

Prep time: 10 minutes | Cook time: 4 minutes | Serves 2 to 4

1 cup water
1½ pounds (680 g) carrots, peeled and sliced into 1-inch pieces
1 tablespoon honey
1 tablespoon soy butter, softened
½ teaspoon kosher salt
Brown sugar (optional)

1. Prepare the Instant Pot by adding the water to the pot and placing a steamer basket in it. 2. Put the carrots in the basket. Close and lock the lid. 3. Select the Manual setting and set the cooking time for 4 minutes at High pressure. 4. Once timer goes off, use a quick release. Carefully unlock the lid. 5. Using a potato masher or electric beater, slowly blend the carrots until smooth and creamy. 6. Add the honey and butter and stir well. Season with salt and stir. 7. If desired, add sugar to taste. Serve.

Root Veggie Tagine

Prep time: 5 minutes | Cook time: 4 minutes | Serves 4

2 cups diced sweet potatoes
2 cups diced carrots
1 cup cubed turnips
½ teaspoon ground ginger
½ teaspoon ground cumin
½ teaspoon ground cinnamon
½ teaspoon saffron strands
1 teaspoon coconut sugar
½ cup orange juice
½ cup water
½ teaspoon sea salt

1. Place all the ingredients in the pressure cooker. Stir well, covering the vegetables with the orange juice and water. Cover and bring to pressure. Cook at high pressure for 3 to 4 minutes. Use a quick release. Remove the lid, stir, and serve.

Butternut and Apple Mash

Prep time: 15 minutes | Cook time: 8 minutes | Serves 4 to 6

1 cup water
1 butternut squash, peeled, deseeded, and cut into medium chunks
1 yellow onion, thinly sliced
2 apples, peeled and sliced
2 tablespoons brown butter
Salt, to taste
½ teaspoon apple pie spice

1. Pour the water into the Instant Pot and insert a steamer basket. 2. Place the squash, onion, and apples in the basket. 3. Close and lock the lid. Select Manual and cook at High pressure for 8 minutes. 4. When the timer goes off, use a quick release. Carefully open the lid. 5. Transfer the squash, onion, and apples to a bowl. Using a potato masher or electric beater, mash them until smooth. 6. Add the butter, salt and apple pie spice. Mix well. Serve.

Flea Market Kettle Corn

Prep time: 5 minutes | Cook time: 10 minutes | Serves 2

2 tablespoons unsalted butter
2 tablespoons coconut oil
½ cup popcorn kernels
¼ cup powdered sugar
2 tablespoons granulated sugar
Kosher salt, to taste

1. Preheat the pressure cooker on Sauté mode. When the display reads hot, add the butter and coconut oil to the pot and melt them completely, until they start to sizzle. Add 3 popcorn kernels (as a test), wait for one or two to pop, then add the rest of the kernels. 2. Place a glass lid on top of the pot, or loosely set your pressure cooker lid on top. In 2 to 3 minutes, the popcorn will begin popping. Using pot holders, remove the inner pot and shake it occasionally as the popcorn pops rapidly, then return it to the cooker. Do this a few times and listen for the popping to slow after 3 to 5 minutes, then select Cancel to turn off the cooker. Sprinkle the popcorn with the powdered sugar and granulated sugar, cover, and shake the pot until the popping stops completely. 3. Using pot holders, carefully remove the pot from the cooker. Lift the lid and season the popcorn with salt. Replace the lid and, using the pot holders to hold the pot, shake to distribute the salt and pop any remaining kernels. 4. Pour the popped corn into a large bowl and serve.

Delectable Swiss Fondue

Prep time: 10 minutes | Cook time: 2 minutes | Serves 4 to 6

1½ cups shredded Gruyère cheese
1½ cups shredded Emmental or Swiss cheese
1 cup shredded white cheddar or Gouda cheese
2 tablespoons gluten-free all-purpose flour
1 cup milk
1 cup quality dry white wine
1 tablespoon fresh lemon juice
1 teaspoon Dijon mustard
1 teaspoon garlic powder
¾ teaspoon sea salt

1. In a large bowl, combine the shredded cheeses and sprinkle the flour on the top. Use a spoon to stir until the cheeses are coated with the flour. Set aside. 2. Pour the milk and wine into the Instant Pot. 3. Secure the lid with the steam vent in the sealed position. Press Manual and set on High Pressure for 2 minutes. 4. Once the timer sounds, press Keep Warm/Cancel. Using an oven mitt, do a quick release. When the steam venting stops and the silver dial drops, carefully open the lid. 5. Add the cheese mixture, lemon juice, Dijon, garlic powder and salt, whisking or stirring constantly until everything is fully incorporated and the cheeses have melted into a smooth fondue consistency. Allow to rest, uncovered, for 5 minutes before serving. 6. Stir and serve immediately with your favorite fondue dipping ingredients, such as cubed gluten-free bread or steamed and then blanched veggies, such as broccoli, cauliflower and so on.

Sesame Green Beans

Prep time: 5 minutes | Cook time: 1 minute | Serves 4

1 pound (454 g) green beans, trimmed and cut into 1-inch pieces
1 tablespoon extra-virgin olive oil
2 cloves garlic, minced
1½ teaspoons toasted sesame oil
¼ teaspoon red pepper flakes
Fine sea salt
1 tablespoon sesame seeds

1. Pour 1 cup water into the Instant Pot and arrange a steamer basket in the bottom. Add the green beans to the basket, making sure the beans don't touch the water. Secure the lid and move the steam release valve to Sealing. Select Manual or Pressure Cook and cook at High pressure for 0 minutes. 2. When the pot beeps and the screen reads L0:00, quickly release the pressure by moving the steam release valve to Venting. When the floating valve drops, remove the lid and press Cancel to stop the cooking cycle. Use oven mitts to remove the steamer basket full of beans and set them aside. Drain the water from the pot. 3. Press Sauté and add the olive oil to the Instant Pot. Once the oil is hot but not smoking, add the garlic, sesame oil, and red pepper flakes. Stir briefly, about 30 seconds, then add the steamed green beans and stir well to coat the beans in the fragrant oil, about 30 seconds more. 4. Season with salt to taste (I use ½ teaspoon), and serve warm with a sprinkling of sesame seeds on top. Store leftovers in an airtight container in the fridge for 5 days; they make a great chilled topping for salads.

Gingered Sweet Potatoes

Prep time: 10 minutes | Cook time: 10 minutes | Serves 6

2½ pounds (1.1 kg) sweet potatoes, peeled and diced large
2 cups water
1 tablespoon minced fresh ginger
½ teaspoon sea salt
1 tablespoon pure maple syrup
1 tablespoon butter
¼ cup milk

1. Add potatoes and water to Instant Pot. Lock lid. 2. Press the Manual button and adjust time to 10 minutes. When the timer beeps, let the pressure release naturally until the float valve drops and then unlock lid. 3. Drain water from the Instant Pot. Add remaining ingredients to the potatoes. Using an immersion blender directly in the Instant Pot, cream the potatoes until desired consistency. Serve warm.

French Fries

Prep time: 10 minutes | Cook time: 5 minutes | Serves 4

1¼ cups water
¼ teaspoon baking soda
8 medium potatoes, peeled and cut into ½-inch sticks
Salt, to taste
3 to 4 tablespoons olive oil

1. In the Instant Pot, combine the water, baking soda and salt. Mix well. 2. Put the trivet in the pot and place the potatoes on the trivet. 3. Close and lock the lid. Select Manual and cook at High pressure for 3 minutes. 4. When the timer beeps, use a quick release. Carefully unlock the lid. 5. Transfer the potatoes to a serving bowl. Pat dry with paper towels. 6. Carefully pour the water out of the pot and completely dry the pot before replacing it. 7. Preheat the Instant Pot by selecting Sauté on High heat. Add the oil and heat it up. 8. Put the potato sticks in the pot and sauté, stirring occasionally, until the potatoes turn golden brown. 9. Season with salt and serve.

The Best Damn Ratatouille

Prep time: 20 minutes | Cook time: 35 minutes | Serves 8

1 pound (454 g) eggplant, cut into ¾-inch cubes
1 tablespoon kosher salt, plus more to taste
¼ cup olive oil
1 large sweet onion, diced
8 garlic cloves, chopped
2 medium summer squash or zucchini, cut into pieces roughly the same size as the eggplant
2 medium red or yellow bell peppers, cut into pieces roughly the same size as the eggplant
½ to 1 teaspoon crushed red pepper flakes, to taste
½ teaspoon freshly cracked black pepper
1 cup fresh basil leaves
2 tablespoons capers, drained
1 bay leaf
6 sprigs fresh thyme
1 pound (454 g) heirloom or Campari tomatoes, roughly chopped, or 1 (14½-ounce / 411-g) can diced San Marzano tomatoes
2 tablespoons tomato paste
½ tablespoon high-quality balsamic vinegar
½ cup fresh Italian flat-leaf parsley, finely chopped

1. Place the eggplant cubes on a cutting board or plate and sprinkle with 1 tablespoon salt. Toss to evenly coat, then place the eggplant in a colander to drain. 2. Select the Sauté setting on the Instant Pot and let the pot heat up for a few minutes before adding the oil. Once the oil is hot, add the onion. Cook until the onion is soft and almost translucent, 4 to 5 minutes. Add the garlic, squash, and a pinch of salt and cook until the vegetables are slightly softened, about 3 minutes. 3. Add the bell peppers, pepper flakes, black pepper, and ½ cup of the basil (leaves kept whole). Cook for 4 minutes, tossing occasionally. Transfer the vegetable mixture to a bowl and set aside. 4. Add the remaining 2 tablespoons olive oil to the Instant Pot, followed by the drained eggplant. Stir gently and frequently to prevent the eggplant from sticking to the bottom of the pot. Cook until the eggplant is soft and starting to turn golden, 4 to 5 minutes. Select the Cancel setting. 5. Return the vegetable mixture to the Instant Pot, along with the capers, bay leaf, and thyme sprigs. Stir all of the ingredients to combine. Top the mixture with the tomatoes and tomato paste, but do not stir, allowing the tomatoes and tomato paste to sit on top (this prevents the tomatoes from blocking the Instant Pot's heat sensor and burning). 6. Secure the lid and set the Pressure Release to Sealing. Select the Pressure Cook setting at high pressure and set the cook time to 9 minutes. 7. While the ratatouille is cooking, make a chiffonade of the remaining ½ cup basil by stacking the leaves on top of one another, rolling them up, and slicing thinly into strips. 8. Once the 9-minute timer has completed and beeps, perform a quick pressure release by carefully switching the Pressure Release knob from Sealing to Venting. 9. Open the pot and check the ratatouille—it should be a bit soupy and the vegetables should be very tender. Discard the thyme sprigs and bay leaf. 10. Select the Sauté setting on the Instant Pot and bring the ratatouille to a boil to reduce the liquid and thicken the sauce. This should take 5 to 8 minutes. 11. Select the Cancel setting and stir in the vinegar, parsley, and sliced basil. Taste for salt and adjust accordingly. Use a slotted spoon to transfer the ratatouille to a serving platter.

Veggie Stewed Tomatoes

Prep time: 5 minutes | Cook time: 15 minutes | Serves 4

1 tablespoon olive oil
2 cloves garlic, minced
1 cup diced onion
½ cup chopped carrot
½ cup chopped celery
4 cups quartered tomatoes
1 tablespoon dried basil
1 tablespoon dried oregano
1 tablespoon dried parsley
1 teaspoon red pepper flakes
1 teaspoon salt
½ cup water
2 to 3 tablespoons tomato paste (optional)
Ground black pepper

1. In an uncovered pressure cooker, heat the oil on medium-high. Add the garlic, onion, carrot, and celery and sauté for about 3 minutes, until the onion is soft. Add the tomatoes, basil, oregano, parsley, red pepper flakes, salt, and water and mix well. 2. Cover and bring to pressure. Cook at high pressure for 5 minutes. Use a quick release. 3. Remove the lid. With a potato masher, crush the tomatoes. If a thicker consistency is desired, stir in the tomato paste and simmer, uncovered, for about 5 minutes. Add the ground black pepper to taste.

Miso-Dressed Eggplant

Prep time: 5 minutes | Cook time: 6 minutes | Serves 4

¼ cup white or red miso paste
3 tablespoons water
1 tablespoon unrefined sugar
1 tablespoon tomato paste
1 teaspoon toasted sesame oil
1 eggplant, cubed

1. In a large bowl, stir together the miso, water, sugar, tomato paste, and sesame oil until smooth and creamy. Add the eggplant and toss to coat with the dressing. Transfer the eggplant to a heat-proof dish that fits inside your electric pressure cooker's cooking pot. 2. Put a trivet in the pot, pour in a cup or two of water, and set the dish on the trivet. If it's a tight fit, use a foil sling to lower the dish onto the trivet. Close and lock the lid and ensure the pressure valve is sealed, then select High Pressure and set the time for 6 minutes. 3. Once the cook time is complete, let the pressure release naturally, about 10 minutes. 4. Once all the pressure has released, carefully unlock and remove the lid. Using oven mitts, lift the dish out of the pot and serve.

Buttery Sour Cream Cabbage

Prep time: 5 minutes | Cook time: 5 minutes | Serves 4 to 6

1 cup water
1 medium-large green or savoy cabbage, sliced
4 tablespoons grass-fed butter
½ cup sour cream
¾ teaspoon sea salt
4 ounces (113 g) cooked crispy bacon or turkey bacon, crumbled, for garnish (optional)

1. Pour the water into the Instant Pot and insert a steamer basket. Layer the sliced cabbage in the steamer basket. 2. Secure the lid with the steam vent in the sealed position. Press Manual and set on High Pressure for 2 minutes. 3. Once the timer sounds, press Keep Warm/Cancel. Using an oven mitt, do a quick release. When the steam venting stops and the silver dial drops, carefully open the lid. 4. Carefully remove the cabbage and steamer basket, setting the cabbage aside. Pour out and discard the water that remains in the pot. 5. Place the butter in the Instant Pot and press Sauté. Once the butter has melted, return the cabbage to the pot and sauté for 1 minute, stirring occasionally. Add the sour cream and salt and sauté for 2 minutes, stirring occasionally. Press Keep Warm/Cancel. 6. Serve immediately, garnished with the crumbled crispy bacon (if using).

Cranberry-Orange Sauce

Prep time: 5 minutes | Cook time: 1 minute | Serves 8

4 cups fresh cranberries
½ cup canned crushed pineapple
Juice from 1 orange
2 teaspoons orange zest
½ cup pure maple syrup
¼ teaspoon cinnamon
Pinch of salt
2 tablespoons sugar

1. Add all ingredients to Instant Pot. Lock lid. 2. Press the Manual button and adjust time to 1 minute. When timer beeps, let pressure release naturally until float valve drops and then unlock lid. 3. Stir ingredients in the Instant Pot and smash any unpopped cranberries with the back of a wooden spoon. Transfer sauce to a serving dish and serve warm.

Fluffy Garlic Mashed Potatoes

Prep time: 5 minutes | Cook time: 5 minutes | Serves 6

2½ pounds (1.1 kg) russet potatoes and/or Yukon Gold potatoes
6 large garlic cloves, roughly chopped
2½ teaspoons kosher salt, plus more to taste
6 tablespoons vegan butter (use a soy-free variety to keep soy-free), plus more to taste
⅓ cup canned lite or reduced-fat coconut milk
Freshly cracked black pepper
Optional Garnishes:
Finely chopped fresh herbs, such as rosemary, thyme, chives, or Italian flat-leaf parsley
Extra-virgin olive oil, for drizzling

1. Scrub, peel, and dice the potatoes into 1- to 1½-inch pieces and place in the inner pot of the Instant Pot. Add the garlic and 1 teaspoon of the salt. Cover the potatoes with enough water to completely cover the potatoes, 4 to 5 cups. 2. Secure the lid and set the Pressure Release to Sealing. Select the Pressure Cook setting at high pressure and set the cook time to 5 minutes for russet potatoes or 6 minutes for Yukon Gold potatoes (6 minutes if using a mixture of both). 3. Once the timer has completed and beeps, perform a quick pressure release by carefully switching the Pressure Release knob from Sealing to Venting. 4. Open the pot and transfer the potato-garlic mixture to a colander. The potatoes should be very fork-tender and nearly falling apart. Let the potatoes rest for 5 minutes to dry out. 5. If you are using a ricer or a food mill, set it over the inner pot or a large bowl and pass the potato-garlic mixture through. If you are using a potato masher or an electric handheld mixer (on low speed), return the potato-garlic mixture to the inner pot or a large bowl and mash. Add the vegan butter, coconut milk, and remaining 1½ teaspoons salt. Fold gently with a silicone spatula to combine, or, if using an electric handheld mixer, whip lightly until the potatoes are smooth and creamy. 6. Add more salt, vegan butter, and/or pepper to taste. I usually add about ½ teaspoon more salt. If desired, garnish with chopped fresh herbs and a drizzle of extra-virgin olive oil.

Steamed Kabocha Squash

Prep time: 2 minutes | Cook time: 4 minutes | Serves 4

1 kabocha squash

1. Place a trivet in the pressure cooker, place a steamer basket on top of the trivet, and add enough water to come up to, but not in, the basket. Bring the water to a boil. 2. Wash the kabocha squash well, as the skin is edible. Cut in half and scoop out the seeds. Place the squash in the steamer basket, cut-side up. 3. Cover and bring to pressure. Cook at high pressure for 4 minutes. Allow for a natural release; if after 10 minutes the pressure has still not come down fully, manually release. 4. Serve immediately, store in an airtight container in the refrigerator for 3 to 4 days, or freeze in a sturdy bag for 6 to 8 months.

Sweet Potatoes with Pecans

Prep time: 10 minutes | Cook time: 18 minutes | Serves 4 to 6

½ cup brown sugar
1 tablespoon lemon zest
½ teaspoon sea salt
1¼ cup water
4 large sweet potatoes, peeled and sliced
¼ cup butter
¼ cup maple syrup
1 tablespoon cornstarch
1 cup pecans, chopped

1. In the Instant Pot, combine the sugar, lemon zest, salt and water. Stir well. 2. Add the potatoes to the pot. Close and lock the lid. 3. Select Manual and cook at High pressure for 15 minutes. 4. Once timer goes off, use a quick release. Carefully unlock the lid. 5. Transfer the potatoes to a serving bowl. 6. Select the Sauté setting on the Instant Pot, add the butter and melt it. 7. Add the maple syrup, cornstarch, and chopped pecans. Stir to combine and sauté the sauce for 2 minutes. 8. Serve the potatoes with sauce and whole pecans.

Empty-the-Root-Cellar Curry

Prep time: 15 minutes | Cook time: 10 minutes | Serves 6

1 pound (454 g) medium parsnips, peeled and cut into 1-inch sections
1 pound (454 g) yellow beets, peeled and cut into 1-inch cubes
1 pound (454 g) large yellow potatoes, cut into quarters
¾ pound medium carrots, peeled and cut into 1-inch sections
1 medium yellow onion, chopped
2 cups vegetable broth
½ cup whole roasted unsalted almonds
3 tablespoons minced peeled fresh ginger
2 tablespoons yellow curry powder
½ teaspoon table salt
Plain regular or low-fat yogurt, for garnish

1. Mix the parsnips, beets, potatoes, carrots, onion, broth, almonds, ginger, curry powder, and salt in a 6- or 8-quart cooker. Stir well, then lock the lid onto the pot. 2. Select Pressure Cook or Manual, and cook on high for 10 minutes with the Keep Warm setting off. 3. Use the quick-release method to bring the pressure back to normal. Unlatch the lid and open the cooker. Stir well before serving in bowls with dollops of yogurt as a garnish.

Balsamic and Allspice–Pickled Beets

Prep time: 5 minutes | Cook time: 8 minutes | Serves 4 to 8

½ cup balsamic vinegar
¼ cup apple cider vinegar
3 tablespoons unrefined sugar
1 teaspoon salt
½ teaspoon ground coriander or 1 teaspoon coriander seeds
½ teaspoon ground allspice or 1 teaspoon allspice berries
½ cup water
3 or 4 large beets, peeled and sliced

1. In your electric pressure cooker's cooking pot, stir together the vinegars, sugar, salt, coriander, allspice, and water. Add the beets. Close and lock the lid and ensure the pressure valve is sealed, then select High Pressure and set the time for 8 minutes. 2. Once the cook time is complete, quick release the pressure, being careful not to get your fingers or face near the steam release. 3. Once all the pressure has released, carefully unlock and remove the lid. Let cool for a few minutes with the lid off to dissipate the vinegar steam, then scoop out the beets and serve.

Tasty Potato Hash

Prep time: 10 minutes | Cook time: 9 minutes | Serves 4 to 6

1 tablespoon olive oil
5 medium potatoes, peeled and roughly chopped
5 eggs, whisked
1 cup Cheddar cheese, shredded
1 cup ham, chopped
¼ cup water
Salt and ground black pepper, to taste

1. Select the Sauté setting on the Instant Pot and heat the oil. 2. Add the potatoes and sauté for 3 to 4 minutes, until slightly brown. 3. Add eggs, cheese, ham, water, salt and pepper. Stir well. Close and lock the lid. 4. Press the Cancel button to stop the Sauté function, then select the Manual setting and set the cooking time for 5 minutes at High pressure. 5. Once pressure cooking is complete, select Cancel and use a quick release. Carefully unlock the lid. 6. Serve warm.

Loaded Mashed Cauliflower

Prep time: 10 minutes | Cook time: 10 minutes | Serves 6

½ pound (227 g) bacon
1 cup water
2 medium heads cauliflower, cut into florets and core removed
1½ cups shredded sharp cheddar cheese, divided
4 tablespoons unsalted butter (at room temperature)
½ cup heavy cream
2 green onions, chopped

1. Press Sauté to preheat the Instant Pot. Once hot, add the bacon. Cook until the bacon is browned and crispy, then remove it with a slotted spoon and place on paper towels to drain any excess fat. Press Cancel to turn off the Instant Pot. Discard the drippings and wipe the pot clean. 2. Pour the water into the pot and insert a steamer basket. Place the cauliflower in the steamer basket. 3. Secure the lid with the steam vent in the sealed position. Press Manual and immediately adjust the timer to 4 minutes. Check that the display light is beneath high pressure. 4. When the timer sounds, quick release the pressure and carefully remove the lid. Carefully transfer the cauliflower to a large bowl and mash until very smooth. Add 1 cup of the shredded cheese plus the butter and cream, stirring to combine. 5. Place the cauliflower mixture into a 7 x 11–inch baking dish. Sprinkle the remaining ½ cup of cheese on top, the broil until the cheese is melted, about 5 minutes. Crumble the bacon and sprinkle over the top along with the green onions.

Mustard Potato Salad

Prep time: 10 minutes | Cook time: 5 minutes | Serves 8

1 pound (454 g, about 5 medium) red potatoes, cut into ½-inch cubes
½ cup broth
3 large eggs
8 to 10 ice cubes
1 cup water
1 cup mayonnaise
1 teaspoon apple cider vinegar
1 tablespoon yellow mustard
½ cup chopped celery
½ cup peeled and chopped onion
1 tablespoon dill relish
¼ teaspoon fine sea salt
¼ teaspoon celery salt
½ teaspoon smoked paprika
½ teaspoon ground black pepper

1. Place potatoes in the Instant Pot. Add broth. Nestle the eggs in the potatoes. Lock lid. 2. Press the Manual button and adjust time to 5 minutes. When timer beeps, quick-release pressure until float valve drops and then unlock lid. 3. Transfer eggs to an iced water bath by placing 8 to 10 ice cubes in a medium bowl filled with about 1 cup of water leaving enough room to add eggs. Drain potatoes and set aside. 4. In a medium bowl, combine mayonnaise, vinegar, yellow mustard, celery, onion, dill relish, salt, celery salt, smoked paprika, and black pepper. Peel eggs and dice. Add to mayonnaise mixture. Add potatoes. Carefully toss. 5. Refrigerate lidded until ready to serve chilled.

Sweet and Sour Beet Salad

Prep time: 15 minutes | Cook time: 20 minutes | Serves 8

6 medium fresh beets (about 2 pounds / 907 g)
1½ cups water
¼ cup extra-virgin olive oil
3 tablespoons lemon juice
2 tablespoons cider vinegar
2 tablespoons honey
¼ teaspoon salt
¼ teaspoon pepper
2 large ruby red grapefruit, peeled and sectioned
2 small red onions, halved and thinly sliced

1. Scrub beets, trimming tops to 1 inch. Place beets on trivet of a 6-quart electric pressure cooker. Add 1½ cups water. Lock lid; make sure vent is closed. Select Manual setting; adjust pressure to High and set time to 20 minutes. 2. When finished cooking, let pressure release naturally before opening; remove beets and cool completely before peeling, halving and thinly slicing them. Place in a serving bowl. Whisk together next six ingredients. Pour over beets; add grapefruit and onion. Toss gently to coat.

Crustless Veggie Potpie

Prep time: 10 minutes | Cook time: 12 minutes | Serves 4

1 large head cauliflower, cut into florets
3 cups vegetable or chicken stock
1 cup frozen peas
2 cups sliced carrot
2 medium Yukon gold potatoes, peeled and diced
3 celery ribs, diced
1 medium yellow onion, diced
3 cloves garlic, minced
2 bay leaves
1½ teaspoons sea salt, plus more to taste
½ teaspoon dried marjoram
2 tablespoons fresh thyme, for garnish (optional)

1. In the Instant Pot, combine the cauliflower florets and stock. 2. Secure the lid with the steam vent in the sealed position. Select Manual or Pressure Cook, and cook on high for 5 minutes. 3. Use a quick release and remove the lid. Using an immersion blender or blender, purée the cauliflower mixture to form the base of your potpie. (Place the mixture back in the pot if it was removed to blend.) 4. Add the frozen peas, carrot, potatoes, celery, onion, garlic and bay leaves to the cauliflower mixture. Sprinkle with the salt and marjoram and give the mixture a stir. 5. Secure the lid with the steam vent in the sealed position. Select Manual or Pressure Cook, and cook on high for 7 minutes. Use a quick release and remove the lid. 6. Serve hot and garnish with fresh thyme (if using), and additional salt to taste (if needed).

Eggplant, Tomato and Chickpea Tagine

Prep time: 15 minutes | Cook time: 15 minutes | Serves 4 to 6

¼ cup extra-virgin olive oil, plus more to serve
4 medium garlic cloves, finely chopped
1 medium yellow onion, roughly chopped
2 pints grape or cherry tomatoes, halved
4 teaspoons finely grated fresh ginger
1½ teaspoons ground cumin
1 teaspoon sweet paprika
¼ teaspoon ground cinnamon
Kosher salt and ground black pepper
2 pounds (907 g) eggplant, trimmed and cut into 1-inch chunks
1 (15½-ounce / 439-g) can chickpeas, rinsed and drained
1 tablespoon lemon juice, plus lemon wedges to serve
1 cup lightly packed fresh cilantro, finely chopped

1. On a 6-quart Instant Pot, select Normal/Medium Sauté. Add the oil and garlic, then cook, stirring often, until the garlic is golden brown, about 4 minutes. 2. Add the onion, tomatoes, ginger, cumin, paprika, cinnamon, 2½ teaspoons salt and 1 teaspoon pepper. Cook, stirring occasionally, until the tomatoes begin to release some of their juices, 2 to 4 minutes. 3. Press Cancel, then stir in ¼ cup water, scraping up any browned bits. Gently stir in the eggplant, then distribute in an even layer. Fast: 4. Lock the lid in place and move the pressure valve to Sealing. Select Pressure Cook or Manual; adjust the pressure level to Low. Set the cooking time for 3 minutes. When pressure cooking is complete, quick-release the steam by moving the pressure valve to Venting. Press Cancel, then carefully open the pot. Slow: Select More/High Sauté and bring the mixture to a boil. Press Cancel, lock the lid in place and move the pressure valve to Venting. Select Slow Cook and set the temperature to Less/Low. Set the cooking time for 5 to 6 hours; the tagine is done when the tomatoes have broken down and the eggplant is very tender. Press Cancel, then carefully open the pot. 5. Gently stir in the chickpeas and lemon juice, then taste and season with salt and pepper. Stir in the cilantro. Serve drizzled with additional oil and with lemon wedges on the side.

Mashed Yukon Gold Potatoes

Prep time: 5 minutes | Cook time: 30 minutes | Serves 4

2 pounds (907 g) unpeeled Yukon Gold potatoes
6 tablespoons (¾ stick) salted butter, cut into 6 pieces, divided
Kosher salt and ground black pepper
½ cup Half-and-Half

1. Fill a large bowl with water. Quarter the potatoes lengthwise, then slice about ½ inch thick; add the slices to the water as you go. After all the potatoes have been sliced, drain in a colander set in the sink and rinse briefly under cool water. Drain well, shaking the colander to remove as much water as possible. 2. On a 6-quart Instant Pot, select More/High Sauté. Add 4 tablespoons of butter and let melt. Add the potatoes and 1 teaspoon salt, then stir until the potatoes are well coated. Stir in ½ cup water, then distribute in an even layer. 3. Press Cancel, lock the lid in place and move the pressure valve to Sealing. Select Pressure Cook or Manual; make sure the pressure level is set to High. Set the cooking time for 9 minutes. 4. When pressure cooking is complete, quick-release the steam by moving the pressure valve to Venting. Press Cancel, then carefully open the pot. 5. If there is liquid remaining in the pot, select More/High Sauté and cook, stirring often, until no moisture remains. Press Cancel to turn off the pot. 6. Using a potato masher, mash the potatoes directly in the pot until mostly smooth with some large bits. Add the half-and-half and continue to mash to the desired consistency. Fold in the remaining 2 tablespoons butter until melted. Taste and season with salt and pepper.

Mixed Vegetables with Peanut Sauce

Prep time: 20 minutes | Cook time: 6 minutes | Serves 4

Peanut Sauce:
3 tablespoons peanut butter
1 tablespoon balsamic vinegar
1 tablespoon maple syrup
1 tablespoon tamari
2 teaspoons grated or minced fresh ginger
2 to 3 cloves garlic, minced
Pinch of crushed red pepper flakes, or ½ teaspoon Chinese chili paste with garlic (optional)

Vegetables:
1 cup sliced onion (cut from top to bottom)
1 cup diced sweet potato
1 cup ½-inch sliced carrot (cut on the diagonal)
⅓ cup vegetable stock or water, plus an additional ¼ cup if needed
1½ cups broccoli florets
Chopped cilantro, for garnish

1. Mix the peanut sauce ingredients and set aside. 2. Set the Instant Pot to Sauté. Add the onion and dry sauté for 2 minutes. 3. Add the sweet potato, carrot, and ⅓ cup stock. Lock the lid on the cooker. Bring to high pressure; cook for 2 minutes. Quick release the pressure. Remove the lid, carefully tilting it away from you. 4. Add the broccoli and ¼ cup more stock if there is no liquid left in the cooker. Stir. Lock on the lid. Bring to low pressure; cook for 2 minutes. Quick release the pressure. Remove the lid, carefully turning it away from you. 5. Stir in the peanut sauce. Transfer the vegetable mixture to a plate. Garnish with cilantro and serve.

Two-Corn Chowder with Green Chili and Scallions

Prep time: 10 minutes | Cook time: 20 minutes | Serves 4 to 6

3 ears fresh corn, husks and silk removed
4 tablespoons (½ stick) salted butter
1 bunch scallions, thinly sliced, white and green parts reserved separately
2 medium garlic cloves, finely chopped
1 poblano chili, stemmed, seeded and chopped
1 (28-ounce / 794-g) can hominy, rinsed and drained
1 pound (454 g) Yukon Gold potatoes, unpeeled, cut into 1-inch chunks
3 cups low-sodium chicken broth
Kosher salt and ground black pepper
½ cup heavy cream

1. One at a time, stand each cob in a wide bowl. Using a chef's knife, cut the kernels from the ears of corn; you should have about 3 cups. Use the back of the knife to scrape each cob from top to bottom all around, allowing the liquid to fall into the bowl. Cut each cob in half and reserve separately. 2. On a 6-quart Instant Pot, select More/High Sauté. Add the butter and let melt. Add the scallion whites, garlic, chili, and corn kernels and liquid. Cook, stirring occasionally, until the chili is softened, about 7 minutes. 3. Stir in the hominy, potatoes, broth, 1½ teaspoons salt and ½ teaspoon pepper, then distribute in an even layer. Add the corn cobs to the pot. Fast: 4. Press Cancel, lock the lid in place and move the pressure valve to Sealing. Select Pressure Cook or Manual; make sure the pressure level is set to High. Set the cooking time for 7 minutes. When pressure cooking is complete, allow the pressure to reduce naturally for 10 minutes, then release the remaining steam by moving the pressure valve to Venting. Press Cancel, then carefully open the pot. Slow: With the pot still on More/High Sauté, bring the mixture to a boil. Press Cancel, lock the lid in place and move the pressure valve to Venting. Select Slow Cook and set the temperature to More/High. Set the cooking time for 2½ to 3 hours; a skewer inserted into a piece of potato should meet no resistance. Press Cancel, then carefully open the pot. 5. Remove and discard the corn cobs. Select More/High Sauté, then stir in the cream and half the scallion greens and cook, stirring occasionally, until heated through, about 3 minutes. Taste and season with salt and pepper. Serve sprinkled with the remaining scallion greens and pepper.

Veggie Queen's Broccoli Raab with Shiitake Mushrooms

Prep time: 10 minutes | Cook time: 5 minutes | Serves 4

Sauté:
1 tablespoon olive oil (or water sauté to make oil-free)
6 shiitake mushrooms, stems removed and saved for stock, sliced thinly
Pressure Cooker:
5 cloves garlic, minced

1 bunch broccoli raab, chopped (4 cups)
Pinch of red pepper flakes (optional)
¼ cup broth, mushroom or vegetable
Salt, to taste

1. Turn your Instant Pot to Sauté. Heat the olive oil and add the mushrooms. Sauté for 2 minutes or until they start wilting. 2. Add the garlic, broccoli raab, red pepper flakes (if using) and broth. Set the timer for 2 minutes, on High Pressure. 3. When time is up, quick release the pressure and remove the lid, carefully tilting it away from you. Remove the finished dish to a plate and add salt, to taste. Serve hot.

Creamy Polenta

Prep time: 2 minutes | Cook time: 7 minutes | Serves 6

4 cups water
1 cup uncooked polenta
½ teaspoon sea salt
Freshly ground black pepper, to taste
½ cup shredded vegan Parmesan cheese (such as Follow Your Heart)

1. Add 4 cups water to the inner pot. Gently sprinkle the polenta, salt, and a pinch of pepper over the water, without stirring. If stirred, the polenta will often trigger the burn warning on the Instant Pot. 2. Lock the lid and ensure the steam release valve is set to the Sealing position. Select Pressure Cook (High), and set the cook time for 7 minutes. 3. Once the cook time is complete, allow the pressure to release naturally for 10 minutes, then quick release any remaining pressure. Whisk until smooth and stir in the Parmesan. Season to taste with additional salt and pepper. The polenta will firm up as it cools, but if it doesn't seem cooked enough, put the lid back on and let it sit for 10 minutes more. 4. Serve warm right away because polenta will solidify if left at room temperature too long.

No-Drain Mashed Potatoes

Prep time: 10 minutes | Cook time: 10 minutes | Serves 4 to 6

2½ pounds (1.1 kg) yellow potatoes, cut into halves or quarters
1¼ cups vegetable or chicken broth
3 tablespoons butter
½ teaspoon table salt
⅓ cup heavy cream, half-and-half, or whole milk
¼ cup regular or low-fat sour cream
1 tablespoon Dijon mustard
Ground black pepper, for garnish

1. Stir the potatoes, broth, butter, and salt in a 6- or 8-quart cooker. Secure the lid with the steam vent in the sealed position. 2. Select Pressure Cook or Manual, and cook on high for 10 minutes with the Keep Warm setting off. 3. When the machine has finished cooking, turn it off and let its pressure return to normal naturally, about 20 minutes. Unlatch the lid and open the cooker. Add the cream, sour cream, and mustard. Use a potato masher right in the pot to mash the potatoes to your liking, chunky or smooth. Grind black pepper over individual servings, if desired.

Spicy White and Sweet Potatoes

Prep time: 10 minutes | Cook time: 9 minutes | Serves 4 to 6

1 medium onion, sliced
2 teaspoons minced fresh ginger
3 garlic cloves, minced
1 medium hot chile, such as jalapeño or serrano, seeded and finely chopped
¾ cup vegetable stock
1 pound (454 g) Yukon Gold or other thin-skinned potatoes, cut into ½-inch slices
1 pound (454 g) sweet potatoes, peeled and sliced ½ inch thick
Grated zest and juice of 1 lemon
½ cup nondairy yogurt (optional)
1 tablespoon tamarind paste
Salt and freshly ground black pepper
4 scallions, sliced

1. Set the Instant Pot to Sauté. Add the onion and dry sauté for 3 minutes. 2. Add the ginger, garlic, and chile and sauté another minute. 3. Add the stock and Yukon Gold and sweet potatoes. Lock the lid on the cooker. Bring to low pressure; cook for 5 minutes. Quick release the pressure. Remove the lid, carefully tilting it away from you. 4. Transfer the potatoes to a dish. 5. In a small bowl, whisk together the lemon zest and juice, yogurt, if using, and tamarind paste. Drizzle over the potatoes. Add salt and pepper to taste, sprinkle with the scallions, and serve.

Eggplant Spread

Prep time: 10 minutes | Cook time: 11 minutes | Serves 4 to 6

4 tablespoons olive oil
2 pounds (907 g) eggplant, sliced
4 cloves garlic, sliced
1 teaspoon kosher salt
1 cup water
1 lemon, juiced
1 tablespoon tahini
1 teaspoon extra-virgin olive oil
¼ cup black olives, pitted and sliced
2 sprigs of thyme

1. Preheat the Instant Pot by selecting Sauté. Add and heat the oil. 2. Put the eggplant in the pot and sauté for 3 minutes on both sides. 3. Add the garlic and cook for 1 to 2 minutes more, until fragrant. 4. Sprinkle with salt and pour in the water. 5. Press the Cancel button to stop the Sauté function. 6. Close and lock the lid. Select Manual and cook at High pressure for 6 minutes. 7. Once cooking is complete, let the pressure release naturally for 5 minutes. Release any remaining steam manually. Uncover the pot. 8. Place the mixture in a blender or food processor; add the lemon juice and tahini. Blend until the texture is smooth. 9. Transfer to a serving bowl and drizzle with extra-virgin olive oil. 10. Serve with olives and thyme.

Thai Red Curry

Prep time: 15 minutes | Cook time: 10 minutes | Serves 4 to 6

1 cup sliced onion
3 cloves garlic, minced
1 teaspoon or more minced hot chile, or ½ teaspoon crushed red pepper
½ cup chana dal or split red lentils
2 pieces dried galangal slices
2 kaffir lime leaves
1¾ cups vegetable stock
½ cup regular or light coconut milk
2 teaspoons Thai red curry paste
4 to 5 cups (or more) peeled cubed winter squash
4 ounces (113 g) oyster mushrooms, sliced
1 cup broccoli florets, or 2 cups thinly sliced kale, collard greens, or Swiss chard
1 to 2 tablespoons lime juice
Chopped cilantro, for garnish

1. Set the Instant Pot to Sauté. Add the onion and dry sauté for 1 minute. Add the garlic and chile and cook 1 minute longer. 2. Add the chana dal, galangal, lime leaves, ¾ cup of the stock, the coconut milk, and curry paste. Lock the lid on the cooker. Bring to high pressure; cook for 3 minutes. Let the pressure come down naturally. Remove the lid, carefully tilting it away from you. 3. Add the squash, mushrooms, and remaining 1 cup stock. Lock the lid back on the cooker. Bring to high pressure; cook for 3 minutes. Quick release the pressure. Remove the lid, carefully tilting it away from you. 4. Stir in the broccoli. Lock the lid back on and let sit for 2 minutes. Carefully open the lid. Remove the galangal slices. 5. Transfer the contents to a large bowl. Add lime juice to taste, sprinkle with cilantro, and serve.

Braised Savoy Cabbage

Prep time: 5 minutes | Cook time: 7 minutes | Serves 4

1 tablespoon olive oil
¼ cup shallots, minced
¼ cup white wine
4 cups savoy cabbage
1 cup vegetable broth

1. Add the olive oil to the Instant Pot and select the Sauté setting. 2. Once the oil is hot, add in the shallots and sauté for 3 minutes. 3. Next, add the white wine and cook for 1 to 2 minutes, or until the wine reduces. 4. Add the savoy cabbage and the vegetable broth to the cooker. 5. Seal the cooker and, using the Pressure Cook option, cook on high for 3 minutes. 6. Use the natural release method to release the steam from the cooker. 7. Carefully remove the lid and serve immediately.

Creamy Black-Eyed Peas

Prep time: 15 minutes | Cook time: 28 minutes | Serves 6

¼ cup (½ stick) butter, cut into chunks
1 medium yellow onion, chopped
1 medium red bell pepper, stemmed, cored, and chopped
2 medium garlic cloves, peeled and minced
1 teaspoon dried thyme
1 teaspoon dried sage
1 teaspoon mild paprika
½ teaspoon table salt
¼ teaspoon celery seeds
¼ teaspoon grated nutmeg
3 cups vegetable or chicken broth
2 cups dried black-eyed peas
½ cup heavy cream

1. Press the Sauté button, and set on Medium or Normal for 5 minutes. 2. Melt the butter in a 6- or 8-quart cooker. Add the onion and bell pepper; cook, stirring occasionally, until the onion softens, about 3 minutes. Stir in the garlic, thyme, sage, paprika, salt, celery seeds, and nutmeg until fragrant, just a few seconds. 3. Pour in the broth and scrape up any browned bits on the pot's bottom. Turn off the Sauté function and stir in the black-eyed peas. Lock the lid onto the cooker. 4. Select Pressure Cook or Manual, and cook on high for 23 minutes with the Keep Warm setting off. 5. Use the quick-release method to bring the pressure back to normal. Unlatch the lid and open the cooker. Stir well, then transfer 2 cups of the pea and liquid mixture in the pot to a blender. Add the cream, cover, remove the center knob in the blender's lid, place a clean kitchen towel over the opening, and blend until a smooth purée. Pour this mixture into the remaining black-eyed peas and stir well before serving.

Creamy or Crispy Parmesan Polenta

Prep time: 5 minutes | Cook time: 26 minutes | Serves 4

2 tablespoons olive oil
2 medium garlic cloves, thinly sliced
4 cups store-bought chicken or vegetable broth, or homemade, warmed
1 bay leaf
Salt and freshly ground black pepper
1 cup polenta (not quick-cooking)
½ cup grated Parmesan cheese

1. Place the oil in the pot, select Sauté, and adjust to Normal/Medium heat. When the oil is hot, add the garlic and cook, stirring frequently, until fragrant, 30 seconds. Add the broth, bay leaf, and ½ teaspoon salt. When the liquid comes to a simmer, gradually whisk in the polenta. Press Cancel. 2. Lock on the lid, select the Pressure Cook function, and adjust to Low pressure for 9 minutes. Make sure the steam valve is in the Sealing position. 3. When the cooking time is up, let the pressure come down naturally for 10 minutes and then quick-release the remaining pressure. Unlock the lid. It will look watery at first, but will come together and thicken as it stands. Whisk in the cheese and season with salt and pepper. Discard the bay leaf before serving. 4. For solid polenta to pan-fry or broil, transfer the polenta to a storage container and refrigerate, uncovered, until solid, at least 2 hours. Cut into squares and pan-fry in a nonstick sauté pan with a few tablespoons of olive oil over medium heat until golden brown, about 5 minutes per side. To broil, spread squares of polenta on a foil-lined baking sheet, drizzle with oil, sprinkle with a little Parmesan cheese, and broil 4 inches from the broiler element until the cheese is bubbly, 6 minutes.

Creamy Bacon-Corn Casserole

Prep time: 10 minutes | Cook time: 17 minutes | Serves 4

6 slices bacon, quartered
1 small red bell pepper, seeded and diced
¼ cup whole milk
2 tablespoons gluten-free all-purpose flour
2 tablespoons melted unsalted butter
2 ounces (57 g) cream cheese
½ teaspoon salt
½ teaspoon ground black pepper
2 (15¼-ounce / 432-g) cans corn, drained
2 tablespoons Parmesan cheese
1 cup water

1. Press the Sauté button on the Instant Pot. Add bacon to pot and cook 5 minutes until crisp. Transfer bacon to a paper towel-lined plate. Crumble when cooled. 2. Add bell pepper to pot and cook 5 minutes in bacon drippings until tender. 3. In medium bowl, whisk together milk and flour. Add butter, cream cheese, salt, and pepper. Add crumbled bacon, bell pepper, and corn. 4. Transfer to a 7-cup glass dish. Sprinkle with Parmesan cheese. 5. Add water to the Instant Pot. Lock lid. 6. Press the Manual or Pressure Cook button and adjust cook time to 7 minutes. When timer beeps, let pressure release naturally for 5 minutes. Quick-release any additional pressure until float valve drops and then unlock lid. 7. Remove dish from the Instant Pot and let cool for 10 minutes. Serve warm.

Vegetable Tian

Prep time: 10 minutes | Cook time: 30 minutes | Serves 4

1 tablespoon olive oil
½ medium yellow onion, peeled and diced
2 cloves garlic, minced
1 cup water
1 medium yellow squash, cut into ½-inch-thick slices
1 medium zucchini, cut into ½-inch-thick slices
2 Roma tomatoes, cut into ½-inch-thick slices
1 large russet potato, cut into ½-inch-thick slices
¼ teaspoon salt
⅛ teaspoon black pepper
½ cup shredded Mozzarella cheese
¼ cup grated Parmesan cheese

1. Press Sauté button on Instant Pot. 2. Add oil and onion. Let cook 4 minutes or until onion is soft. 3. Add garlic and cook an additional 30 seconds until fragrant. 4. Remove garlic and onion and spread in the bottom of a 7-inch cake pan. 5. Clean inner pot and place back inside Instant Pot. Add water and trivet to pot. 6. Arrange sliced vegetables in a pattern of squash, zucchini, tomato, and potato around the edge of the cake pan. Continue in the center of the pan until the vegetables are all used. 7. Top with a paper towel and cover top of pan tightly with foil. Create a foil sling and carefully lower cake pan into Instant Pot. 8. Close lid and set pressure release to Sealing. 9. Press Manual or Pressure Cook button and adjust time to 30 minutes. 10. When the timer beeps, allow pressure to release naturally for 10 minutes. Quick release remaining pressure and then unlock lid and remove it. 11. Remove pan from Instant Pot using foil sling. Sprinkle salt, pepper, Mozzarella, and Parmesan on top. Serve warm.

Blueberry Dijon Sprouted Wheatberry Salad

Prep time: 10 minutes | Cook time: 25 minutes | Serves 4

1½ cups wheat berries, soaked overnight	½ teaspoon salt
4 cups water	½ teaspoon black pepper
¼ cup walnut oil	½ cup red onion, minced
¼ cup apple cider vinegar	1 cup fresh blueberries
1 tablespoon Dijon mustard	½ cup sliced almonds

1. Drain the excess water off the soaked wheat berries and place them in the Instant Pot. 2. Add in the water and stir. 3. Seal the cooker and, using the Pressure Cook setting, cook on high for 25 minutes. 4. Use the natural release method to release the steam from the cooker. 5. While the steam is releasing, combine the walnut oil, apple cider vinegar, Dijon mustard, salt and black pepper. Whisk together until thoroughly combined. 6. Remove the cooked wheatberries from the cooker. Add the dressing and stir. 7. Cover and place in the refrigerator for at least 1 hour to chill. 8. Remove the wheat berries from the cooker and fluff with a fork. 10. Add the blueberries and almonds and stir gently before serving.

Orange Juice Beets

Prep time: 5 minutes | Cook time: 10 minutes | Serves 6

1 cup water	2 teaspoons unsalted butter
6 medium beets, ends trimmed	1 teaspoon salt
Juice of 1 medium orange	

1. Add water to the Instant Pot and insert steamer basket. Add beets to basket. Lock lid. 2. Press the Manual or Pressure Cook button and adjust cook time to 10 minutes. When timer beeps, quick-release pressure until float valve drops and then unlock lid. 3. Let beets rest 5 minutes. Once cool, peel off their outer skin with your hands. Cut beets into quarters and transfer to a serving dish. 4. Add orange juice, butter, and salt to dish. Toss and serve warm.

Polenta and Kale

Prep time: 5 minutes | Cook time: 23 minutes | Serves 4 to 6

1 tablespoon olive oil	1 cup polenta
2 bunches kale, stemmed, leaves chopped	1 quart vegetable stock
3 or 4 garlic cloves, minced	2 tablespoons nutritional yeast
1 teaspoon salt, divided, plus more as needed	2 to 3 tablespoons vegan butter
	Freshly ground black pepper

1. On your Instant Pot, select Sauté Low. When the display reads Hot, add the oil and heat until it shimmers. Add the kale, garlic, and ½ teaspoon of salt. Cook for about 2 minutes, stirring frequently so nothing burns, until the kale is soft and the garlic is fragrant. (You can always turn off the Instant Pot if it gets too hot.) Transfer the garlicky kale to a bowl and set aside. 2. In your Instant Pot, combine the polenta, stock, and remaining ½ teaspoon of salt. Lock the lid and turn the steam release handle to Sealing. Using the Manual function, set the cooker to High Pressure for 20 minutes. 3. When the cook time is complete, let the pressure release naturally for 15 minutes; quick release any remaining pressure. 4. Carefully remove the lid and stir well (some liquid may have accumulated on top of the polenta). Add the nutritional yeast and butter along with any additional salt and pepper. Serve in bowls topped with the kale.

Chow-Chow Relish

Prep time: 15 minutes | Cook time: 20 minutes | Serves 8

2 large green bell peppers, seeded and diced small	2 teaspoons red pepper flakes
1 large red bell pepper, seeded and diced small	2 teaspoons celery seed
2 large green tomatoes, diced small	2 teaspoons ground ginger
2 cups finely diced cabbage	1 teaspoon ground turmeric
1 large sweet onion, peeled and diced small	1 tablespoon sea salt
1 tablespoon ground mustard	½ cup granulated sugar
	½ cup packed dark brown sugar
	1 cup apple cider vinegar
	1 cup water

1. Place all ingredients into Instant Pot. Lock lid. 2. Press the Manual button and adjust time to 20 minutes. When timer beeps, let pressure release naturally until float valve drops and then unlock lid. Stir. 3. Use a slotted spoon to transfer relish to a serving dish. Serve warmed or chilled.

Garlicky Kale and Potatoes

Prep time: 5 minutes | Cook time: 10 minutes | Serves 4

½ cup vegetable broth	kale
3 cloves garlic, minced	1 tablespoon almond or other plant-based milk
2 medium russet potatoes, diced, or other favorite mashing potato	Salt, to taste (optional)
4 cups loosely packed chopped	Ground black pepper, to taste (optional)

1. Heat vegetable broth and garlic in the Instant Pot on Sauté (adjust to less heat) for 3 minutes. Add the potatoes. Place a trivet over the potatoes and set a steamer basket on top. Add the kale to the steamer basket. 2. Cover the pot, move the steam release handle to sealing, select Manual, toggle the Pressure button to low pressure, and set to 7 minutes. Use a quick release once done. 3. Remove the cover and pull the steam basket with the kale out of the pot with tongs or silicone gloves. Set aside. Add the almond milk, salt, and pepper to the potatoes, and mash with a hand masher. If there's too much liquid, set the Instant Pot on Sauté, adjust to less heat, and mash until the liquid is absorbed. Transfer the cooked kale into the pot and stir to combine.

Chapter 7 Stews and Soups

Chapter 7 Stews and Soups

Spice Trade Beans and Bulgur

Prep time: 30 minutes | Cook time: 30 minutes | Serves 10

3 tablespoons canola oil, divided
1½ cups bulgur
2 medium onions, chopped
1 medium sweet red pepper, chopped
5 garlic cloves, minced
1 tablespoon ground cumin
1 tablespoon paprika
2 teaspoons ground ginger
1 teaspoon pepper
½ teaspoon ground cinnamon
½ teaspoon cayenne pepper
1 (32-ounce / 907-g) carton vegetable broth
2 tablespoons soy sauce
1 (28-ounce / 794-g) can crushed tomatoes
1 (14½-ounce / 411-g) can diced tomatoes, undrained
1 (15-ounce / 425-g) can garbanzo beans or chickpeas, rinsed and drained
½ cup golden raisins
2 tablespoons brown sugar
Minced fresh cilantro (optional)

1. Select Sauté setting on a 6-quart electric pressure cooker. Adjust for medium heat; add 1 tablespoon oil. When oil is hot, cook and stir bulgur until lightly browned, 2 to 3 minutes. Remove from pressure cooker. 2. Heat remaining 2 tablespoons oil in pressure cooker. Cook and stir onions and red pepper until crisp-tender, 2 to 3 minutes. Add garlic and seasonings; cook 1 minute longer. Press Cancel. Add broth, soy sauce and bulgur to pressure cooker. 3. Lock lid; close pressure-release valve. Adjust to Pressure Cook on low for 12 minutes. Quick-release pressure. Press Cancel. 4. Select Sauté setting and adjust for low heat. Add the tomatoes, beans, raisins and brown sugar; simmer, uncovered, until mixture is slightly thickened and heated through, about 10 minutes, stirring occasionally. If desired, sprinkle with the minced cilantro.

Mom's Corn Chowder

Prep time: 10 minutes | Cook time: 11 minutes | Serves 4 to 6

1 tablespoon olive oil
1 small sweet onion, diced
3 celery stalks, sliced
2 garlic cloves, minced
1 teaspoon dried thyme
½ teaspoon ground coriander
½ to 1 teaspoon salt
¼ teaspoon freshly ground black pepper
3 medium to large russet potatoes, peeled and cut into large dice
3½ cups vegetable stock
6 tablespoons vegan butter
½ cup all-purpose flour
1 cup nondairy milk
12 ounces (340 g) frozen sweet corn
1 carrot, grated
Sliced scallion, green and light green parts, for garnishing (optional)

1. On your Instant Pot, select Sauté Low. When the display reads Hot, add the oil and heat until it shimmers. Add the onion. Cook for 2 to 3 minutes, stirring frequently. Turn off the Instant Pot and add the celery, garlic, thyme, coriander, salt, and pepper. Cook for another minute or so (the inner pot is still hot). 2. Stir in the potatoes and stock. Lock the lid and turn the steam release handle to Sealing. Using the Manual function, set the cooker to High Pressure for 6 minutes. 3. While the chowder cooks, in a small pan over medium-low heat on the stovetop, melt the butter. Whisk in the flour and cook for 3 to 4 minutes. Whisk in the milk, getting rid of any lumps to finish the roux. 4. When the cook time is complete, quick release the pressure. 5. .Carefully remove the lid and select Sauté Low again. Add the corn and carrot. Stir in the roux and let warm through and thicken. Taste and season with salt and pepper, as desired. Garnish with scallion (if using) before serving.

Sausage and Kale Soup

Prep time: 10 minutes | Cook time: 18 minutes | Serves 8

1 tablespoon olive oil
1 pound (454 g) hot Italian sausage, casings removed
4 cups chicken broth
4 cups water
6 medium russet potatoes, peeled and cubed
4 cups kale, stems removed
1 small yellow onion, peeled and chopped
3 cloves garlic, minced
½ teaspoon salt
⅛ teaspoon black pepper
1 cup heavy whipping cream
1 tablespoon flour

1. Set Instant Pot to Sauté. Put oil and sausage into Instant Pot. Cook sausage 8 minutes until brown, breaking it up into pieces while cooking. Turn Instant Pot off. 2. Add broth, water, potatoes, kale, onion, garlic, salt, and pepper and stir to combine. 3. Close lid and set pressure release to Sealing. 4. Press Manual or Pressure Cook button and adjust time to 10 minutes. 5. When the timer beeps, quick release pressure and then unlock lid and remove it. 6. Whisk in heavy cream and flour. Serve.

Turkey Rice Soup

Prep time: 10 minutes | Cook time: 15 minutes | Serves 4 to 6

1 pound (454 g) turkey cutlets, cut into 1-inch pieces
1½ quarts chicken broth
1 medium red onion, chopped
1 small green bell pepper or medium Cubanelle pepper, stemmed, cored, and chopped
2 medium garlic cloves, peeled and minced
¾ cup raw long-grain white rice
2 tablespoons fresh thyme leaves
2 teaspoons finely grated lemon zest
1 teaspoon ground black pepper
½ teaspoon table salt
1 tablespoon fresh lemon juice

1. Stir the turkey, broth, onion, bell pepper, garlic, rice, thyme, zest, pepper, and salt in a 6- or 8-quart cooker. Secure the lid with the steam vent in the sealed position. 2. Select Soup/Broth, Pressure Cook or Manual, and cook on high for 15 minutes with the Keep Warm setting off. 3. Use the quick-release method to bring the pressure back to normal. Unlatch the lid and open the pot. Stir in the lemon juice before serving.

Chicken Potpie Soup

Prep time: 15 minutes | Cook time: 15 minutes | Serves 6

3 tablespoons vegetable oil
2 stalks celery, chopped
1 medium onion, peeled and chopped
1 medium carrot, peeled and chopped
2 cloves garlic, peeled and minced
½ teaspoon salt
½ teaspoon ground black pepper
¼ teaspoon dried thyme
3 tablespoons all-purpose flour
3 cups chicken stock
3 cups shredded cooked chicken breast
½ cup heavy whipping cream
1 cup frozen peas
12 round butter crackers, such as Ritz

1. Press the Sauté button on the Instant Pot and heat oil. Add celery, onion, and carrot and cook until tender, about 8 minutes. Add garlic, salt, pepper, and thyme and cook until fragrant, about 30 seconds. 2. Sprinkle flour over vegetables and cook, stirring well, until flour is completely moistened, about 1 minute. Slowly whisk in stock, making sure to scrape any bits off the bottom of the pot. Press the Cancel button and stir in chicken. Close lid, set steam release to Sealing, press the Manual button, and adjust cook time to 5 minutes. 3. When the timer beeps, quick-release the pressure. Open lid, stir soup well, and stir in cream and peas. Let stand on the Keep Warm setting for 10 minutes, or until peas are hot and tender. Ladle into bowls and top each bowl with 2 crackers. Serve immediately.

Roma Vieja

Prep time: 45 minutes | Cook time: 40 minutes | Serves 6

2½ pounds (1.1 kg) boneless chuck roast or brisket, cut into 4-inch pieces
1 teaspoon salt
1 teaspoon ground black pepper
1 tablespoon olive oil
2 medium yellow onions, peeled and chopped
2 medium red bell peppers, seeded and chopped
6 cloves garlic, peeled and minced
2 teaspoons dried oregano
2 teaspoons ground cumin
2 teaspoons smoked paprika
½ teaspoon cayenne pepper
½ cup white wine
1 (14½-ounce / 411-g) can diced tomatoes
1 bay leaf
½ cup halved Spanish olives
2 teaspoons distilled white vinegar

1. Season meat with salt and pepper on all sides. Set aside. 2. Press the Sauté button on the Instant Pot and heat oil. Brown half the meat until well browned, about 7 minutes on each side. Transfer browned meat to a platter and set aside. Repeat with remaining meat. 3. Add onions and bell peppers to pot. Cook until vegetables are just tender, about 5 minutes. Add garlic, oregano, cumin, paprika, and cayenne pepper. Cook 1 minute until fragrant. Add wine and cook until liquid is reduced by half, about 2 minutes. Add tomatoes, bay leaf, and meat back to pot. Press the Cancel button. 4. Close lid and set steam release to Sealing, then press the Manual button and adjust cook time to 40 minutes. When the timer beeps, quick-release the pressure. Open lid and discard bay leaf. Stir in olives and vinegar, then shred meat with two forks. Serve hot.

Creamy Winter Squash Soup

Prep time: 15 minutes | Cook time: 7 minutes | Serves 6 to 8

Topping:
1 red tart sweet apple such as Gala or Pink Lady, cored and finely chopped
1 tablespoon orange juice
½ teaspoon grated lime or lemon zest
2 teaspoons fresh lime or lemon juice
Pinch of ground cardamom
2 tablespoons chopped cilantro or flat-leaf parsley
¼ cup pumpkin seeds (pepitas), toasted

Soup:
2 cups finely chopped onion
2 to 3 teaspoons (or more) curry powder
1 medium to large kabocha-type or butternut squash, peeled, seeded, and cubed
1 apple (any kind), peeled and diced
4 cups vegetable stock
1½ cups coconut milk or coconut water
½ teaspoon salt
Freshly ground black pepper

Make the Topping: 1. Mix the chopped apple, orange juice, lemon or lime zest and juice, and cardamom in a small bowl. Cover and set aside. Keep the cilantro and pumpkin seeds separate. Make the Soup: 2. Set the Instant Pot to Sauté. Add the onion and dry sauté for 3 minutes. Add the curry powder, squash, diced apple, stock, coconut milk, and salt. 3. Lock the lid on the cooker. Bring to high pressure; cook for 4 minutes. Let the pressure come down naturally. Remove the lid, carefully tilting it away from you. 4. Using an immersion blender, blender, or food processor, blend the soup until it is smooth and creamy. Add freshly ground black pepper to taste. 5. Just before serving, top each bowl with apple topping, cilantro, and pumpkin seeds.

Red Lentil Curry Soup

Prep time: 15 minutes | Cook time: 8 minutes | Serves 4 to 5

1 tablespoon avocado oil or extra-virgin olive oil
1 medium yellow onion, diced
2 cloves garlic, minced
1 tablespoon chopped fresh ginger
1 red bell pepper, seeded and diced
2 cups split red lentils
6 cups vegetable or chicken stock
1 (14½-ounce / 411-g) can diced tomatoes
2 tablespoons red curry paste
2 teaspoons garam masala
1 teaspoon curry powder
1 teaspoon sea salt, plus more to taste
1 (13½-ounce / 383-g) can full-fat coconut milk
Juice of 1 lime
¼ cup chopped fresh cilantro, for garnish (optional)

1. Select Sauté on the Instant Pot. Once the pot is hot, coat the pan with the oil. Add the onion, garlic, ginger and bell pepper. Sauté for about 3 minutes, then select Cancel. 2. Add the lentils, stock, tomatoes, curry paste, garam masala, curry powder and salt. Give the mixture a quick stir. 3. Secure the lid with the steam vent in the sealed position. Select Manual or Pressure Cook, and cook on high for 5 minutes. 4. Use a quick release and remove the lid. Pour in the coconut milk and lime juice and stir. 5. Enjoy hot, topping with fresh cilantro and additional salt to taste.

Tofu and Miso Soup

Prep time: 10 minutes | Cook time: 7 minutes | Serves 4

1 cup silken tofu, cubed
½ onion, diced
1 carrot, chopped
2 celery stalks, chopped
4 cups water
1 tablespoon tamari sauce
2 tablespoons miso paste
Salt, to taste

1. Combine all of the ingredients, except for the miso and salt, in the Instant Pot and stir to mix. 2. Close and lock the lid. Select the Poultry setting and set the cooking time for 7 minutes. 3. When the timer goes off, use a quick release. Carefully open the lid. 4. Whisk together the miso paste with some of the soup. 5. Pour the mixture in the soup and stir. Season with salt. Serve.

Butternut Squash Chickpea Tagine

Prep time: 20 minutes | Cook time: 30 minutes | Serves 4

1 cup dried chickpeas
2 teaspoons kosher salt
Spicy Pickled Raisins:
⅓ cup golden raisins
2½ tablespoons organic cane sugar
⅓ cup apple cider vinegar or white wine vinegar
¼ to ½ teaspoon crushed red pepper flakes, to taste
Tagine:
2 tablespoons olive oil
1 large yellow onion, diced
2 medium carrots, diced
5 garlic cloves, minced
2 teaspoons ground cinnamon
2 teaspoons ground coriander
1 teaspoon cumin seeds or ground cumin
1 teaspoon sweet paprika
¼ to ½ teaspoon cayenne pepper, to taste (optional)
2 bay leaves
1½ teaspoons kosher salt, plus more to taste
1¼ cups low-sodium vegetable broth or water
3 cups peeled and finely diced peeled butternut squash (from one 1½-pound / 680-g butternut squash)
¼ cup finely diced dried apricots (about 8 apricots)
1 (14½-ounce / 411-g) can crushed tomatoes
3 to 4 ounces (85 to 113 g) Tuscan (lacinato) kale, stems and midribs removed, roughly chopped
¼ cup roughly chopped fresh cilantro, plus more for garnish (optional)
Grated zest and juice of 1 small lemon

1. Cover the chickpeas with 6 cups water and stir in the 2 teaspoons salt. Soak for 8 hours or overnight, then drain and rinse them under cold water. 2. Make the spicy pickled raisins: Place the raisins in a glass jar. In a small saucepan, combine the sugar, vinegar, and pepper flakes and bring to a boil over medium-high heat, whisking until the sugar is dissolved. Remove from the heat and carefully pour the hot vinegar mixture over the raisins. Leave the jar uncovered and allow the mixture to come to room temperature. 3. Cook the tagine: Select the Sauté setting on the Instant Pot and let the pot heat up for a few minutes before adding the olive oil. Once the oil is hot, add the onion and carrots. Cook until the vegetables have softened, 4 to 5 minutes. Add the garlic and cook for 1 minute, stirring frequently. 4. Add the cinnamon, coriander, cumin seeds, paprika, cayenne (if using), bay leaves, and salt. Stir the spices into the vegetables for 30 seconds until the mixture is fragrant. Select the Cancel setting. 5. Pour in the broth, followed by the drained chickpeas, butternut squash, and dried apricots. Stir to combine all of the ingredients. Pour the crushed tomatoes on top, but do not stir, allowing the tomatoes to sit on top (this prevents the tomatoes from blocking the Instant Pot's heat sensor and burning). 6. Secure the lid and set the Pressure Release to Sealing. Select the Pressure Cook setting at high pressure and set the cook time to 12 minutes. 7. Once the 12-minute timer has completed and beeps, allow a natural pressure release. 8. Open the pot, discard the bay leaves, and stir in the kale. Select the Sauté setting and cook for 2 to 3 minutes to wilt the kale. Select the Cancel setting. 9. Add the cilantro and a bit of the lemon zest and half of the lemon juice. Stir and give it a taste. Add more lemon juice and/or lemon zest as desired. Taste for seasonings and add more salt as needed. 10. Transfer the tagine to bowls and add a few spoons of the spicy pickled raisins to each bowl. Garnish with fresh cilantro if desired.

Chik'n Lentil Noodle Soup

Prep time: 5 minutes | Cook time: 15 minutes | Serves 6

1 teaspoon extra-virgin olive oil
3 cloves garlic, finely diced
1 large onion, diced
2 cups fresh or frozen green beans, snapped into bite-size pieces
1 cup chopped carrots
1 cup chopped celery
2 teaspoons vegan chicken-flavored seasoning
1 bay leaf
½ teaspoon dried sage
1 cup dried brown lentils, rinsed and drained
4 ounces (113 g) soba noodles
4 cups vegetable broth
1 to 1½ cups water

1. In an uncovered pressure cooker, heat the oil on medium-high. Add the garlic, onions, green beans, carrots, and celery and sauté for about 3 minutes. Add the chicken-flavored seasoning, bay leaf, and sage and sauté for another 2 minutes. Add the lentils, noodles, vegetable both, and water. Stir to combine. 2. Cover and to bring to pressure. Cook at high pressure for 8 minutes. Use a quick release. 3. Sample both the lentils and the noodles. If they are not cooked through, simmer on low in the uncovered pressure cooker until done, adding more water if necessary. Remove the bay leaf before serving.

Instant Pot Miso Soup

Prep time: 5 minutes | Cook time: 6 minutes | Serves 4

1 small onion, cut into half-moon slices
2 medium carrots, chopped
2 medium stalks celery, chopped
½ cup fresh or frozen corn
1 teaspoon wakame flakes
1 cup silken tofu (lite firm or firm), cubed
4 cups water
2 tablespoons white or yellow miso paste
Soy sauce, to taste

1. Combine the onion, carrots, celery, corn, wakame flakes, tofu, and water in the Instant Pot. Cover the pot, move the steam release handle to sealing, select Manual, toggle the pressure cooker button to low pressure, and set for 6 minutes. Use a quick release once done. 2. Remove the lid and spoon about one cup of the broth into a bowl or measuring cup. Add the miso paste to the hot broth and whisk until dissolved. Pour the miso broth back into the pot. Stir and serve. Add soy sauce to taste.

Curried Pumpkin Bisque

Prep time: 20 minutes | Cook time: 22 minutes | Serves 6

1 sugar or pie pumpkin, cut in half, stem and seeds removed
1 cup water
¼ cup unsalted butter
1 medium yellow onion, peeled and finely chopped
1 medium carrot, peeled and finely chopped
2 cloves garlic, peeled and minced
1 teaspoon garam masala
½ teaspoon ground cinnamon
½ teaspoon ground cumin
½ teaspoon ground coriander
3 cups vegetable broth or chicken stock
2 cups heavy cream
3 tablespoons chopped fresh cilantro

1. Place pumpkin and water in the Instant Pot. Close lid, set steam release to Sealing, press the Manual button, and adjust time to 12 minutes. When the timer beeps, let pressure release naturally, about 20 minutes. Open lid, transfer pumpkin to cutting board, and drain off liquid. Scoop out pumpkin flesh into a large bowl and set aside. 2. Return pot to machine, making sure it is wiped dry. Press the Sauté button and melt butter. Add onion and carrot and cook until tender, about 5 minutes. Add garlic, garam masala, cinnamon, cumin, and coriander and cook until fragrant and the spices are darker in color, about 1 minute. Press the Cancel button. 3. Add pumpkin and broth and stir well. Close lid and set steam release to Sealing, then press the Manual button and adjust cook time to 5 minutes. 4. When the timer beeps, let pressure release naturally, about 15 minutes. Remove lid and stir well. Use an immersion blender, or work in batches with a blender, to purée soup until smooth. 5. Add cream to pot. Let stand on the Keep Warm setting to warm cream, about 5 minutes. Serve hot with cilantro for garnish.

Creamy Asparagus Soup with Basil

Prep time: 15 minutes | Cook time: 5 minutes | Serves 8

4 tablespoons unsalted butter
2 cups chopped asparagus
1 stalk celery, chopped
1 medium onion, peeled and chopped
1 clove garlic, peeled and minced
3 tablespoons chopped fresh basil
½ teaspoon salt
¼ teaspoon ground black pepper
¼ cup all-purpose flour
4 cups chicken broth or water
1 cup whole milk
¾ cup heavy whipping cream

1. Press the Sauté button on the Instant Pot and melt butter. Add asparagus, celery, and onion. Cook until tender, about 5 minutes, then add garlic, basil, salt, and pepper. Cook until fragrant, about 1 minute. 2. Add flour and cook for 1 minute, making sure all flour is moistened. Press the Cancel button, then slowly add broth and mix well, scraping the bottom of pot well. Close lid, set steam release to Sealing, press the Manual button, and set time for 5 minutes. 3. When the timer beeps, let pressure release naturally for 10 minutes, then quick-release the remaining pressure. Press the Cancel button, open lid, and stir in milk. Purée soup with an immersion blender or blend soup in batches in a blender. Stir in cream. Serve hot.

Irish Stew

Prep time: 20 minutes | Cook time: 40 minutes | Serves 4

2 tablespoons olive oil
2 pounds (907 g) boneless leg of lamb, fat trimmed, cut into 1-inch pieces
Salt and freshly ground black pepper
1 medium yellow onion, thinly sliced through the root end
½ cup Guinness or Murphy's Irish stout
1½ cups store-bought beef broth, or homemade
3 medium carrots, peeled and cut into 1-inch-thick coins
1 large (16-ounce /454-g) russet potato, peeled and cut into ½-inch slices
2 tablespoons cornstarch

1. Put the oil in the pot, select Sauté, and adjust to More/High heat. Season the lamb all over with salt and pepper. Add 1 cup of the meat (or the chops, in batches) to the pot and cook, stirring occasionally, until browned, 8 minutes. Do not overcrowd the meat or it will simmer in its juices instead of browning. 2. Add the onion to the pot and cook, stirring occasionally, until the onion begins to brown, 5 minutes. Add the stout and cook for 1 minute, scraping up the browned bits on the bottom of the pot. Press Cancel. 3. Add the remaining lamb, the broth, and the carrots and stir to combine. Place the potatoes on the top, but don't stir them into the lamb mixture. Lock on the lid, select Pressure Cook, and adjust to High pressure for 25 minutes. Make sure the steam valve is in the Sealing position. When the cooking time is up, let the pressure come down naturally for 10 minutes and then quick-release the remaining pressure. 4. Select Sauté, and adjust to More/High heat. Mix the cornstarch with 2 tablespoons water and gently stir the mixture into the stew. Simmer until bubbly, 1 minute. Season with salt and pepper. Serve.

Kidney Bean and Sausage Soup

Prep time: 15 minutes | Cook time: 30 minutes | Serves 6

½ pound (227 g) bulk Italian sausage
1 large yellow onion, peeled and chopped
2 cups roughly chopped cabbage
2 cloves garlic, peeled and minced
1 teaspoon ground fennel
½ teaspoon dried oregano
1 teaspoon smoked paprika
1 pound (454 g) dried kidney beans, soaked overnight in water to cover and drained
4 sprigs fresh thyme
¼ cup roughly chopped fresh flat-leaf parsley
8 cups water
½ teaspoon salt

1. Press the Sauté button on the Instant Pot and add sausage. Cook, crumbling into ½-inch pieces, until sausage is browned, about 8 minutes. Add onion and cook, stirring often, until tender, about 5 minutes. Add cabbage, garlic, fennel, oregano, and paprika and cook 2 minutes until garlic and spices are fragrant. 2. Add beans, thyme, and chopped parsley to pot and toss to coat in onion and spices. Add water, then press the Cancel button. Close lid, set steam release to Sealing, press the Bean/Chili button, and cook for the default time of 30 minutes. 3. When the timer beeps, let pressure release naturally, about 15 minutes. Uncover, remove thyme sprigs, stir in salt, and serve hot.

Turkey Chili Verde

Prep time: 10 minutes | Cook time: 28 minutes | Serves 6

2 tablespoons olive oil
2 medium green bell peppers, stemmed, seeded, and chopped
1 medium yellow onion, chopped
2 fresh jalapeño chiles, stemmed, seeded, and chopped
2 medium garlic cloves, peeled and minced
2 pounds (907 g) ground turkey
1 pound (454 g) fresh tomatillos, husked if necessary and chopped
1 cup chicken broth
½ cup loosely packed fresh cilantro leaves, chopped
2½ teaspoons dried oregano
1 teaspoon table salt
2 tablespoons yellow cornmeal

1. Press the Sauté button, and set on Medium or Normal for 15 minutes. 2. Warm the oil in a 6- or 8-quart cooker for a minute or two. Add the bell pepper, onion, jalapeño, and garlic. Cook, stirring often, until the onion begins to soften, about 5 minutes. 3. Crumble in the ground turkey. Cook, stirring once in a while and breaking up any large chunks, until the turkey begins to brown, about 4 minutes. Stir in the tomatillos, broth, cilantro, oregano, and salt. Turn off the Sauté function and lock the lid onto the pot. 4. Press the button Bean/Chili, Pressure Cook or Manual, and set on High for 8 minutes with the Keep Warm setting off. 5. When the machine has finished cooking, use the quick-release method to bring the pressure back to normal. 6. Unlatch the lid and open the cooker. 7. Press the Sauté button, and set on Medium or Normal for 5 minutes. 8. Bring the chili to a full simmer. Stir in the cornmeal. Cook, stirring constantly, until slightly thickened, about 4 minutes. Turn off the Sauté function, set the lid loosely over the pot, and set aside to continue to thicken without any heat for 5 minutes.

Chili Dog Soup

Prep time: 20 minutes | Cook time: 20 minutes | Serves 8

1 pound (454 g) 80% lean ground beef
1 medium white onion, peeled and chopped
2 cloves garlic, peeled and minced
¼ cup chili powder
1 teaspoon ground cumin
½ teaspoon ground coriander
2 tablespoons light brown sugar
½ teaspoon salt
½ teaspoon ground black pepper
1 (14½-ounce / 411-g) can diced tomatoes
2 cups beef broth
8 all-beef hot dogs, chopped
1 cup shredded Cheddar cheese
½ cup finely chopped Vidalia onion

1. Press the Sauté button on the Instant Pot and brown ground beef until no pink remains, about 10 minutes. Add white onion, garlic, chili powder, cumin, coriander, brown sugar, salt, and pepper and cook until the onions are just tender, about 10 minutes. 2. Add tomatoes, broth, and hot dogs and stir well. Press the Cancel button, close lid, set steam release to Sealing, press the Manual button, and set time to 20 minutes. 3. When the timer beeps, let pressure release naturally, about 20 minutes. Open lid and stir well. Serve hot with cheese and Vidalia onion for garnish.

French Dip Soup

Prep time: 30 minutes | Cook time: 30 minutes | Serves 6

3 tablespoons vegetable oil
1 pound (454 g) bottom round roast, cut into 3-inch pieces
3 medium yellow onions, peeled and sliced
4 cloves garlic, peeled and minced
1 teaspoon dried thyme
½ teaspoon dried oregano
½ teaspoon salt
½ teaspoon black pepper
½ cup sherry
3 cups beef broth
1 teaspoon Worcestershire sauce
1 bay leaf
2 cups plain croutons
1 cup shredded provolone cheese

1. Press the Sauté button on the Instant Pot and heat oil. Add half the beef, leaving space between each piece to avoid steaming, browning for 3 minutes per side. Transfer beef to a plate and repeat with remaining beef. 2. To pot add onions and cook until tender, about 5 minutes. Add garlic, thyme, oregano, salt, and pepper and cook until fragrant, about 1 minute. Add sherry, scraping bottom of pot well, and cool until reduced by half, about 1 minute. 3. Add browned beef, broth, Worcestershire sauce, and bay leaf to pot and stir well. Press the Cancel button, close lid, set steam release to Sealing, press the Manual button, and set time to 30 minutes. 4. When the timer beeps, let pressure release naturally, about 20 minutes. Open lid and remove bay leaf. Remove beef from pot and shred with two forks. Return to pot and stir well. Serve hot with croutons and cheese for garnish.

Shrimp and White Bean Soup

Prep time: 15 minutes | Cook time: 35 minutes | Serves 4

2 tablespoons unsalted butter
2 stalks celery, finely chopped
1 medium sweet onion, peeled and finely chopped
1 medium green bell pepper, seeded and finely chopped
1 clove garlic, peeled and minced
½ teaspoon seafood seasoning
½ teaspoon dried thyme
½ teaspoon ground black pepper
1 bay leaf
1 cup dried cannellini beans, soaked overnight in water to cover and drained
4 cups chicken broth
1 pound (454 g) small peeled and deveined shrimp
1 cup frozen or fresh corn kernels
¼ teaspoon hot sauce

1. Press the Sauté button on the Instant Pot and melt butter. Add celery, onion, and green pepper and cook until just tender, about 5 minutes. Add garlic, seafood seasoning, thyme, black pepper, and bay leaf and cook until garlic is fragrant, about 1 minute. 2. Press the Cancel button and add beans and broth to pot. Close lid, set steam release to Sealing, press the Bean/Chili button, and cook for the default time of 30 minutes. 3. When the timer beeps, let pressure release naturally, about 15 minutes. Open lid, remove bay leaf, and stir in shrimp and corn. Press the Cancel button, then press the Sauté button and simmer until shrimp are opaque and curled into C shapes, about 5 to 8 minutes. Drizzle with hot sauce before serving.

Curried Lentil Soup

Prep time: 10 minutes | Cook time: 15 minutes | Serves 6

- 2 tablespoons salted butter
- 1 medium white onion, peeled and chopped
- 1 tablespoon red curry paste
- ½ teaspoon garam masala
- ½ teaspoon turmeric
- ½ teaspoon brown sugar
- 2 cloves garlic, minced
- 2 teaspoons grated fresh ginger
- 3 tablespoons tomato paste
- 1 cup red lentils
- 4 cups chicken stock or vegetable broth
- ½ cup full-fat canned coconut milk, shaken well

1. Press the Sauté button on the Instant Pot and melt butter. Add onion and cook until just tender, about 3 minutes. Add curry paste, garam masala, turmeric, brown sugar, garlic, and ginger and cook until fragrant, about 30 seconds. Stir in tomato paste and cook for 30 seconds. Press the Cancel button. 2. Add lentils and stock, close lid, set steam release to Sealing, press the Manual button, and adjust time to 15 minutes. When the timer beeps, let pressure release naturally, about 15 minutes. Remove lid and stir in coconut milk. Serve warm.

Vietnamese-Style Chicken and Glass Noodle Soup

Prep time: 10 minutes | Cook time: 15 minutes | Serves 4

- 1 star anise pod
- 2 large shallots, root end intact, halved
- 1 (1-inch) piece fresh ginger, peeled and thinly sliced
- 5 dried shiitake mushrooms
- 1 bunch fresh cilantro, stems and leaves reserved separately
- 2 boneless, skinless chicken breasts
- 7 cups low-sodium chicken broth
- Kosher salt and ground black pepper
- 4 ounces (113 g) glass noodles
- 1 tablespoon fish sauce, plus more if needed
- Lime wedges, to serve

1. In a 6-quart Instant Pot, combine the star anise, shallots, ginger, mushrooms, cilantro stems, chicken breasts, broth and 1 teaspoon each salt and pepper. Fast: 2. Lock the lid in place and move the pressure valve to Sealing. Select Pressure Cook or Manual; make sure the pressure level is set to High. Set the cooking time for 5 minutes. When pressure cooking is complete, allow the pressure to reduce naturally for 5 minutes, then release the remaining steam by moving the pressure valve to Venting. Press Cancel, then carefully open the pot. Slow: Select More/High Sauté and bring to a boil. Press Cancel, lock the lid in place and move the pressure valve to Venting. Select Slow Cook and set the temperature to More/Low. Set the cooking time for 3 to 3½ hours; the chicken and broth are done when a skewer inserted into the breasts meets no resistance. Press Cancel, then carefully open the pot. 3. Using tongs, transfer the chicken and mushrooms to a plate and set aside. Using a slotted spoon, scoop out and discard the remaining solids in the broth. Thinly slice the mushrooms, discarding any tough stems. Using two forks, shred the chicken into bite-size pieces. 4. Select More/High Sauté and bring the broth to a boil. Stir in the noodles and fish sauce, then cook, stirring occasionally, until tender, 3 to 6 minutes. 5. Press Cancel to turn off the pot. Using kitchen shears, snip the noodles a few times directly in the pot to cut them into shorter lengths. Stir in the sliced mushrooms and chicken, then taste and season with additional fish sauce, if needed, and pepper. 6. Serve sprinkled with additional pepper and cilantro leaves and with lime wedges on the side.

Vegetable Chowder

Prep time: 15 minutes | Cook time: 5 minutes | Serves 8

- 4 tablespoons unsalted butter
- 2 stalks celery, chopped
- 2 medium carrots, peeled and chopped
- 1 medium yellow onion, peeled and diced
- 2 cloves garlic, peeled and minced
- ½ teaspoon ground black pepper
- ¼ teaspoon dried thyme
- ¼ teaspoon dried marjoram
- ⅓ cup all-purpose flour
- 4 cups vegetable broth
- 1 bay leaf
- 1 pound (454 g) new potatoes, diced
- 2 cups fresh broccoli florets
- 1 cup fresh cauliflower florets
- 2 cups heavy cream
- ⅓ cup chopped fresh chives

1. Press the Sauté button on the Instant Pot and melt butter. Add celery, carrots, and onion and cook until tender, about 5 minutes. Add garlic, pepper, thyme, and marjoram and cook until fragrant, about 30 seconds. 2. Sprinkle flour over vegetables and mix well, then cook 1 minute until no dry flour remains. Slowly add broth, whisking constantly until smooth, then add bay leaf, potatoes, broccoli, and cauliflower. Press the Cancel button. 3. Close lid and set steam release to Sealing, then press the Manual button and adjust cook time to 5 minutes. 4. When the timer beeps, let pressure release naturally, about 15 minutes. Open lid and stir in cream. Discard bay leaf and serve immediately with chives for garnish.

Wild Rice Soup

Prep time: 15 minutes | Cook time: 48 minutes | Serves 8

- 2 tablespoons unsalted butter
- 4 medium carrots, peeled and chopped
- 4 stalks celery, chopped
- 1 medium onion, peeled and chopped
- 1 (8-ounce / 227-g) container sliced mushrooms
- 2 cloves garlic, peeled and minced
- ½ teaspoon dried thyme
- 1 teaspoon salt
- ½ teaspoon black pepper
- 1 cup uncooked wild rice
- 4 cups chicken broth
- ⅓ cup water
- 2 tablespoons cornstarch
- ½ cup heavy cream

1. Press the Sauté button on the Instant Pot and melt butter. Add carrots, celery, and onion. Cook until vegetables are just tender, about 4 to 5 minutes, then add mushrooms and cook until they start to release liquid, about 3 minutes. 2. Add garlic, thyme, salt, pepper, and rice and cook until garlic is fragrant, about 1 minute. Press the Cancel button, add broth, and close lid. Set steam release to Sealing, press the Manual button, and set time to 45 minutes. 3. When the timer beeps, quick-release the pressure, open lid, and stir well. Press the Cancel button, then press the Sauté button. Whisk together water and cornstarch and stir into pot. Bring to a boil, stirring constantly, until thickened, about 3 to 4 minutes. Press the Cancel button and stir in cream. Serve hot.

Ground Turkey Stew with Black-Eyed Peas

Prep time: 10 minutes | Cook time: 15 minutes | Serves 4

1 large jarred roasted red bell pepper
6 sun-dried tomatoes packed in oil
¼ cup dry but light red wine
1 tablespoon mild paprika
½ teaspoon ground cinnamon
½ teaspoon table salt
¼ teaspoon red pepper flakes
2 tablespoons butter
1 pound (454 g) lean ground turkey
1 (15-ounce / 425-g) can black-eyed peas, drained and rinsed
1 (14-ounce / 397-g) can diced tomatoes
½ cup chicken broth
2 tablespoons loosely packed fresh dill fronds, finely chopped

1. Put the roasted pepper, sun-dried tomatoes, wine, paprika, cinnamon, salt, and red pepper flakes in a food processor. Cover and pulse to create a coarse but thin sauce, stopping the machine at least once to scrape down the inside. 2. Press the Sauté button, and set on Medium or Normal for 10 minutes. 3. Melt the butter in a 3- or 6-quart cooker. Crumble in the ground turkey and cook, stirring often to break up any clumps, until lightly browned, about 4 minutes. Scrape every bit of the red pepper paste into the cooker and cook, stirring all the while, for 1 minute. 4. Turn off the Sauté function. Stir in the black-eyed peas, tomatoes, broth, and dill until uniform. Secure the lid with the steam vent in the sealed position. 5. Select Meat/Stew, Pressure Cook or Manual, and cook on high for 5 minutes with the Keep Warm setting off. 6. Use the quick-release method to bring the pressure back to normal. Unlatch the lid and open the cooker. Stir well before serving.

Spiced Green Lentil and Coconut Milk Soup

Prep time: 10 minutes | Cook time: 20 minutes | Serves 6

2 tablespoons olive oil
2 stalks celery, sliced
1 medium white onion, peeled and chopped
2 medium carrots, peeled and sliced
2 cloves garlic, minced
1 teaspoon minced ginger
1 tablespoon Thai red curry paste
½ teaspoon ground coriander
½ teaspoon ground cumin
¼ teaspoon cayenne pepper
¼ teaspoon smoked paprika
½ teaspoon salt
2 cups dried green lentils
1 large russet potato, peeled and cubed
4 cups vegetable stock
1 (13.66-ounce / 387-g) can full-fat coconut milk
2 tablespoons fresh lime juice
2 tablespoons chopped fresh cilantro
½ teaspoon black pepper

1. Press the Sauté button on the Instant Pot and heat oil. Add celery, onion, and carrots and cook until just tender, about 3 minutes. Add garlic, ginger, curry paste, coriander, cumin, cayenne pepper, paprika, and salt. Cook until fragrant, about 30 seconds. Press the Cancel button. 2. Add lentils, potato, stock, and coconut milk to pot and stir well. Close lid, set steam release to Sealing, press the Manual button, and adjust time to 20 minutes. When the timer beeps, let pressure release naturally, about 15 minutes. Remove lid and stir in lime juice. Serve warm with cilantro and black pepper for garnish.

Lentil Minestrone

Prep time: 10 minutes | Cook time: 10 minutes | Serves 6

1 tablespoon extra-virgin olive oil
1 yellow onion, chopped
1½ cups chopped carrots (about 3 carrots)
1 cup chopped celery (about 3 stalks)
3 cloves garlic, minced
Heaping 1 cup chopped zucchini (about 1 squash)
1 cup green lentils
1 (28-ounce / 794-g) can diced tomatoes
2 teaspoons dried basil
1 teaspoon dried oregano
1 teaspoon dried thyme
3 cups water
Freshly ground black pepper
2 teaspoons fine sea salt
Lemon wedges, for serving (optional)

1. Press Sauté and add the olive oil to the Instant Pot. Once the oil is hot but not smoking, add the onion, carrots, and celery and sauté for 5 minutes, until softened. Press Cancel and stir in the garlic while the pot is still hot. 2. Add the zucchini, lentils, tomatoes with their juices, basil, oregano, thyme, water, and several grinds of pepper. Give the mixture a stir to ensure the lentils are covered in liquid for even cooking. Secure the lid and move the steam release valve to Sealing. Select Manual or Pressure Cook and cook on High pressure for 5 minutes. 3. When the cooking cycle is complete, let the pressure naturally release for 10 minutes, then move the steam release valve to Venting to release any remaining pressure. When the floating valve drops, remove the lid. Stir in the salt, then taste and adjust the seasonings as needed. Serve immediately, with a squeeze of fresh lemon to brighten the flavors. Store leftovers in an airtight container in the fridge for 5 days.

Spicy Beef and Broccoli Zoodle Soup

Prep time: 15 minutes | Cook time: 12 minutes | Serves 4 to 5

2 tablespoons avocado oil
3 tablespoons minced fresh ginger
2 cloves garlic, minced
1½ pounds (680 g) top sirloin steak tips, about 1-inch pieces
3 level cups fresh broccoli florets
8 ounces (227 g) sliced cremini mushrooms
6 cups beef stock
¼ cup rice vinegar
¼ cup coconut aminos or soy sauce
¼ cup buffalo hot sauce or sriracha
1 large zucchini, spiralized into noodles
⅓ cup chopped fresh green onion

1. Select Sauté on the Instant Pot. Once hot, add the oil, ginger, garlic and steak tips. Cook for a few minutes, until the beef is lightly browned on each side and the garlic and ginger are fragrant. Select Cancel. 2. Add the broccoli, mushrooms, beef stock, vinegar, coconut aminos and hot sauce and stir. At this point, you can remove and set aside the broccoli and add with the zoodles after the soup has cooked, if you want the broccoli to be crisper. 3. Secure the lid with the steam vent in the sealed position. Select Manual or Pressure Cook, and cook on high for 8 minutes. 4. Use a quick release to let the steam out, then open the lid and add more hot sauce if you desire a spicier broth. Add the spiralized zucchini, top with fresh green onion and serve hot.

Ginger and Spice Carrot Soup

Prep time: 10 minutes | Cook time: 20 minutes | Serves 6

2 tablespoons coconut oil
1 cup Vidalia onion, chopped
2 tablespoons freshly grated ginger root
1 tablespoon jalapeño pepper, minced
5 cups carrots, coarsely grated
1 teaspoon coriander
1 teaspoon curry powder
4 cups vegetable broth
1 cup couscous

1. Set the Instant Pot to the Sauté setting and add the coconut oil. 2. Next, add in the Vidalia onion, ginger and jalapeño pepper. Sauté for 2 minutes or until highly fragrant. 3. Add the carrots, coriander, and curry powder to the cooker and sauté for 5 minutes before adding in the vegetable broth. 4. Seal the cooker and set it to the Pressure Cook setting. Cook on high for 5 minutes. 5. Using the quick release option, release the steam from the cooker. 6. At this point, if you prefer a creamier textured soup, you can remove the lid and blend the soup using an immersion blender. For a chunkier soup, leave as is. 7. Add the couscous to the Instant Pot and seal. 8. Pressure Cook for 7 minutes. 9. Using the quick release option, release the steam from the cooker. 10. Stir before serving.

Toscana Soup

Prep time: 10 minutes | Cook time: 30 minutes | Serves 4 to 6

2 tablespoons olive oil
1 onion, diced
4 cloves garlic, minced
1 pound (454 g) Italian sausages, chopped
3 large russet potatoes, unpeeled and sliced thickly
¼ cup water
6 cups chicken broth
Salt and ground black pepper, to taste
2 cups kale, chopped
¾ cup heavy cream

1. Set your Instant Pot on Sauté mode, add the oil and heat it up. 2. Add the onion, garlic, and Italian sausages. Stir and sauté for 4 to 5 minutes, until the sausages have turned light brown. 3. Add the potatoes, water, and chicken broth and stir. 4. Sprinkle with salt and pepper. 5. Press the Cancel button to stop the Sauté function. 6. Close and lock the lid. Select Manual and cook at High pressure for 20 minutes. 7. When the timer goes off, use a quick release. Carefully open the lid. 8. Set your Instant Pot on Sauté mode, add the kale and heavy cream. 9. Simmer for 3 to 4 minutes. Press the Cancel button and let it sit for 5 minutes. 10. Serve.

Middle Eastern Lentil and Spinach Soup

Prep time: 10 minutes | Cook time: 15 minutes | Serves 4

1 tablespoon olive oil
1 large yellow onion, chopped
1 large carrot, chopped
2 teaspoons shawarma spice blend
4 cups store-bought vegetable or chicken broth, or homemade
1 (15-ounce / 425-g) can fire-roasted diced tomatoes with green chilies, with juice
1 cup dried brown lentils
Salt and freshly ground black pepper
2 cups baby spinach, large stems discarded

1. Put the oil in the pot, select Sauté, and adjust to More/High heat. When the oil is hot, add the onion, carrot, and seasoning blend and cook, stirring frequently, until the onion begins to brown, 4 minutes. Press Cancel. 2. Add the broth, tomatoes, lentils, 1 teaspoon salt, and several grinds of pepper. Lock on the lid, select the Pressure Cook function, and adjust to High pressure for 10 minutes. Make sure the steam valve is in the Sealing position. 3. When the cooking time is up, let the pressure come down naturally for 10 minutes and then quick-release the remaining pressure. Add the spinach and stir until wilted, 1 minute. Season with salt and pepper and serve.

Spicy Chicken Chili

Prep time: 15 minutes | Cook time: 40 minutes | Serves 8

1 tablespoon olive oil
1 pound (454 g) ground chicken
1 medium yellow onion, peeled and diced
3 cloves garlic, minced
3 canned chipotle chilies in adobo sauce
1 (15-ounce / 425-g) can dark red kidney beans, drained and rinsed
1 (15-ounce / 425-g) can black beans, drained and rinsed
1 teaspoon Worcestershire sauce
1 (30-ounce / 850-g) can diced tomatoes, including liquid
1 (4-ounce / 113-g) can diced green chilies, including liquid
1 teaspoon sea salt
2 teaspoons hot sauce
1 teaspoon smoked paprika
1 teaspoon chili powder

1. Press the Sauté button on the Instant Pot. Heat oil. Add the ground chicken and onion and stir-fry approximately 5 minutes until chicken is no longer pink. 2. Stir in the remaining ingredients. Lock lid. 3. Press the Meat/Stew button and cook for the default time of 35 minutes. 4. When timer beeps, let pressure release naturally until float valve drops and then unlock lid. 5. Ladle into individual bowls and serve warm.

Basic Vegetable Broth

Prep time: 5 minutes | Cook time: 30 minutes | Serves 6

1 peach, quartered
2 apples, quartered
1 medium onion, quartered
4 cloves garlic, chopped (peel and all)
8 carrots, halved
6 stalks celery, halved
1 tomato, quartered
6 whole romaine lettuce leaves
1 teaspoon avocado oil (optional)
8 cups water
½ teaspoon dried oregano
½ teaspoon dried sage
½ teaspoon dried sweet basil
½ teaspoon dried whole (rubbed) rosemary
1 teaspoon sea salt (optional)

1. Place all the ingredients in the pressure cooker. Stir to combine. 2. Cover and bring to pressure. Cook at high pressure for 15 to 30 minutes (for a richer broth, opt for 30 minutes). 3. Remove from the heat and allow for a natural release. Remove the lid from the pressure cooker. 4. Strain the broth through a fine-mesh strainer or cheesecloth. Use immediately or store in an airtight glass jar or container for up to 1 week; freeze in a heavy-duty freezer bag for 3 to 6 months.

Jamaican-Style Yellow Split Pea Soup

Prep time: 20 minutes | Cook time: 35 minutes | Serves 4 to 6

2 tablespoons (preferably unrefined) coconut oil
1 large yellow onion, finely chopped
6 medium garlic cloves, finely chopped
1 teaspoon dried thyme
1 teaspoon ground allspice
1 habanero or Scotch bonnet chili, stemmed
1½ quarts low-sodium chicken broth
1½ cups yellow split peas, rinsed and drained
3 medium carrots, peeled, halved lengthwise and thinly sliced
Kosher salt and ground black pepper
1 tablespoon ground turmeric
¼ cup finely chopped fresh cilantro
Lime wedges, to serve

1. On a 6-quart Instant Pot, select More/High Sauté. Add the oil and heat until shimmering. Add the onion and cook, stirring often, until softened and golden brown at the edges, 5 to 7 minutes. 2. Stir in the garlic, thyme and allspice, then cook until fragrant, about 30 seconds. Add the chili, broth and split peas; stir to combine, then distribute in an even layer. Fast: 3. Press Cancel, lock the lid in place and move the pressure valve to Sealing. Select Pressure Cook or Manual; make sure the pressure level is set to High. Set the cooking time for 18 minutes. When pressure cooking is complete, quick-release the steam by moving the pressure valve to Venting. Press Cancel, then carefully open the pot. Slow: With the pot still on More/High Sauté, bring the mixture to a boil. Press Cancel, lock the lid in place and move the pressure valve to Venting. Select Slow Cook and set the temperature to More/High. Set the cooking time for 6 to 7 hours; the soup is done when the split peas have completely broken down. Press Cancel, then carefully open the pot. 4. Stir the split pea mixture, scraping the bottom of the pot, then stir in the carrots. Select More/High Sauté and cook, stirring occasionally, until the carrots are tender, about 5 minutes. 5. Press Cancel to turn off the pot. Let stand for 10 minutes, then whisk in the turmeric and cilantro. Remove and discard the chili. Taste and season with salt and pepper.

Wild Rice and Mushroom Stew

Prep time: 10 minutes | Cook time: 25 minutes | Serves 6

1 yellow onion, chopped
5 carrots, peeled and chopped
5 celery stalks, chopped
3 cloves garlic, minced
8 ounces (227 g) cremini mushrooms, roughly chopped
1 teaspoon dried thyme
1 teaspoon ground sage
1 cup wild rice and brown rice blend, or wild rice
4 cups water
Fine sea salt
½ cup full-fat coconut milk
Freshly ground black pepper
Lemon wedges, for serving
Fresh thyme, for garnish

1. Combine the onion, carrots, celery, garlic, mushrooms, thyme, sage, rice, 4 cups of the water, and 2 teaspoons salt in the Instant Pot and secure the lid. Move the steam release valve to Sealing and select Manual or Pressure Cook to cook on High pressure for 25 minutes. 2. When the cooking cycle is complete, let the pressure naturally release for 10 minutes, then move the steam release valve to Venting to release any remaining pressure. When the floating valve drops, remove the lid. Stir in the coconut milk. 3. Season with additional salt and pepper, to taste, and serve immediately with a squeeze of fresh lemon to brighten the flavors and a few sprigs of thyme. Store leftovers in an airtight container in the fridge for 5 days.

Cream of Fennel Soup

Prep time: 20 minutes | Cook time: 3 minutes | Serves 8

2 tablespoons unsalted butter
2 bulbs fennel, tops trimmed and bulbs diced
2 stalks celery, diced
1 medium onion, peeled and chopped
1 clove garlic, peeled and minced
½ teaspoon dried dill
½ teaspoon salt
¼ teaspoon ground black pepper
¼ cup all-purpose flour
4 cups chicken broth
1 cup heavy whipping cream

1. Press the Sauté button on the Instant Pot and melt butter. Add fennel, celery, and onion. Cook until tender, about 8 minutes, then add garlic, dill, salt, and pepper. Cook until fragrant, about 1 minute. 2. Add flour and cook for 1 minute, making sure all flour is moistened. Press the Cancel button, then slowly add broth and mix well, scraping the bottom of pot well. Close lid, set steam release to Sealing, press the Manual button, and set time for 3 minutes. 3. When the timer beeps, let pressure release naturally for 10 minutes, then quick-release the remaining pressure. Press the Cancel button, open lid, and purée soup with an immersion blender or in batches in a blender. Stir in cream. Serve hot.

Anasazi Bean and Winter Vegetable Stew

Prep time: 15 minutes | Cook time: 11 minutes | Serves 4

1 cup diced onion
1 cup ½-inch-thick sliced carrot
½ cup sliced peeled parsnip (about 1 medium)
4 cloves garlic, minced
1½ tablespoons Italian seasoning
2 bay leaves
1 cup Anasazi beans, soaked and drained
1½ cups vegetable stock
1½ cups diced peeled rutabaga
or unpeeled small turnips
1¼ cups diced peeled butternut or other winter squash
1 (15-ounce / 425-g) can diced tomatoes or fire-roasted tomatoes
1 cup finely sliced kale leaves or baby spinach
Salt and freshly ground black pepper
¼ cup chopped fresh flat-leaf parsley, for garnish

1. Set the Instant Pot to Sauté. Add the onion and dry sauté for 2 minutes. Add the carrot, parsnip, and garlic and cook another minute. Add the seasoning, bay leaves, beans, and stock. 2. Lock the lid on the cooker, bring to high pressure, and cook for 6 minutes. Let the pressure come down naturally. Remove the lid, carefully tilting it away from you. 3. Add the rutabaga and squash. Lock on the lid and bring the cooker back to high pressure; cook for 3 minutes. Quick release the pressure. Remove the lid carefully. 4. Add the tomatoes and greens. Stir. Lock the lid on the pot and let sit for 2 minutes. Remove the lid carefully. Remove and discard the bay leaves. Add salt and pepper to taste, garnish with the parsley, and serve.

Creamy Butternut Spinach Soup

Prep time: 10 minutes | Cook time: 13 minutes | Serves 4

10 cups butternut squash, peeled and cubed (approximately 4 pounds)
1 tablespoon coconut oil
1 cup red onion, chopped
4 cups fresh spinach, chopped
2 cloves garlic, crushed and minced
½ teaspoon nutmeg
1 teaspoon dried thyme
½ teaspoon salt
1 teaspoon coarse ground black pepper
4 cups vegetable stock
1 cup plain soy yogurt
¼ cup toasted pumpkin seeds (optional)

1. Add the coconut oil to the Instant Pot and turn it to the Sauté setting. 2. Add in the red onions, spinach, garlic, nutmeg, thyme, salt and black pepper. Sauté for 5 minutes. 3. Next, add in the butternut squash and the vegetable stock. 4. Seal the cooker and select the Pressure Cook setting. 5. Cook for 8 minutes. 6. Release the steam from the cooker using the quick release option. 7. Carefully remove the cover and release any remaining steam. 8. Add the plain soy yogurt to the cooker. 9. Using an immersion blender, blend the soup until creamy. 10. Serve garnished with toasted pumpkin seeds (optional).

Pork and Tofu Soup with Miso and Cabbage

Prep time: 20 minutes | Cook time: 50 minutes | Serves 4

½ cup white miso
6 medium garlic cloves, smashed and peeled
1 (3-inch) piece fresh ginger, peeled and thinly sliced
2 tablespoons grapeseed or other neutral oil
⅔ cup sake
1 pound (454 g) boneless pork shoulder, trimmed and cut across the grain into ½-inch slabs
Kosher salt and ground white pepper
½ medium head napa cabbage, halved lengthwise, then cut crosswise into 1-inch pieces
1 (14-ounce / 397-g) container firm tofu, drained and cut into 1-inch cubes
3 tablespoons soy sauce
4 scallions, thinly sliced on the diagonal
Toasted sesame oil, to serve

1. On a 6-quart Instant Pot, select Normal/Medium Sauté. Add the miso, garlic, ginger and oil. Cook, stirring constantly, until the miso sticks to the bottom of the pot and browns evenly, 3 to 4 minutes. 2. Add the sake and 4 cups water, scraping up the browned bits. Add the pork and 1 teaspoon white pepper; stir, then distribute in an even layer. Fast: 3. Press Cancel, lock the lid in place and move the pressure valve to Sealing. Select Pressure Cook or Manual; make sure the pressure level is set to High. Set the cooking time for 27 minutes. When pressure cooking is complete, let the pressure reduce naturally for 15 minutes, then release the remaining steam by moving the pressure valve to Venting. Press Cancel, then carefully open the pot. Slow: With the pot still on Normal/Medium Sauté, bring the mixture to a boil. Press Cancel, lock the lid in place and move the pressure valve to Venting. Select Slow Cook and set the temperature to More/High. Set the cooking time for 4 to 5 hours; the soup is done when a skewer inserted into a piece of pork meets no resistance. Press Cancel, then carefully open the pot. 4. Using a large spoon, skim off and discard the fat from the surface. Select Normal/Medium Sauté and bring to a simmer. Add the cabbage and tofu, then cook, stirring gently, until the leaves are wilted and the stems are crisp-tender, 2 to 4 minutes. 5. Press Cancel to turn off the pot. Stir in the soy sauce, then taste and season with salt and pepper. Serve sprinkled with the scallions and drizzled with sesame oil.

King Ranch Chicken Soup

Prep time: 20 minutes | Cook time: 5 minutes | Serves 6

4 tablespoons salted butter
1 medium onion, peeled and chopped
1 small jalapeño pepper, seeded and chopped
2 cloves garlic, peeled and minced
1 tablespoon chili powder
½ teaspoon salt
½ teaspoon ground black pepper
3 tablespoons all-purpose flour
3 cups chicken stock
1 (10-ounce / 283-g) can diced tomatoes with green chilies
3 cups shredded cooked chicken breast
½ cup heavy whipping cream
2 cups shredded Cheddar cheese
¼ cup chopped fresh cilantro
3 ounces (85 g) tortilla chips

1. Press the Sauté button on the Instant Pot and melt butter. Add onion, jalapeño, and garlic and cook until tender, about 8 minutes. Add chili powder, salt, and pepper and cook until fragrant, about 30 seconds. 2. Sprinkle flour over vegetables and cook, stirring well, until flour is completely moistened, about 1 minute. Slowly whisk in stock, making sure to scrape any bits off the bottom of the pot. Press the Cancel button and stir in tomatoes and chicken. Close lid, set steam release to Sealing, press the Manual button, and adjust cook time to 5 minutes. 3. When the timer beeps, quick-release the pressure. Open lid and stir soup well, then stir in cream. Add cheese ½ cup at a time, allowing the first addition to melt before adding the next. Serve hot with cilantro and tortilla chips for garnish.

Dark Vegetable Stock

Prep time: 10 minutes | Cook time: 20 minutes | Makes 2 quarts

1 tablespoon oil (optional)
2 red onions, peeled and quartered
3 cloves garlic, smashed
2 carrots, peeled and coarsely chopped
½ cup shiitake mushroom stems, or 4 whole dried shiitake mushrooms
6 ounces (170 g) crimini or shiitake mushrooms, sliced
2 celery stalks with leaves, chopped
8 cups water
1 sprig rosemary
3 sprigs thyme
2 bay leaves
¼ teaspoon whole black peppercorns
½ teaspoon salt

1. Set the Instant Pot to Sauté; add the oil, if using. Add the onions and cook for 4 minutes. Add the garlic and cook 6 minutes longer, until the onions start turning brown. Add all the remaining ingredients except the salt. 2. Lock the lid on the cooker and bring to high pressure; cook for 10 minutes. Let the pressure come down naturally. Remove the lid, carefully tilting it away from you. 3. Strain the stock by pouring through a strainer and pressing on the solids with a spoon to extract all the liquid and flavor. Add the salt to the stock. 4. The stock will keep for a week in the refrigerator or 3 months in the freezer.

Pepperoni Pizza Stew

Prep time: 15 minutes | Cook time: 6 minutes | Serves 6

2 tablespoons vegetable oil
1 medium onion, peeled and chopped
2 cups sliced button mushrooms
1 green bell pepper, seeded and chopped
2 cloves garlic, peeled and minced
1 tablespoon Italian seasoning
2 (14½-ounce / 411-g) cans diced tomatoes
2 cups beef stock
¼ pound (113 g) sliced pepperoni
1 (9-ounce / 255-g) package refrigerated cheese ravioli
1 cup shredded Mozzarella cheese

1. Press the Sauté button on the Instant Pot and heat oil. Add onion, mushrooms, and bell pepper and cook until vegetables are tender, about 8 minutes. Add garlic and Italian seasoning and cook until fragrant, about 30 seconds. 2. Add tomatoes, stock, and pepperoni to pot and stir well. Press the Cancel button, close lid, set steam release to Sealing, press the Manual button, and adjust cook time to 5 minutes. 3. When the timer beeps, quick-release the pressure. Press the Cancel button, open lid, stir in ravioli, close lid, set steam release to Sealing, press the Manual button, and set time to 1 minute. 4. When the timer beeps, quick-release the pressure, open lid, and stir soup. Serve hot with shredded cheese for garnish.

Loaded Cauliflower Soup

Prep time: 15 minutes | Cook time: 11 minutes | Serves 4 to 5

2 tablespoons unsalted butter
1 cup diced leeks
2 celery ribs, diced
3 cloves garlic, crushed
1 large head cauliflower, cut into florets
3 cups vegetable or chicken stock
1 teaspoon sea salt, plus more to taste
3 tablespoons cream cheese
½ cup half-and-half or milk
4 strips cooked bacon, crumbled
¾ cup shredded sharp cheddar cheese
Diced green onion, for garnish (optional)
Sour cream, for garnish (optional)

1. Select Sauté on the Instant Pot. Once hot, melt the butter. Toss in the leeks. Sauté for 2 to 3 minutes, or until fragrant, then add the celery and garlic. Cook for another 2 minutes. Select Cancel. 2. Add the cauliflower, then pour the stock on top. Stir in the salt. 3. Secure the lid with the steam vent in the sealed position. Select Manual or Pressure Cook, and cook on high for 6 minutes. 4. Use a quick release, and remove the lid once the steam is completely released. 5. Add the cream cheese and half-and-half. Using a blender or immersion blender, blend until smooth. 6. Pour into individual bowls and top with the bacon, cheddar and optional green onion and sour cream.

Crab Bisque

Prep time: 15 minutes | Cook time: 15 minutes | Serves 6

¼ cup unsalted butter
3 stalks celery, finely chopped
1 large carrot, peeled and finely chopped
1 medium yellow onion, peeled and finely chopped
½ medium red bell pepper, seeded and finely chopped
1 clove garlic, peeled and minced
¼ teaspoon seafood seasoning
¼ cup all-purpose flour
3 cups seafood stock
2 sprigs fresh thyme
1 bay leaf
4 cups lump crab meat
1½ cups heavy cream
1 tablespoon dry sherry

1. Press the Sauté button on the Instant Pot and melt butter. Add celery, carrot, onion, and bell pepper. Cook until tender, about 5 minutes. Add garlic and seafood seasoning and cook until fragrant, about 30 seconds. 2. Sprinkle flour over vegetables and stir to combine, then cook 1 minute, making sure all flour is moistened. Slowly add 1 cup stock, scraping bottom of pot well. Whisk in remaining stock, thyme, and bay leaf. Press the Cancel button. 3. Close lid and set steam release to Sealing, then press the Manual button and adjust cook time to 5 minutes. 4. When the timer beeps, let pressure release naturally, about 15 minutes. Uncover, stir well, and remove thyme and bay leaf. Use an immersion blender, or work in batches with a blender, to purée soup until smooth. 5. Add crab, cream, and sherry to pot. Let stand on the Keep Warm setting until crab is cooked through, about 10 minutes. Serve hot.

Navy Bean, Spinach, and Bacon Soup

Prep time: 10 minutes | Cook time: 25 minutes | Serves 6

3 (15-ounce / 425-g) cans navy beans, rinsed and drained
1 cup water
4 slices bacon, chopped
1 onion, chopped
1 large carrot, chopped
1 large celery stalk, chopped
2 tablespoons tomato paste
1 sprig fresh rosemary
2 bay leaves
4 cups chicken broth
3 cups baby spinach
Salt and ground black pepper, to taste

1. Combine the 1 can beans with 1 cup of water. 2. With an immersion blender, blend the mixture. 3. Set your Instant Pot on Sauté mode, add the bacon and sauté until crisp. 4. Transfer the bacon to a plate lined with paper towel. 5. Add the onion, carrot, and celery to the pot and sauté for 5 minutes, until softened. 6. Add the tomato paste and stir. 7. Add 2 cans beans, puréed beans, rosemary, bay leaves, and broth. Close and lock the lid. 8. Press the Cancel button to stop the Sauté function. 9. Close and lock the lid. Select Manual and cook at High pressure for 15 minutes. 10. Once cooking is complete, let the pressure release naturally for 10 minutes. Release any remaining steam manually. Uncover the pot. 11. Remove the rosemary and bay leaves. Add the spinach, season with salt and pepper and stir well. 12. Let the dish sit for 5 minutes. Serve.

Cheesy Potato Soup

Prep time: 10 minutes | Cook time: 20 minutes | Serves 8

3 pounds (1.4 kg) red potatoes, quartered
4 cups vegetable broth
4 cups water
2 teaspoons salt
½ teaspoon garlic powder
½ teaspoon onion powder
½ teaspoon dried oregano
¼ teaspoon black pepper
2 (15-ounce / 425-g) cans Cheddar cheese sauce

1. Combine potatoes, broth, water, salt, garlic powder, onion powder, oregano, and pepper in Instant Pot. 2. Close lid and set pressure release to Sealing. 3. Press Manual or Pressure Cook button and adjust time to 10 minutes. 4. When the timer beeps, quick release pressure and then unlock lid and remove it. 5. Blend soup using an immersion blender until smooth. 6. Press Sauté button and mix in Cheddar cheese sauce. Let cook, stirring occasionally, 10 minutes. Serve.

Split Pea Soup with Old Bay Croutons

Prep time: 10 minutes | Cook time: 26 minutes | Serves 8

Soup:
2 tablespoons extra-virgin olive oil, plus more for serving
1 yellow onion, diced
2 carrots, peeled and diced
2 celery stalks, diced
1 tablespoon Old Bay seasoning
1 teaspoon smoked paprika
½ teaspoon freshly ground black pepper
2⅓ cups green split peas
4 cups low-sodium vegetable broth
4 cups water
1 bay leaf
Croutons:
4 slices crusty bread, cut into ½-inch cubes
2 tablespoons extra-virgin olive oil
1 teaspoon Old Bay seasoning
Smoked paprika, for serving

Make the Soup: 1. Select the Sauté setting on the Instant Pot, add the oil, and heat for 1 minute. Add the onion, carrots, and celery and sauté for 5 minutes, until the onion softens. Add the Old Bay, smoked paprika, pepper, split peas, broth, water, and bay leaf. Stir to combine. 2. Secure the lid and set the pressure release to Sealing. Press the Cancel button to reset the cooking program. Then select the Manual or Pressure Cook setting and set the cooking time for 20 minutes at high pressure. (The pot will take about 25 minutes to come up to pressure before the cooking program begins.) 3. When the cooking program ends, let the pressure release naturally (this will take about 45 minutes). Open the pot, then remove and discard the bay leaf. Make the Croutons: 4. When you're ready to serve the soup, toss the cubed bread with the oil and Old Bay in a bowl, until the bread is evenly coated. Spread out the bread in an even layer on a foil-lined baking sheet, and toast in a toaster oven or under a broiler for about 3–5 minutes, until lightly browned. 5. Ladle the soup into bowls and serve piping hot, with the croutons and smoked paprika sprinkled on top and a drizzle of oil.

Lentil Stew

Prep time: 45 minutes | Cook time: 20 minutes | Serves 8

2 tablespoons canola oil
2 large onions, thinly sliced, divided
8 plum tomatoes, chopped
2 tablespoons minced fresh ginger root
3 garlic cloves, minced
2 teaspoons ground coriander
1½ teaspoons ground cumin
¼ teaspoon cayenne pepper
3 cups vegetable broth
2 cups dried lentils, rinsed
2 cups water
1 (4-ounce / 113-g) can chopped green chiles
¾ cup heavy whipping cream
2 tablespoons butter
1 teaspoon cumin seeds
6 cups hot cooked basmati or jasmine rice
Sliced green onions (optional)
Minced fresh cilantro (optional)

1. Select Sauté setting on a 6-quart electric pressure cooker. Adjust for medium heat; add oil. When oil is hot, cook and stir half the onions until crisp-tender, 2 to 3 minutes. Add tomatoes, ginger and garlic, coriander, cumin and cayenne; cook and stir 1 minute longer. Press Cancel. Stir in broth, lentils, water, green chiles and remaining onion. 2. Lock lid; close pressure-release valve. Adjust to pressure cook on high for 15 minutes. Let pressure release naturally. Just before serving, stir in the cream. In a small skillet, heat butter over medium heat. Add cumin seeds; cook and stir until golden brown, for 1 to 2 minutes. Add to lentil mixture. 3. Serve with rice. If desired, sprinkle with sliced green onions or minced cilantro.

Macaroni and Cheese Soup

Prep time: 15 minutes | Cook time: 9 minutes | Serves 8

3 tablespoons unsalted butter
2 medium carrots, peeled and finely chopped
2 stalks celery, diced
1 medium onion, peeled and diced
1 clove garlic, minced
1 teaspoon dried mustard
3 cups chicken broth
8 ounces (227 g) elbow macaroni
1 cup heavy cream
2 cups shredded sharp Cheddar cheese
1 cup shredded American cheese

1. Press the Sauté button on the Instant Pot and melt butter. Add carrots, celery, and onion. Cook, stirring often, until softened, about 5 minutes. Add garlic and cook until fragrant, about 30 seconds, then add mustard and stir well. Add broth, then press the Cancel button. 2. Close lid, set steam release to Sealing, press the Manual button, and set time to 5 minutes. When the timer beeps, let pressure release naturally, about 15 minutes. Press the Cancel button, open lid, and stir in pasta. Close lid, set steam release to Sealing, press the Manual button, and set time to 4 minutes. 3. When the timer beeps, quick-release the pressure. Open lid and stir soup well. Stir in cream, then stir in cheese 1 cup at a time, stirring each addition until completely melted before adding another. Serve hot.

Spring Split Pea Soup

Prep time: 15 minutes | Cook time: 14 minutes | Serves 6

1 tablespoon oil (optional)
2 cups coarsely chopped onion or leek
2 carrots, peeled and diced
2 large stalks celery, diced
6 cups water or vegetable stock, or a combination
2 cups yellow or green split peas, picked over and rinsed
1 piece smoked or regular dulse, or ¼ to ½ teaspoon dulse granules
2 large bay leaves
½ to 1 teaspoon dried thyme (optional)
½ cup fresh English peas or frozen (not thawed) peas
Juice of 1 lemon
Sprinkle of smoked or regular salt (optional)

1. Set the Instant Pot to Sauté; add the oil, if using. Add the onion, carrot, and celery and cook for a minute or two. Add the water or stock, split peas, dulse, and bay leaves. 2. Lock the lid in place. Bring to high pressure; cook for 10 minutes. Allow the pressure to come down naturally. Remove the lid, tilting it away from you. 3. With long tongs, remove and discard the bay leaves. Add the thyme, if using, using the Sauté function, for 1 to 2 minutes, until the thyme flavor pervades the soup. Stir well, taking care to blend in the peas that have sunk to the bottom of the cooker. 4. Add the fresh peas. Lock the lid on the cooker and let sit for 5 minutes. Remove the lid carefully. Add the lemon juice and season with salt to taste (as much as 1 teaspoon), if desired.

Chapter 8 Desserts

Chapter 8 Desserts

Apple Dumplings

Prep time: 10 minutes | Cook time: 12 minutes | Serves 8

1 (8-ounce / 227-g) can refrigerated crescent rolls
1 large apple, peeled, cored, and cut into 8 wedges
4 tablespoons (½ stick) unsalted butter
½ cup brown sugar
2 teaspoons ground cinnamon
¼ teaspoon ground nutmeg
1 teaspoon vanilla extract
¾ cup orange juice

1. Open the can of crescent rolls and flatten the dough. Separate the 8 triangles. Place 1 apple wedge on each crescent roll triangle and fold the dough around the apple to enclose it. 2. Select Sauté and adjust the heat to Medium. Add the butter to the inner cooking pot. When it has melted, press Cancel and add the sugar, cinnamon, nutmeg, and vanilla, stirring until melted. Place the dumplings in the Instant Pot (they should fit side by side) and drizzle with the orange juice. 3. Lock the lid into place and turn the valve to Sealing. Select Manual or Pressure Cook and adjust the pressure to High. Set the time for 10 minutes. When cooking ends, let the pressure release naturally for 5 minutes, then turn the valve to Venting to quick release any remaining pressure. Unlock and remove the lid.

Blueberry Cheesecake

Prep time: 10 minutes | Cook time: 6 minutes | Serves 6

Coconut oil or vegan margarine, for greasing
1¼ cups soft pitted Medjool dates, divided
1 cup gluten-free rolled oats
2 cups cashews
1 cup fresh blueberries
3 tablespoons freshly squeezed lemon juice or lime juice
¾ cups water
Pinch salt

1. Grease a 6-inch springform pan or pie dish with coconut oil. 2. In a food processor, combine 1 cup of dates and the oats. Pulse until they form a sticky mixture. Press this into the prepared pan. 3. In a high-speed blender, combine the remaining ¼ cup of dates, the cashews, blueberries, lemon juice, water, and a pinch of salt. Blend on high speed for about 1 minute, until smooth and creamy, stopping a couple of times to scrape down the sides. Pour this mixture over the crust. Cover the pan with aluminum foil. 4. Put a trivet in the bottom of the pressure cooker and pour in another cup or two of water. Using a foil sling to lower the pan onto the trivet. Close and lock the lid and ensure the pressure valve is sealed, then select High Pressure and set the time for 6 minutes. 5. Once the cook time is complete, let the pressure release naturally, about 10 minutes. 6. Once all the pressure has released, carefully unlock and remove the lid. Let cool for a few minutes before carefully lifting out the pan with oven mitts. 7. Let the cake cool to room temperature, or refrigerate until cooled and set.

Mini Crustless Pumpkin Pies

Prep time: 5 minutes | Cook time: 10 minutes | Serves 2

Butter, at room temperature, for greasing
½ cup pumpkin purée
3 tablespoons packed brown sugar
1 teaspoon cornstarch
Pinch kosher salt
½ teaspoon pumpkin pie spice
1 egg, lightly beaten
¼ cup plus 2 tablespoons heavy cream

1. Add 1 cup of water to your pressure cooker and place the trivet in the bottom. Butter two 1-cup ramekins. 2. In a medium bowl, whisk together the pumpkin, brown sugar, cornstarch, salt, pumpkin pie spice, and egg. Add the cream and stir to combine. 3. Divide the pumpkin mixture between the prepared ramekins. Set the ramekins on the trivet, placing a third empty ramekin next to them to ensure that they don't jostle during cooking. 4. Secure the cooker lid and cook on High pressure for 10 minutes, then allow the pressure to naturally release, about 10 minutes. Open the vent at the top and remove the lid. 5. Using tongs, remove the ramekins from the cooker, transfer to a heatproof surface, and let cool for 5 to 10 minutes before serving with a dollop of whipped cream and crumbled gingersnap cookies, if you're looking for some crunch. The pie can also be refrigerated for up to 2 days; let cool completely first and cover with plastic wrap.

Spiced Red Wine-Poached Pears

Prep time: 15 minutes | Cook time: 13 minutes | Serves 4

4 ripe but still firm pears
2 tablespoons fresh lemon juice
4 cups dry red wine
½ cup freshly squeezed orange juice
2 teaspoons grated orange zest
¼ cup sugar
1 cinnamon stick
½ teaspoon ground cloves
½ teaspoon ground ginger
1 sprig fresh mint

1. Rinse and peel the pears leaving the stem. Using a corer or melon baller, remove the cores from underneath without going through the top so you can maintain the stem. Brush the pears inside and out with the lemon juice. 2. Combine the wine, orange juice, orange zest, sugar, cinnamon stick, cloves, and ginger in Instant Pot. Press the Sauté button and then hit the Adjust button to change the temperature to More. Bring to a slow boil in about 3 to 5 minutes; stir to blend and dissolve the sugar. Carefully place the pears in liquid. Press Adjust button to change temperature to Less and simmer unlidded for 5 additional minutes. Lock lid. 3. Press Manual button and adjust time to 3 minutes. Use the Pressure button to set the pressure to Low. When the timer beeps, quick-release pressure until float valve drops and then unlock lid. 4. Use a slotted spoon to transfer the pears to a serving platter. Garnish with mint sprig.

Sweet Coconut Rice with Mango

Prep time: 5 minutes | Cook time: 25 minutes | Serves 6

1 (14-ounce / 397-g) can full-fat coconut milk or coconut cream
½ cup granulated white sugar
½ teaspoon vanilla extract
½ teaspoon table salt
3½ cups water
1½ cups raw, sweet, glutinous white rice
3 medium ripe mangos, peeled, pitted, and cut into bite-size chunks

1. Press the Sauté button, and set on Medium or Normal for 10 minutes. 2. Mix the coconut milk, sugar, vanilla, and salt in a 6- or 8-quart cooker. Cook, stirring often, until bubbling, about 4 minutes. Turn off the Sauté function, remove the hot insert from the machine, and scrape every drop of the coconut mixture into a heat-safe, large bowl. Set aside. 3. Clean the insert and return it to the machine. Pour 1½ cups water into the pot, then set a heat- and pressure-safe trivet in the pot. Mix the rice and the remaining 2 cups water in a 2-quart, high-sided, round soufflé dish. Set this dish on the trivet and lock the lid onto the pot. 4. Select Pressure Cook or Manual, and cook on high for 15 minutes with the Keep Warm setting off. 5. Use the quick-release method to bring the pressure back to normal—but do not open the pot. Set aside for 10 minutes, then unlatch the lid and open the cooker. Remove the hot bowl from the trivet. 6. Stir all but ⅓ cup of the coconut milk mixture into the cooked rice. Serve the rice warm in bowls with mango pieces all over the top and drizzle the portions with as much of the remaining coconut milk mixture as desired.

Chocolate Cake with Peanut Butter Ganache

Prep time: 15 minutes | Cook time: 20 minutes | Serves 6

2 large eggs, whisked
1 teaspoon vanilla extract
⅓ cup gluten-free all-purpose flour
2 tablespoons unsweetened cocoa powder
⅓ cup granulated sugar
2 teaspoons gluten-free baking powder
1 teaspoon baking soda
⅛ teaspoon salt
4 tablespoons melted unsalted butter
2 tablespoons whole milk
⅓ cup semisweet chocolate chips
1 cup water
¼ cup heavy cream
½ cup peanut butter chips

1. In a large bowl, combine eggs, vanilla, flour, cocoa powder, sugar, baking powder, baking soda, and salt. Stir in melted butter and milk and then fold in chocolate chips. Do not overmix. Pour batter into a 6-inch cake pan greased with either oil or cooking spray. 2. Add water to the Instant Pot. Insert steam rack. Place cake pan on top of the steam rack. Lock lid. 3. Press the Pressure Cook or Manual button and adjust cook time to 20 minutes. When timer beeps, let pressure release naturally. Quick-release any additional pressure until float valve drops and then unlock lid. 4. Remove cake pan from pot and transfer to a rack to cool 10 minutes. Flip cake onto a serving platter. Let cool completely 30 minutes. 5. In a small saucepan, bring heavy cream to a light rolling boil over medium heat (do not overheat, as it will scorch). Remove from heat. Add peanut butter chips to heated cream and stir until melted. Gently pour ganache over cake. Let set for 30 minutes. Serve.

Mango Cardamom Tapioca Pudding

Prep time: 5 minutes | Cook time: 20 minutes | Serves 4

Pressure Cooker:
1 (13½-ounce / 383-g) can full-fat coconut milk
½ cup small tapioca pearls (not quick-cooking)
2 cups mango chunks, cut small or diced
½ cup water
1 teaspoon ground cardamom
For Serving:
Sweetener of choice, to taste (optional)

1. Add water to the bottom of your electric pressure cooker. In a Pyrex or stainless steel bowl that fits into your electric pressure cooker, add the coconut milk, tapioca, mango, water and cardamom. Whisk until thoroughly combined. 2. Cover the bowl with foil. You can lower the bowl down using the rack that came with your Instant Pot. I also recommend using an OXO sling or making handles out of aluminum foil to make it easier to get it out later. 3. Cook on High Pressure for 20 minutes. Release the pressure naturally for 5 minutes, then manually release the rest of the pressure. Remove the bowl from the electric pressure cooker and set it on a trivet. 4. The pudding will be liquid at this point. Don't worry, it will get firm and set up after it's refrigerated for a few hours. 5. Taste the pudding. If the mangos you used are very ripe you will not need any additional sweetener. If it's not sweet enough for you, stir in the sweetener of your choice until it's the way you like it. Do this before the pudding is completely cool to ensure that the sweetener gets totally combined. 6. Transfer the pudding to single-serving cups if you like. Chill the pudding in the refrigerator for at least 2 hours before serving.

Lava Cake

Prep time: 15 minutes | Cook time: 20 minutes | Serves 8

1 cup all-purpose flour
1 cup packed brown sugar, divided
5 tablespoons baking cocoa, divided
2 teaspoons baking powder
¼ teaspoon salt
½ cup fat-free milk
2 tablespoons canola oil
½ teaspoon vanilla extract
⅛ teaspoon ground cinnamon
1¼ cups hot water
Optional Toppings:
Fresh raspberries
Ice cream

1. In a large bowl, whisk the flour, ½ cup brown sugar, 3 tablespoons cocoa, baking powder and salt. In another bowl, whisk milk, oil and vanilla until blended. Add to flour mixture; stir just until moistened. 2. Spread into a 1½-quart baking dish coated with cooking spray. In a small bowl, mix cinnamon and remaining ½ cup brown sugar and 2 tablespoons cocoa; stir in hot water. Pour over batter (do not stir). 3. Place trivet insert and 1 cup water in a 6-quart electric pressure cooker. Cover the baking dish with foil. Fold a (18 x 12 inch) piece of foil lengthwise into thirds, making a sling. Use the sling to lower the dish onto the trivet. Lock lid; close pressure-release valve. Adjust to Pressure Cook on high for 20 minutes. Quick-release pressure. 4. Using the foil sling, carefully remove baking dish. Let stand 15 minutes. A toothpick inserted in cake portion should come out clean.

Salted Date Caramel Sauce

Prep time: 2 minutes | Cook time: 1 minute | Makes about 1 cup

1 cup Medjool dates (about 10)
1 cup water
1 cup full-fat coconut milk
1 teaspoon pure vanilla extract
¼ teaspoon sea salt
Options for Serving:
Granny Smith apple slices and chopped walnuts
Strawberries
Pretzels
Vegan vanilla ice cream

1. Add the dates and 1 cup water to the inner pot. Lock the lid and ensure the steam release valve is set to the Sealing position. Select Pressure Cook (High), and set the cook time for 1 minute. 2. Once the cook time is complete, immediately quick release the pressure. Carefully remove the lid. Use a slotted spoon to remove the dates and place on a cutting board. Carefully remove and discard the pits. (A knife and fork can make this easier when the dates are hot.) 3. Transfer the pitted dates to a blender or food processor. Add ½ cup coconut milk, vanilla, and salt. Blend, adding more coconut milk or water, as needed, to thin into a thick but pourable consistency. Continue blending until very smooth, scraping down the sides as needed—this will take several minutes. 4. Transfer the caramel to a small bowl or jar and serve immediately with the desired serving options, or store in an airtight container in the refrigerator for up to 5 days.

Lemony Blueberry Buckle Dessert Sauce

Prep time: 5 minutes | Cook time: 15 minutes | Serves 4

2 cups frozen blueberries
¼ cup coconut sugar
½ teaspoon cinnamon
½ cup lemonade

1. Combine all the ingredients in the Instant Pot and stir. 2. Seal the cooker and, using the Pressure Cook option, cook on high for 7 minutes. 3. Use the natural release option to release the steam from the cooker. 4. Carefully open the lid and stir the sauce. 5. Turn the cooker to the Sauté setting and continue cooking the sauce, stirring occasionally, until the desired consistency is reached.

Pear and Sweet Potato Applesauce

Prep time: 10 minutes | Cook time: 10 minutes | Serves 4 to 6

5 Honeycrisp apples, cored and chopped
1 sweet potato, peeled and chopped
1 Bartlett pear, cored and chopped
Pinch of salt
1 cup water
½ teaspoon cinnamon
1 tablespoon pure maple syrup

1. In the Instant Pot, combine all the ingredients and mix well. 2. Secure the lid with the steam vent in the sealed position. Press Pressure Cook until the display light is beneath high pressure. Use the plus and minus buttons to adjust the time until the display reads 10 minutes. 3. When the timer sounds, quick release the pressure. Remove the lid and use an immersion blender to purée until smooth.

Pumpkin Flans

Prep time: 20 minutes | Cook time: 35 minutes | Serves 6

1 cup sugar, divided
¼ cups water
1½ cups fat-free evaporated milk
3 large eggs
1 large egg white
¼ teaspoon salt
¼ teaspoon ground ginger
¼ teaspoon cinnamon
¼ teaspoon cloves
1 cup canned pumpkin
1 teaspoon vanilla extract

1. In a small heavy skillet over medium-low heat, combine ⅓ cup sugar and ¼ cup water. Cook, stirring occasionally, until sugar begins to melt. Cook without stirring until amber, about 20 minutes. Quickly pour into 6 (6-ounce / 170-g) ungreased ramekins or custard cups, tilting to coat bottoms of dishes. Let stand for 10 minutes. 2. In a small saucepan, heat milk until bubbles form around the sides of pan; remove from heat. In a large bowl, whisk eggs, egg white, salt, spices and remaining ⅔ cup sugar until blended but not foamy. Slowly stir in hot milk. Stir in pumpkin and vanilla. Slowly pour into prepared ramekins. 3. Cover each ramekin with foil. Place trivet insert and 1 cup water in pressure cooker. Set ramekins on trivet. Lock lid; close pressure-release valve. Adjust to Pressure Cook on high for 13 minutes. Quick-release pressure. 4. Centers should just be set (the mixture will jiggle) and a thermometer inserted in flan should read at least 160°F (71°C). Carefully remove ramekins. Cool 10 minutes; refrigerate, covered, at least 4 hours. Carefully run a knife around the edges of ramekins to loosen; invert each dish onto a rimmed serving dish. If desired, sprinkle with additional cinnamon. Serve immediately.

Spiced Peaches with Cinnamon Whipped Cream

Prep time: 15 minutes | Cook time: 8 minutes | Serves 6

1½ cups heavy whipping cream
2 tablespoons powdered sugar
1 teaspoon ground cinnamon
½ teaspoon vanilla extract
2 (15-ounce / 425-g) cans sliced peaches in syrup
¼ cup water
2 tablespoons packed light brown sugar
1 tablespoon white wine vinegar
⅛ teaspoon ground allspice
1 teaspoon ground ginger
1 cinnamon stick
4 whole cloves
Pinch of cayenne pepper
3 whole black peppercorns

1. Pour whipping cream into a metal bowl. Whisk until soft peaks form. Slowly add powdered sugar, cinnamon, and vanilla and continue whipping until firm. Set aside and refrigerate. 2. Add remaining ingredients to Instant Pot. Stir to mix. Lock lid. 3. Press the Manual button and adjust time to 3 minutes. When timer beeps, quick-release pressure until float valve drops and then unlock lid. Remove and discard the cinnamon stick, cloves, and peppercorns. Press Sauté button on Instant Pot, press Adjust button to change the temperature to Less, and simmer for 5 minutes to thicken the syrup. Serve warm or chilled, topped with cinnamon whipped cream.

Mini Pumpkin Cheesecakes

Prep time: 15 minutes | Cook time: 13 minutes | Serves 4

1 cup water
12 gingersnap cookies
½ cup plus 1 tablespoon granulated sugar, divided
¼ teaspoon salt, divided
2 tablespoons unsalted butter, melted
12 ounces (340 g) cream cheese, softened
½ cup pure canned pumpkin
1 teaspoon vanilla extract
¼ teaspoon ground cinnamon
⅛ teaspoon ground nutmeg
⅛ teaspoon allspice
1 large egg plus 1 large egg yolk, room temperature

1. Pour water into Instant Pot and add trivet. Grease four ramekins and set aside. 2. Place gingersnap cookies, 1 tablespoon sugar, and ⅛ teaspoon salt in a gallon-sized zip-top bag and seal. Roll with a rolling pin until small crumbs are formed. 3. In a small bowl, mix crushed cookies and melted butter together. 4. Press cookie crust into bottom of ramekins. Place ramekins in freezer while preparing cheesecake batter. 5. With an electric mixer, cream together cream cheese and remaining ½ cup sugar. Beat until light and fluffy, about 2 minutes. 6. Mix in pumpkin, vanilla, cinnamon, nutmeg, allspice, and remaining ⅛ teaspoon salt. Mix an additional 2 minutes. 7. Add in egg and egg yolk, one at a time, and beat until just combined. Do not overmix. 8. Divide batter evenly among four ramekins. Cover each ramekin tightly with foil. 9. Place each ramekin in Instant Pot, three on bottom and the fourth on top, stacked in the center of the three. 10. Close lid and set pressure release to Sealing. 11. Press Manual or Pressure Cook button and adjust time to 13 minutes. 12. When the timer beeps, allow pressure to release naturally and then unlock lid and remove it. 13. Carefully remove ramekins from Instant Pot, using an oven mitt. Place on a cooling rack and let cool to room temperature. 14. Refrigerate at least 8 hours before serving.

Butterscotch Pudding

Prep time: 5 minutes | Cook time: 20 minutes | Serves 4

3 tablespoons butter
½ cup packed dark brown sugar
1½ cups whole milk
½ cup heavy cream
6 large egg yolks
¼ teaspoon vanilla extract
⅛ teaspoon salt
1½ cups water

1. Press the Sauté button, and set on Medium or Normal for 10 minutes. 2. Melt the butter in a 6- or 8-quart cooker. Stir in the brown sugar until smooth and cook until constantly bubbling, about 3 minutes. Stir in the milk and cream until the sugar mixture melts again and becomes smooth. Turn off the Sauté function and pour the mixture from the hot insert into a nearby large bowl. Cool for 15 minutes. Meanwhile, clean and dry the insert; return it to the machine. 3. Whisk the egg yolks, vanilla, and salt into the milk mixture until smooth. Divide this mixture evenly among four heat- and pressure-safe 1-cup ramekins. Cover each with aluminum foil. 4. Pour the water into the cooker and set a heat- and pressure-safe trivet in the machine. Stack the ramekins on the trivet, balancing a second layer on the edge of more than one ramekin below. Secure the lid with the steam vent in the sealed position. 5. Select Pressure Cook or Manual, and cook on high for 10 minutes with the Keep Warm setting off. 6. When the machine has finished cooking, turn it off and let its pressure return to normal naturally, about 20 minutes.

Unlatch the lid and open the cooker. Transfer the hot covered ramekins to a wire rack, uncover, and cool for 15 minutes. Serve warm or cover again and refrigerate for at least 2 hours or up to 4 days.

Cinnamon-Vanilla Applesauce

Prep time: 10 minutes | Cook time: 5 minutes | Serves 6 to 8

3 pounds (1.4 kg) apples, cored and quartered, no need to peel
⅓ cup water
1 teaspoon vanilla extract
1 teaspoon ground cinnamon, plus more as needed
1 teaspoon freshly squeezed lemon juice
½ teaspoon salt

1. In your Instant Pot, combine the apples, water, vanilla, cinnamon, lemon juice, and salt. Lock the lid and turn the steam release handle to Sealing. Using the Manual function, set the cooker to High Pressure for 5 minutes. 2. When the cook time is complete, let the pressure release naturally for 10 minutes; quick release any remaining pressure. 3. Carefully remove the lid. Using an immersion blender, blend the applesauce until smooth. Taste and add more cinnamon, as desired.

Turtle Brownie Pudding

Prep time: 5 minutes | Cook time: 25 minutes | Serves 4

Nonstick cooking spray
½ cup (1 stick) unsalted butter
8 ounces (227 g) dark chocolate chips
1 cup granulated sugar
2 teaspoons vanilla extract
2 large eggs
¾ cup all-purpose flour
¾ cup pecans, chopped, divided
1 (12-ounce / 340-g) jar caramel sauce, divided
1 cup hot water, for steaming
1 (12-ounce / 340-g) jar hot fudge sauce

1. Grease a 7-inch round cake pan with nonstick cooking spray. Combine the butter and chocolate chips in a medium bowl and melt them together in the microwave, stirring occasionally. 2. Add the sugar and vanilla and stir until combined. Mix in the eggs, one at a time, stirring until no streaks of egg remain. Stir in the flour. Fold in ½ cup of pecans. Transfer the batter to the prepared pan. Add ¼ cup of caramel sauce and use a spoon to swirl it into the brownie batter. Cover the pan with aluminum foil. 3. Place a trivet in the inner cooking pot and add the water. Using a sling, lower the pan onto the trivet. Lock the lid into place and turn the valve to Sealing. Select Manual or Pressure Cook and adjust the pressure to High. Set the time for 25 minutes. When cooking ends, carefully turn the valve to Venting to quick release the pressure. 4. Unlock and remove the lid. Using the sling, remove the pan and then remove foil. The center will look undercooked, but it's okay. The consistency is going to be somewhere between a cake-like brownie and chocolate pudding. Allow it to cool. Drizzle with the remaining caramel sauce and the hot fudge and garnish with the remaining ¼ cup of pecans.

Pumpkin Cheesecake

Prep time: 10 minutes | Cook time: 30 minutes | Serves 6

Crust:
20 gingersnaps
3 tablespoons melted butter
Cheesecake Filling:
1 cup pumpkin purée
8 ounces (227 g) cream cheese, cubed and room temperature
2 tablespoons sour cream, room temperature
½ cup sugar
Pinch of salt
2 large eggs, room temperature
¼ teaspoon ground cinnamon
⅛ teaspoon ground nutmeg
½ teaspoon vanilla extract
2 cups water

1. Grease a 7-inch springform pan and set aside. 2. For Crust: Add gingersnaps to a food processor and pulse to combine. Add in melted butter and pulse to blend. Transfer crumb mixture to springform pan and press down along the bottom and about ⅓ of the way up the sides of the pan. Place a square of aluminum foil along the outside bottom of the pan and crimp up around the edges. 3. For Cheesecake Filling: With a hand blender or food processor, cream together pumpkin, cream cheese, sour cream, sugar, and salt. Pulse until smooth. Slowly add eggs, cinnamon, nutmeg, and vanilla. Pulse for another 10 seconds. Scrape the bowl and pulse until batter is smooth. 4. Transfer the batter into springform pan. 5. Pour water into the Instant Pot. Insert the trivet. Set the springform pan on the trivet. Lock lid. 6. Press the Manual button and adjust time to 30 minutes. When timer beeps, quick-release pressure until float valve drops and then unlock lid. Lift pan out of Instant Pot. Let cool at room temperature for 10 minutes. 7. The cheesecake will be a little jiggly in the center. Refrigerate for a minimum of 2 hours to allow it to set. Release side pan and serve.

Cherry Chocolate Poke Cake

Prep time: 20 minutes | Cook time: 32 minutes | Serves 6

1 cup water
¾ cup vegetable oil
¾ cup granulated sugar
2 large eggs
2 teaspoons vanilla extract, divided
1¼ cups cake flour
6 tablespoons unsweetened cocoa powder, divided
½ teaspoon salt
½ cup buttermilk
1 teaspoon baking soda
1 teaspoon white vinegar
1 (10-ounce / 283-g) jar maraschino cherries, chopped and divided with juice reserved
1 cup powdered sugar, sifted
¼ cup unsalted butter, softened
⅛ cup whole milk

1. Pour water into Instant Pot and add trivet. Grease a 6-cup Bundt pan and set aside. 2. With an electric mixer, cream together oil and sugar. Mix 2 minutes. 3. Add eggs and 1 teaspoon vanilla, one at a time, beating after each addition. 4. In a medium bowl, whisk together flour, 3 tablespoons cocoa powder, and salt. 5. Slowly add flour mixture and buttermilk to the egg mixture, alternating between the two until fully combined. 6. In a small bowl, combine baking soda and vinegar. Give it a quick stir (it will start to bubble) and pour into cake batter. Mix an additional 10 seconds. 7. Fold in half of the chopped maraschino cherries. Pour cake batter into greased Bundt pan. Create a foil sling and carefully lower Bundt pan into Instant Pot. 8. Close lid and set pressure release to Sealing. 9. Press Manual or Pressure Cook button and adjust time to 32 minutes. 10. When the timer beeps, quick release pressure and then unlock lid and remove it. Carefully remove Bundt pan using foil sling. 11. Use a straw to poke twenty holes in cake. Pour cherry juice into holes. Place cake on cooling rack and let cool, about 30 minutes. 12. With an electric mixer, mix together powdered sugar, butter, remaining 3 tablespoons cocoa powder, milk, and remaining 1 teaspoon vanilla. Mix until light and fluffy, about 2 minutes. 13. Once cake is cooled, run a butter knife around inner and outer edges of cake. Turn cake over onto a plate and wiggle to remove Bundt pan. 14. Spread chocolate frosting on top of cake and top with remaining cherries.

Peanut Butter Cup Cheesecake

Prep time: 15 minutes | Cook time: 40 minutes | Serves 6

1 cup water
16 cream-filled chocolate sandwich cookies
2 tablespoons unsalted butter, melted
16 ounces (454 g) cream cheese, softened
¾ cup packed light brown sugar
½ cup heavy whipping cream, divided
½ cup creamy peanut butter
1¼ teaspoons vanilla extract, divided
2 large eggs, room temperature
24 mini peanut butter cups, divided and chopped
½ cup semisweet chocolate chips

1. Pour water into Instant Pot and add trivet. Grease a 7-inch PushPan and set aside. 2. Place chocolate cookies in a gallon-sized zip-top bag and seal. Roll with a rolling pin until small crumbs are formed. 3. In a small bowl, mix crushed cookies and melted butter together. Press cookie crust into bottom and halfway up sides of greased PushPan. Place pan in freezer while preparing cheesecake batter. 4. With an electric mixer, cream together cream cheese and brown sugar. Beat until light and fluffy, about 2 minutes. 5. Mix in ¼ cup cream, peanut butter, and 1 teaspoon vanilla. Mix an additional 2 minutes. 6. Add in eggs, one at a time, beating until just combined. Do not overmix. 7. Fold in half of the chopped peanut butter cups. Pour batter into PushPan. 8. Create a foil sling and carefully lower pan into Instant Pot. 9. Close lid and set pressure release to Sealing. 10. Press Manual or Pressure Cook button and adjust time to 40 minutes. 11. When the timer beeps, allow pressure to release naturally and then unlock lid and remove it. 12. Carefully remove pan from Instant Pot using foil sling. Place on a cooling rack and let cool to room temperature.

Citrus-Infused Sweet Bean Paste

Prep time: 5 minutes | Cook time: 25 minutes | Serves 12

2 cups adzuki beans
3 cups water
1 cup orange juice
1 teaspoon pure vanilla extract
1 tablespoon orange zest
¾ cup coconut sugar

1. Begin by picking through the adzuki beans. Place the beans in a bowl of water and soak them for 15 minutes, then rinse and drain them thoroughly 2. Combine all the ingredients, except for the sugar, in the Instant Pot. 3. Seal the cooker, and using the Pressure Cook option, cook on high for 25 minutes. 4. Use the natural release option to release the steam from the cooker. 5. Remove the lid from the cooker and allow the beans to cool for 15 minutes. 6. Remove the beans, being careful if they are still warm, and place them in a colander. Drain off any excess liquid. 7. Transfer the beans to a blender or food processor and add the sugar. Blend until smooth. 8. Use this sweet bean paste to top cookies, wafers, or as a filling for dumplings.

Banana Cheesecake

Prep time: 10 minutes | Cook time: 25 minutes | Serves 6 to 8

- ⅔ cup sliced almonds
- ⅔ cup graham cracker crumbs
- ½ cup plus 2 tablespoons granulated white sugar
- 3 tablespoons butter, melted and cooled, plus additional butter for greasing
- 1 pound (454 g) regular cream cheese
- 1 small very ripe banana
- ⅓ cup packaged, dehydrated, crisp, unsweetened, and unsalted banana chips
- 2 large eggs
- 1 tablespoon all-purpose flour
- ½ teaspoon almond extract
- 1½ cups water

1. Generously butter the inside of a 7-inch round springform pan. Mix the sliced almonds, graham cracker crumbs, 2 tablespoons sugar, and the melted butter in a medium bowl until uniform; then pour into the prepared pan. Press this mixture evenly across the bottom and about halfway up the sides of the pan to make a crust. 2. Put the remaining ½ cup sugar, the cream cheese, banana, and banana chips (if using) in a food processor, cover, and process until smooth, about 1 minute. Add the eggs one at a time, processing each until smooth. 3. Open the machine, scrape down the inside, and add the flour and almond extract. Cover and process until smooth. Pour this mixture into the prepared crust in the pan (it will rise above the crust on the sides). Do not cover the pan with foil. 4. Pour the water into a 6- or 8-quart cooker. Set a heat- and pressure-safe trivet in the cooker. Make an aluminum foil sling, set the filled springform pan on it, and use it to lower the pan into the pot. Fold down the ends of the sling so that they do not touch the cheesecake batter in the pan. Secure the lid with the steam vent in the sealed position. 5. Select Pressure Cook or Manual, and cook on high for 25 minutes with the Keep Warm setting off. 6. When the machine has finished cooking, turn it off and let its pressure return to normal naturally, about 20 minutes. Unlatch the lid and open the cooker. Use the sling to transfer the hot springform pan to a wire rack. Cool for 15 minutes, then refrigerate for 1 hour. Cover and continue refrigerating for at least 1 more hour or up to 2 days. 7. To serve, uncover and run a thin knife between the pan and the cake. Unlatch the sides of the pan and open it to remove the cake inside. If desired, use a long, thin knife to slice the cake off the pan's base and use a large metal spatula to transfer the cheesecake to a serving platter.

Bananas Foster

Prep time: 5 minutes | Cook time: 2 minutes | Serves 4

- 8 tablespoons (1 stick) salted butter, cubed
- ¼ cup light (clear) rum
- ¼ cup water
- 1 cup dark-brown sugar, packed
- 1 teaspoon cinnamon
- 1 teaspoon vanilla extract
- 6 good-sized bananas, firm but not green, peeled and sliced into 1-inch pieces
- Vanilla ice cream, for serving

1. In the Instant Pot, combine the butter, rum, water, brown sugar, cinnamon, and vanilla. Mix well until the large lumps of the sugar are dissolved and the mixture is the texture of molasses. The butter should remain chunky. 2. Add the bananas and stir gently to coat with the sauce. 3. Secure the lid, move the valve to the sealing position, and hit Manual or Pressure Cook on High Pressure for 2 minutes. When done, allow a 5-minute natural release followed by a quick release. 4. Let cool for a few moments before serving over bowls of vanilla ice cream.

Raspberry Curd

Prep time: 2 minutes | Cook time: 5 minutes | Serves 6 to 8

- 18 ounces (510 g) raspberries
- 1½ cups sugar
- 3 tablespoons lemon juice
- 3 egg yolks
- 3 tablespoons butter

1. In the Instant Pot, combine the raspberries, sugar and lemon juice. 2. Close and lock the lid. Select the Manual setting and set the cooking time for 2 minutes at High pressure. 3. When the timer goes off, let the pressure release naturally for 5 minutes, then release any remaining steam manually. Open the lid. 4. Use the mesh strainer to purée the raspberries and remove the seeds. 5. In a bowl, whisk egg yolks and combine with the raspberries purée. 6. Return the mixture to the pot. Select Sauté and bring the mixture to a boil, stirring constantly. 7. Press the Cancel button to stop the Sauté function. 8. Add the butter and stir to combine. 9. Serve chilled.

Flan in a Jar

Prep time: 25 minutes | Cook time: 6 minutes | Serves 6

- ½ cup sugar
- 1 tablespoon plus 1 cup hot water
- 1 cup coconut milk or whole milk
- ⅓ cup whole milk
- ⅓ cup sweetened condensed milk
- 2 large eggs plus 1 large egg yolk, lightly beaten
- Dash salt
- 1 teaspoon vanilla extract
- 1 teaspoon dark rum, optional

1. In a small heavy saucepan, spread sugar; cook, without stirring, over medium-low heat until it begins to melt. Gently drag melted sugar to center of pan so sugar melts evenly. Cook, stirring constantly, until melted sugar turns a deep amber color, about 2 minutes. Immediately remove from heat and carefully stir in 1 tablespoon hot water. Quickly pour into six hot 4-ounce (113-g) jars. 2. In a small saucepan, heat coconut milk and whole milk until bubbles form around sides of pan; remove from heat. In a large bowl, whisk condensed milk, eggs, egg yolk and salt until blended but not foamy. Slowly stir in hot milk; stir in vanilla and, if desired, rum. Strain through a fine sieve. Pour egg mixture into prepared jars. Center lids on jars; screw on bands until fingertip tight. 3. Add remaining hot water to 6-quart electric pressure cooker and place trivet insert in the bottom. Place jars on trivet, offset-stacking as needed. Lock lid; make sure vent is closed. Select Manual setting; adjust pressure to High and set time for 6 minutes. When finished cooking, allow pressure to naturally release for 10 minutes, then quick-release any remaining pressure according to manufacturer's directions. Cool jars 30 minutes at room temperature. 4. Refrigerate until cold, about 1 hour. Run a knife around the sides of the jars; invert flans onto dessert plates.

Coconut-Gingered Black Bean Brownies

Prep time: 5 minutes | Cook time: 1½ hours | Serves 12

1½ to 2 cups dried black beans, soaked for 12 hours or overnight
6 tablespoons maple, date, or brown rice syrup, divided
1 (15-ounce / 425-g) can organic light coconut milk
¾ cup no-sugar-added applesauce
2 teaspoons pure vanilla extract
1 tablespoon freshly grated ginger or 1 teaspoon ground
½ cup cacao powder
½ cup millet flour (or substitute oat, quinoa, or sorghum flour)
2 tablespoons dark chocolate chunks, chopped from a bar
¼ cup chopped walnuts

1. Preheat the oven to 350ºF (180ºC). Line a 9 x 9-inch baking dish with parchment paper. 2. Rinse and drain the beans. Add the beans, 2 tablespoons of the syrup, and coconut milk to the pressure cooker. Stir to combine. Cover and bring to pressure. Cook at high pressure for 12 minutes. Allow for a natural release. 3. Remove the lid. If beans are not done, simmer uncovered for 5 to 10 minutes, or until cooked through. 4. Pour the cooked beans into a food processor fitted with an S blade and pulse to chop up the beans. Add the applesauce, vanilla, ginger, and remaining 4 tablespoons syrup and blend until smooth. 5. Add the cacao powder and flour, and blend until smooth, resembling a cake batter. Add half of the dark chocolate and half of the chopped walnuts to the food processor and quickly pulse (don't blend) so the pieces are mixed in but still chunky. 6. Pour the batter into the prepared baking dish. Sprinkle the remaining half of the chocolate and walnut pieces on top. Bake for 40 to 50 minutes, or until a toothpick inserted into the center comes out almost clean. These brownies are fudgy, so the toothpick will still have some moist crumbs clinging to it. If necessary, bake for 5 to 10 minutes longer. 7. Remove the brownies and the parchment paper from the baking dish and let cool on a rack for 20 minutes. Slice into squares and serve.

Fudgy Brownies

Prep time: 10 minutes | Cook time: 5 minutes | Makes 3 brownies

3 ounces (85 g) dairy-free dark chocolate
1 tablespoon coconut oil or vegan margarine
½ cup applesauce
2 tablespoons unrefined sugar
⅓ cup all-purpose flour
½ teaspoon baking powder
Pinch salt

1. Put a trivet in your electric pressure cooker's cooking pot and pour in a cup or two of two of water. Select Sauté. 2. In a large heat-proof glass or ceramic bowl, combine the chocolate and coconut oil. Place the bowl over the top of your pressure cooker, as you would a double boiler. Stir occasionally until the chocolate is melted, then turn off the pressure cooker. 3. Stir the applesauce and sugar into the chocolate mixture. Add the flour, baking powder, and salt and stir just until combined. Pour the batter into 3 heat-proof ramekins. Put them in a heat-proof dish and cover with aluminum foil. Using a foil sling to lower the dish onto the trivet. (Alternately, cover each ramekin with foil and place them directly on the trivet, without the dish.) Close and lock the lid and ensure the pressure valve is sealed, then select High Pressure and set the time for 5 minutes. 4. Once the cook time is complete, quick release the pressure, being careful not to get your fingers or face near the steam release. 5. Once all the pressure has released, carefully unlock and remove the lid. Let cool for a few minutes before carefully lifting out the dish, or ramekins, with oven mitts or tongs. Let cool for a few minutes more before serving.

Crumbly Oat Stuffed Peaches

Prep time: 5 minutes | Cook time: 4 minutes | Serves 4

2 medium-sized, just-ripe, firm peaches (white or yellow)
¼ cup almond flour
⅛ cup old-fashioned rolled oats (certified gluten-free, if needed)
⅛ cup chopped pecans
⅛ cup coconut sugar
Pinch of sea salt
1 tablespoon vegan butter (such as Miyoko's or Earth Balance), melted
1 tablespoon pure maple syrup
⅔ cup water
1 pint vegan vanilla ice cream (optional), for serving
Fresh mint (optional), for garnish
Ground cinnamon (optional), for garnish

1. Cut the peaches in half. Carefully remove the pits. If they don't easily come out, use a melon baller, taking care not to remove much of the peach flesh. 2. In a small bowl, stir together the almond flour, oats, pecans, coconut sugar, and salt. Pour in the melted butter and syrup, and stir to combine into a crumbly topping. Top the cut sides of the peaches evenly with the topping mixture. 3. Fit the inner pot with the trivet or steam rack, and add ⅔ cup water. Cover the trivet with a small piece of parchment paper. Place the peaches cut-side up on the parchment. 4. Lock the lid and ensure the steam release valve is set to the Sealing position. Select Pressure Cook (Low), and set the cook time for 2 minutes. 5. Once the cook time is complete, immediately quick release the pressure and carefully remove the lid. Check that the peaches are tender. If not, pressure cook for 1 minute more. 6. To crisp the topping, place the peaches onto a baking sheet and place under the broiler for 2 minutes, or until golden. (This step is optional but encouraged.) 7. Serve the stuffed peaches warm, topped with a scoop of ice cream, if desired, and garnished with fresh mint leaves and cinnamon, if using.

Mango-Coconut Custard

Prep time: 5 minutes | Cook time: 10 minutes | Serves 4

2 cups chopped fresh or frozen mango
½ (13½-ounce / 383-g) can full-fat coconut milk (about ¾ cup)
2 tablespoons cornstarch or arrowroot powder
Unrefined sugar, for sprinkling (optional)

1. In a blender or food processor, purée the mango, coconut milk, and cornstarch. Pour the mixture into 4 heat-proof ramekins. Sprinkle a bit of sugar on top of each, if you like. 2. Put a trivet in the bottom of your electric pressure cooker's cooking pot and pour in a cup or two of water. Lower the ramekins onto the trivet, stacking them if needed (3 on the bottom, 1 on top). Close and lock the lid and ensure the pressure valve is sealed, then select High Pressure and set the time for 10 minutes. 3. Once the cook time is complete, let the pressure release naturally, about 10 minutes. 4. Once all the pressure has released, carefully unlock and remove the lid. Let cool for a few minutes before carefully lifting out the ramekins with oven mitts or tongs. 5. Let the custards cool to room

temperature, or refrigerate until cooled and set.

Sticky Rice and Fresh Fruit

Prep time: 5 minutes | Cook time: 14 minutes | Serves 4

¾ to 1 cup full-fat coconut milk
¼ cup sugar
½ teaspoon salt
2¼ cups water, divided
1 cup sweet rice, rinsed and drained
Sliced fresh fruit, for serving

1. In a small saucepan over low heat, make the coconut sauce by combining the coconut milk, sugar, and salt. Cook for 2 to 3 minutes, stirring frequently—don't let it boil—until the sugar dissolves. Remove from the heat. 2. Pour 1 cup of water into the Instant Pot and place a trivet into the inner pot. In a medium glass or stainless steel bowl, combine the remaining 1¼ cups water and the rice, ensuring the rice is completely covered. Place the bowl atop the trivet. Lock the lid and turn the steam release handle to Sealing. Using the Manual function, set the cooker to High Pressure for 14 minutes. 3. When the cook time is complete, let the pressure release naturally for 10 to 12 minutes; quick release any remaining pressure. 4. Carefully remove the lid and add half the coconut sauce. Cover the cooker and let sit for at least 5 minutes so the rice absorbs the liquid. 5. Top each serving with fruit and additional coconut sauce.

Chocolate Cake with Dark Chocolate Ganache

Prep time: 10 minutes | Cook time: 30 minutes | Serves 10

1 cup water
1 cup whole wheat pastry flour
½ cup unsweetened cocoa powder
½ cup raw turbinado sugar
1 teaspoon baking soda
½ teaspoon baking powder
½ teaspoon instant coffee
¼ teaspoon salt
¾ cup unsweetened almond milk
1 tablespoon apple cider vinegar
1 teaspoon pure vanilla extract
¼ cup melted coconut oil
¼ cup chopped, toasted hazelnuts, for garnish
1 cup fresh raspberries, for garnish
Fresh mint leaves, for garnish
Ganache:
¾ cup chopped dairy-free dark chocolate
¼ to ⅓ cup canned coconut milk, stirred

1. Fit the inner pot with the trivet or steam rack, and add with 1 cup water. Coat a 7-inch springform pan with cooking spray. 2. In a medium bowl, whisk together the flour, cocoa powder, sugar, baking soda, baking powder, instant coffee, and salt. 3. In another medium bowl, whisk together the almond milk, vinegar, vanilla, and oil. Stir the wet ingredients into the dry. Transfer the batter into the prepared pan and smooth into an even layer with the back of a spoon. 4. Cover the pan with foil and place on the trivet. Lock the lid and ensure the steam release valve is set to the Sealing position. Select Cake (High)—if your pot has that function—or Pressure Cook (High), and set the cook time for 30 minutes. 5. Once the cook time is complete, allow the pressure to release naturally for 10 minutes, then quick release any remaining pressure. Carefully remove the lid and the cake pan. Remove the foil and let the cake cool completely on a cooling rack. 6. Meanwhile, make the ganache. Place the chocolate in a small glass bowl. Heat the coconut milk in a small saucepan, or in the Instant Pot on Sauté (Medium), until it just begins to simmer. Carefully pour the coconut milk over the chocolate and stir until all the chocolate has melted and the mixture is smooth. 7. Pour the ganache over the top of the cooled cake, letting it drip down the sides. Garnish by arranging the berries, hazelnuts, and mint over the ganache. (I like to do this in a decorative crescent moon shape!) 8. Serve the cake at room temperature with more of the ganache, raspberries, and hazelnuts on the side, if desired.

Cinnamon Apples

Prep time: 10 minutes | Cook time: 5 minutes | Serves 4

1 cup water
3 medium Granny Smith apples, peeled and sliced
3 medium Gala apples, peeled and sliced
½ cup packed light brown sugar
2 tablespoons lemon juice
2 teaspoons ground cinnamon
½ teaspoon ground nutmeg

1. Pour water into Instant Pot and add trivet. 2. In a 6-cup metal bowl, toss together apples, brown sugar, lemon juice, cinnamon, and nutmeg. 3. Cover bowl tightly with foil. Create a foil sling and carefully lower bowl into Instant Pot. 4. Close lid and set pressure release to Sealing. 5. Press Manual or Pressure Cook button and adjust time to 5 minutes. 6. When the timer beeps, quick release pressure and then unlock lid and remove it. 7. Remove bowl using foil sling. Remove foil lid and stir apples. Serve warm.

Flourless Brownies

Prep time: 10 minutes | Cook time: 15 minutes | Makes 16

¾ cup almond butter
¾ cup coconut sugar
⅓ cup raw cacao powder
1 egg
¼ teaspoon fine sea salt
½ teaspoon baking soda
½ teaspoon pure vanilla extract
½ cup dark chocolate chips (optional)

1. Line a 7-inch round pan with parchment paper. In a large bowl, combine the almond butter, coconut sugar, cacao powder, egg, salt, baking soda, and vanilla and stir well to create a thick batter. 2. Transfer the batter to the prepared pan and use your hands to press it evenly into the pan. Sprinkle with the chocolate chips and gently press them into the batter. Pour 1 cup water into the Instant Pot and arrange the handled trivet on the bottom. Place the pan on top of the trivet and cover it with an upside-down plate or another piece of parchment to protect the brownies from condensation. 3. Secure the lid and move the steam release valve to Sealing. Select Manual or Pressure Cook to cook on High pressure for 15 minutes. When the cooking cycle is complete, let the pressure naturally release for 10 minutes, then move the steam release valve to Venting to release any remaining pressure. When the floating valve drops, remove the lid. 4. Use oven mitts to lift the trivet and the pan out of the pot. Let the brownies cool completely in the pan before cutting and serving, as they will be very fragile when warm. Store leftovers in an airtight container in the fridge for 2 weeks.

Stout-Poached Pears

Prep time: 5 minutes | Cook time: 9 minutes | Serves 2

3 peeled (stem on) firm Bartlett pears
1½ cups (1 bottle) stout beer
1 vanilla bean, split lengthwise and seeds scraped
½ cup packed brown sugar

1. Slice a thin layer from the bottom of each pear so they can stand upright. Using a melon baller, scoop out the seeds and core from the bottom. 2. In the pressure cooker, stir together the beer, vanilla bean and seeds, and brown sugar. Place the pears upright in the pot. 3. Secure the lid and cook on High pressure for 9 minutes, then quick release the pressure in the pot and remove the lid. Press Cancel. 4. Using tongs, carefully remove the pears by their stems and transfer to a plate. Set aside. Select Sauté and simmer the liquid in the pot until reduced by half. 5. Strain the liquid into a bowl through a fine-mesh sieve, then pour over the pears. Serve at room temperature or chilled, plain or with whipped cream and a drizzle of chocolate sauce.

Walnut Brownie Sundaes with Coconut Caramel Sauce

Prep time: 15 minutes | Cook time: 1½ hours | Serves 8

3 tablespoons egg replacer powder
6 tablespoons water
¾ cup vegan shortening, melted and cooled (I recommend Nutiva or Earth Balance brand)
1½ teaspoons instant coffee crystals or espresso powder
1½ teaspoons vanilla extract
1 cup coconut sugar
½ teaspoon fine sea salt
¼ cup unsweetened nondairy milk
¾ cup all-purpose flour
¾ cup cocoa powder
¾ cup chocolate chips
¾ cup walnut halves and pieces, toasted
Coconut Caramel Sauce
1 (11¼-ounce / 319-g) can sweetened condensed coconut milk
Coconut vanilla ice cream, for serving

1. Line the base of a 7-inch round springform or push-up pan with an 8-inch round of parchment paper. If using a springform pan, secure the collar on the pan, closing it onto the base so that the parchment round is clamped in. Lightly grease the sides of the pan with oil or nonstick cooking spray. 2. In a small bowl, stir together the egg replacer and water, using a spoon to mash any lumps of egg replacer against the side of the bowl. Set aside. 3. In a mixing bowl, whisk together the shortening, instant coffee, vanilla, sugar, and salt. Whisk in the nondairy milk and egg replacer mixture. Stir in the flour and cocoa powder, just until the dry ingredients are incorporated. Fold in the chocolate chips and walnuts. 4. Transfer the batter to the prepared pan; it will be very thick. Use a spatula to pat it out into an even layer. Cover the pan tightly with aluminum foil, then place the pan on a long-handled silicone steam rack. 5. Pour 1½ cups water into the Instant Pot. Holding the handles of the steam rack, lower it into the pot. 6. Secure the lid and set the pressure release to Sealing. Select the Cake, Pressure Cook, or Manual setting and set the cooking time for 45 minutes at high pressure. (The pot will take about 10 minutes to come up to pressure before the cooking program begins.) 7. When the cooking program ends, let the pressure release naturally for 10 minutes, then move the pressure release to Venting to release any remaining steam. Open the pot and, wearing heat-resistant mitts, grab the handles of the steam rack, lift the rack out of the pot, and set the pan on a cooling rack. Remove the aluminum foil, taking care not to let any condensation that has settled on the aluminum foil drip onto the brownies. 8. Let the brownies cool for at least 2 hours, or up to 24 hours, before serving. Make the Coconut Caramel Sauce: 9. While the brownies are cooling, pour 1 cup water into the Instant Pot and place a wire metal steam rack inside. Place the unopened can of sweetened condensed coconut milk in the center of the rack. 10. Secure the lid and set the pressure release to Sealing. Select the Steam setting and set the cooking time for 45 minutes, then deselect the Keep Warm setting so that the pot will turn off when the cooking program ends. (The pot will take about 5 minutes to come up to pressure before the cooking program begins.) 11. When the cooking program ends, leave the can in the pot to cool for 2 hours, undisturbed. 12. After 2 hours, open the pot and remove the can; it will still be a bit warm. You can use the caramel while it is still warm, or chill in the refrigerator for a few hours, where it will thicken a bit. After opening the can, transfer the caramel to an airtight container and store, refrigerated, for up to 1 month. 13. When the brownies are cool, slice them into wedges, transfer to serving plates, and serve with a scoop of ice cream and caramel sauce drizzled on top.

Cookies and Cream Cheesecake

Prep time: 15 minutes | Cook time: 40 minutes | Serves 6

1 cup water
26 cream-filled chocolate sandwich cookies, divided
2 tablespoons unsalted butter, melted
16 ounces (454 g) cream cheese, softened
½ cup granulated sugar
1 teaspoon vanilla extract
½ cup full-fat sour cream
2 large eggs, room temperature

1. Pour water into Instant Pot and add trivet. Grease a 7-inch PushPan and set aside. 2. Place 16 chocolate cookies in a gallon-sized zip-top bag and seal. Roll with a rolling pin until small crumbs are formed. 3. In a small bowl, mix crushed cookies and melted butter together. 4. Press cookie crust into bottom and halfway up sides of greased PushPan. Place pan in freezer while preparing cheesecake batter. 5. With an electric mixer, cream together cream cheese, sugar, and vanilla. Beat until light and fluffy, about 2 minutes. 6. Slowly add in sour cream and mix. 7. Add in eggs, one at a time, beating after each addition. Only mix until combined. Do not overmix. 8. Chop remaining cookies and fold half of them into cheesecake batter. Reserve remaining chopped cookies for topping. 9. Pour batter into PushPan. Create a foil sling and carefully lower pan into Instant Pot. 10. Close lid and set pressure release to Sealing. 11. Press Manual or Pressure Cook button and adjust time to 40 minutes. 12. When the timer beeps, allow pressure to release naturally and then unlock lid and remove it. 13. Carefully remove pan from Instant Pot using foil sling. Place on a cooling rack and let cool to room temperature. 14. Cover with plastic wrap and refrigerate for a minimum of 8 hours. 15. Top cheesecake with remaining chopped cookies and serve.

Poached Pears with Spiced Pomegranate Sauce

Prep time: 5 minutes | Cook time: 12 minutes | Serves 4

4 pears, peeled
½ cup pomegranate juice
½ cup orange juice
¼ cup pomegranate seeds
2 star anise pods
1 teaspoon fresh grated ginger
½ teaspoon ground cinnamon
¼ cup coconut sugar

1. Into the Instant Pot, add all the ingredients, except for the pears. Use a whisk or a spoon to mix until the sugar is mostly dissolved. 2. Place the steamer rack into the cooker and place the pears on top. 3. Seal the cooker and, using the Pressure Cook option, cook on high for 7 minutes. 4. Use the quick release method to release the steam from the cooker. 5. Let the cooker sit for 7 to 10 minutes before removing the lid. 6. Carefully open the lid and remove the pears from the cooker. Set aside. 7. Turn the setting on the cooker to the Sauté option. 8. Cook the sauce, stirring frequently, for approximately 5 minutes, or until it reduces and thickens. 9. Place the pears on serving plates and drizzle the pomegranate sauce over the top before serving.

Pearberry Crisp

Prep time: 15 minutes | Cook time: 8 minutes | Serves 4

Pearberry Filling:
6 medium pears, peeled, cored, and diced
1 cup thawed frozen mixed berries
¼ cup water
1 tablespoon fresh lemon juice
2 tablespoons pure maple syrup
1 teaspoon ground cinnamon
¼ teaspoon ground nutmeg
Pinch of salt
Topping:
4 tablespoons melted butter
1 cup old-fashioned oats
⅛ cup all-purpose flour
¼ cup chopped almonds
¼ cup packed light brown sugar
¼ teaspoon sea salt

1. For Pearberry Filling: Place pearberry filling ingredients in Instant Pot. Stir to distribute ingredients. 2. For Topping: Mix topping ingredients together in a small bowl. Spoon drops of topping over the filling. Lock lid. 3. Press the Manual button and adjust time to 8 minutes. When the timer beeps, let pressure release naturally until float valve drops and then unlock lid. Spoon into bowls and enjoy.

Cinnamon Stuffed Peaches

Prep time: 10 minutes | Cook time: 3 minutes | Serves 4

4 medium-sized ripe peaches
2 tablespoons coconut oil
¼ cup coconut sugar
2 tablespoons oat flour
½ teaspoon cinnamon
¼ cup pecans, finely chopped

1. Slice off the top of each peach, remove the pit and scoop out a hollow well into the center. 2. In a bowl, mix together the coconut oil, sugar, oat flour and cinnamon. Once you have a crumbly mixture, add the pecans and mix well. 3. Spoon the filling into the center of each peach. 4. Place approximately 1 cup of water in the Instant Pot and then place the steamer rack inside. 5. Arrange the peaches on the steamer. 6. Seal the cooker and, using the Pressure Cook option, cook on high for 3 minutes. 7. Use the quick release option to release the steam. 8. Carefully open the lid and remove the peaches. 9. Serve as is or with favorite vegan ice cream.

Baked Plums

Prep time: 10 minutes | Cook time: 20 minutes | Serves 4 to 6

1½ pounds (680 g) fresh plums, pitted and halved
1½ cups water
2 tablespoons honey
1 teaspoon vanilla extract
4 cloves
1 star anise
3 cardamom pods
1 teaspoon ground cinnamon

1. Put the plums into the Instant Pot. 2. Add the water, honey, vanilla, cloves, anise, cardamom, and cinnamon. 3. Close and lock the lid. Select Manual and cook at High pressure for 15 minutes. 4. Once cooking is complete, let the pressure release naturally for 10 minutes. Release any remaining steam manually. Uncover the pot. 5. Transfer the plums to a serving bowl. 6. Select the Sauté setting on the Instant Pot on High heat. Reduce the remaining liquid by half. 7. Serve or store the plums with the sauce.

Chocolate-Berry Bread Pudding

Prep time: 10 minutes | Cook time: 20 minutes | Serves 6

6 slices day-old vegan white bread
½ cup raspberry preserves
½ cup diced dried strawberries or prunes
½ cup chopped hazelnuts
½ cup cocoa powder
½ cup granulated sugar
Pinch salt
2 tablespoons vegan margarine
2 medium bananas, mashed
2 cups unsweetened soy milk or almond milk
2 cups vegan sour cream
1 tablespoon vanilla extract
1 cup water

1. If the crusts on the bread are dark, remove them. If using fresh bread, lightly toast it. Spread raspberry preserves over the bread. Treat a 5-cup heatproof soufflé dish with nonstick spray. 2. Tear the bread into chunks. Layer half the bread in the bottom of the soufflé dish. Sprinkle with dried fruit and chopped hazelnuts. Add remaining bread with preserves. 3. In a medium bowl, whisk together the cocoa, sugar, and salt. Add the margarine and mashed bananas; whisk to mix. Whisk in soy milk, sour cream, and vanilla. Pour half the cocoa mixture over the bread. Tap down the dish and wait several minutes for the bread to absorb the liquid. Pour in the remaining cocoa mixture. 4. Pour the water into the Instant Pot and insert the trivet. Set the cake on the trivet. Lock the lid into place, press the Manual button, and adjust timer to 20 minutes. When the timer beeps, let pressure release naturally until float valve drops and then unlock lid. 5. Remove the chocolate-berry bread pudding from the pot and place on a rack until ready to serve or until it's cool enough to cover and refrigerate.

Fruit Compote

Prep time: 8 minutes | Cook time: 15 minutes | Serves 6

1 cup apple juice
1 cup dry white wine
2 tablespoons granulated sugar
1 cinnamon stick
¼ teaspoon ground nutmeg
Zest of 1 medium lemon
Zest of 1 medium orange
3 medium Granny Smith apples, peeled, cored, and chopped
3 medium Bartlett pears, peeled, cored, and chopped
½ cup dried cherries, cranberries, or raisins

1. In the Instant Pot, combine the apple juice and wine, press the Sauté button, and adjust setting to High. Bring to a boil and stir in the sugar until dissolved, about 3 minutes. Add the cinnamon stick, nutmeg, lemon zest, and orange zest. Adjust to Low and simmer 5 minutes. 2. Add the apples and pears to the pot and stir to mix ingredients. Lock the lid into place, press the Manual button, and adjust timer to 3 minutes. When the timer beeps, quick-release pressure until float valve drops and then unlock lid. 3. Use a slotted spoon to transfer the cooked fruit to a serving bowl. Press the Sauté button on the pot and adjust to High to bring juices to a boil; boil and stir until reduced to a syrup that will coat the back of a spoon. 4. Stir the dried cherries, cranberries, or raisins in with the cooked fruit in the bowl and pour the syrup over the fruit mixture. Stir to mix. Allow to cool slightly, then cover with plastic wrap and chill overnight in the refrigerator.

Mexican Chocolate Gelatin Pudding Cups

Prep time: 15 minutes | Cook time: 5 minutes | Serves 5

1½ cups heavy cream
½ cup milk
¾ cup chocolate chips or chopped chocolate
2 large eggs
¼ cup pure maple syrup or honey
1½ tablespoons unsweetened cocoa powder
2 tablespoons grass-fed butter, ghee or coconut oil, melted, divided
1 tablespoon pure vanilla extract
½ teaspoon organic orange extract
½ teaspoon ground cinnamon
⅛ teaspoon ground cayenne
⅛ teaspoon sea salt
1 teaspoon grass-fed bovine gelatin
1 cup water
Homemade whipped cream, for garnish (optional)
Shaved or chopped organic stone-ground Mexican chocolate, for garnish (optional)

1. In a small saucepan, over medium-low heat, gently warm the cream, milk and chocolate, whisking until melted. Remove from the heat and set aside. 2. In a blender, combine the eggs, sweetener of choice, cocoa powder, melted fat of your choice, vanilla, orange extract, cinnamon, cayenne and salt. Process on low speed for 30 seconds until fully blended. 3. While the blender is still blending, remove the vent lid and add the chocolate mixture then the gelatin, and continue to blend for 30 seconds until fully combined. 4. Evenly pour the custard mixture into five half-pint glass jars, leaving at least a ½-inch headspace at the top. Cover and secure the jars with lids. 5. Pour the water into your Instant Pot and insert the steam trivet. Set all five jars on the trivet. They should fit perfectly inside the Instant Pot. Secure the lid with the steam vent in the sealed position. Press Manual, then low pressure and set for 5 minutes. 6. Once the timer sounds, press Keep Warm/Cancel. Using an oven mitt, do a quick release. When the steam venting stops and the silver dial drops, carefully open the lid. 7. Using an oven mitt or tongs, carefully remove the jars and remove their lids. Give each pudding cup a good stir until the mixture becomes smooth, then allow them to cool at room temperature. Once they have cooled, transfer them to the refrigerator to set. Let them chill for a minimum of 6 hours, best overnight for the most authentic solid texture. 8. Serve chilled as is or garnished, if desired, with homemade whipped cream or shaved or chopped organic stone-ground Mexican chocolate.

Pumpkin Pie Cups

Prep time: 5 minutes | Cook time: 6 minutes | Serves 4

1 cup canned pumpkin purée
1 cup nondairy milk
6 tablespoons unrefined sugar or pure maple syrup (less if using sweetened milk), plus more for sprinkling
¼ cup spelt flour or all-purpose flour
½ teaspoon pumpkin pie spice
Pinch salt

1. In a medium bowl, stir together the pumpkin, milk, sugar, flour, pumpkin pie spice, and salt. Pour the mixture into 4 heat-proof ramekins. Sprinkle a bit more sugar on the top of each, if you like. 2. Put a trivet in the bottom of your electric pressure cooker's cooking pot and pour in a cup or two of water. Place the ramekins onto the trivet, stacking them if needed (3 on the bottom, 1 on top). Close and lock the lid and ensure the pressure valve is sealed, then select High Pressure and set the time for 6 minutes. 3. Once the cook time is complete, quick release the pressure, being careful not to get your fingers or face near the steam release. 4. Once all the pressure has released, carefully unlock and remove the lid. Let cool for a few minutes before carefully lifting out the ramekins with oven mitts or tongs. 5. Let cool for at least 10 minutes before serving.

Blackberry Crisp

Prep time: 15 minutes | Cook time: 8 minutes | Serves 4

Blackberry Filling:
2 cups fresh blackberries
¼ cup water
1 tablespoon freshly squeezed orange juice
¼ cup granulated sugar
1 teaspoon cornstarch
1 teaspoon cinnamon
¼ teaspoon ground nutmeg
⅛ teaspoon salt

Topping:
4 tablespoons melted unsalted butter
1 cup old-fashioned oats
⅛ cup gluten-free all-purpose flour
¼ cup chopped almonds
¼ cup packed light brown sugar
¼ teaspoon salt

Make the Blackberry Filling: 1. Add filling ingredients to the Instant Pot. Stir to evenly distribute ingredients. Make the Topping: 1. Mix topping ingredients together in a small bowl. Spoon drops of topping over filling in pot. Lock lid. 2. Press the Manual button and adjust cook time to 8 minutes. When timer beeps, let pressure release naturally until float valve drops and then unlock lid. 3. Spoon crisp into four bowls and enjoy.

Raspberry-Lemon Curd

Prep time: 5 minutes | Cook time: 3 minutes | Makes 1½ cups

12 ounces (340 g) fresh raspberries
¾ cup sugar
2 tablespoons fresh lemon juice
1 teaspoon lemon zest
2 large egg yolks
2 tablespoons unsalted butter

1. In the Instant Pot, combine the raspberries, sugar and lemon juice and zest. 2. Secure the lid with the steam vent in the sealed position. Select Manual or Pressure Cook, and cook on high for 1 minute. 3. Use a natural release for at least 10 minutes. Release any remaining steam. 4. Remove the lid. Use an immersion blender or transfer the mixture to a blender and pulse until smooth. If removed, place the mixture back inside the Instant Pot and select Sauté. 5. Meanwhile, in a small bowl, whisk together the egg yolks. Slowly fold them into the raspberry mixture. Continue to stir while the mixture comes to a boil, then select Cancel. Add the butter. 6. Transfer to a glass or other airtight, heatproof container and let cool to room temperature. Refrigerate until the curd is completely set. Serve chilled. 7. Store this recipe in the fridge for up to 2 weeks.

Peach-Raspberry Crisp

Prep time: 5 minutes | Cook time: 8 minutes | Serves 8 to 10

Peach-Raspberry Filling:
8 firm-ripe medium peaches
Cooking spray or neutral-flavored oil, for the pot
1 pint raspberries (about 2 cups)
2 tablespoons organic cane sugar
1 tablespoon organic brown sugar or organic cane sugar
½ teaspoon ground cinnamon
¼ teaspoon ground ginger
2 whole cloves or ⅛ teaspoon ground cloves (optional)
Pinch of kosher salt or fine sea salt
½ teaspoon pure almond extract (or pure vanilla extract)
1 teaspoon fresh lemon juice
1 tablespoon cornstarch or arrowroot powder
Crisp Topping:
⅓ cup refined coconut oil
1 cup rolled oats (gluten-free if needed)
½ cup almond flour
½ cup walnuts, chopped
½ cup packed organic brown sugar
½ teaspoon ground cinnamon
½ teaspoon kosher salt
For Serving (optional):
Vegan vanilla ice cream

1. Leave the peaches unpeeled and use a serrated knife to slice them into ¾-inch-thick wedges. You will end up with about 6 cups of sliced peaches. 2. Coat the inner pot of the Instant Pot with cooking spray or lightly grease with oil. 3. Add the sliced peaches and raspberries to the inner pot. Top with the cane sugar, brown sugar, cinnamon, ginger, cloves (if using), salt, almond extract, and lemon juice. Stir gently to coat the fruit. 4. Secure the lid and set the Pressure Release to Sealing. Select the Pressure Cook setting at high pressure and set the cook time to 1 minute. 5. Meanwhile, prepare the crisp topping: In a large skillet, heat the coconut oil over medium heat. Once the oil is melted and hot, add the oats, almond flour, walnuts, brown sugar, cinnamon, and salt. Cook, tossing frequently to prevent burning, until toasted and lightly browned, 5 to 7 minutes. Carefully transfer the crisp topping to a large piece of parchment paper and spread out to cool slightly. 6. Once the 1-minute timer has completed and beeps, perform a quick pressure release by carefully switching the Pressure Release knob from Sealing to Venting. 7. In a small bowl, whisk together the cornstarch and 1 tablespoon water until dissolved into a slurry. Open the pot and pour the slurry into the peach-raspberry filling. Select the Sauté setting and bring to a boil, stirring gently until the filling has thickened, 1 to 2 minutes. 8. Transfer the peach-raspberry filling to a large serving bowl or individual dessert bowls and sprinkle generously with the crisp topping. Serve warm with vegan vanilla ice cream if desired.

Refined-Sugar-Free Blueberry Pie

Prep time: 10 minutes | Cook time: 23 minutes | Serves 6

1 cup water
1 pint vegan vanilla ice cream, for serving
Fresh mint leaves, for serving
Filling:
4 cups fresh blueberries
1 tablespoon fresh lemon juice
3 tablespoons corn starch
3 tablespoons coconut sugar
Crust:
2 cups blanched almond flour
¼ cup arrowroot starch
¼ teaspoon sea salt
4 tablespoons melted coconut oil
2 tablespoons pure maple syrup

1. To make the filling, in a medium bowl, toss together all ingredients. Transfer to a baking dish that will fit inside the inner pot, such as a glass Pyrex or soufflé dish. A 7 × 3-inch soufflé dish is ideal. Cover with foil. 2. Fit the inner pot with the trivet or steam rack, and add 1 cup water. Place the dish on the trivet. Lock the lid and ensure the steam release valve is set to the Sealing position. Select Pressure Cook (High), and set the cook time for 13 minutes. 3. Once the cook time is complete, immediately quick release the pressure. Carefully remove the lid and the dish from the pot and discard the foil. Stir the filling if you'd like to break up the berries more. Let the filling cool for at least 15 minutes to thicken up. 4. Meanwhile, make the crust. In a medium bowl, whisk together the almond flour, arrowroot, and salt. Make a well in the middle and add the coconut oil and syrup. Stir into the dry ingredients until the dough comes together. On a piece of parchment or a silicone baking mat, roll the dough into a ¼-inch-thick circle slightly smaller than the dish containing the filling. Use a small, 1- to 3-inch cookie cutter to cut a piece out of the center (optional) and cut more shapes from the remaining dough. Slide the parchment or silicone mat onto a cookie sheet. Transfer to the freezer for 10 minutes. Preheat the oven to 370ºF (188ºC). 5. Bake the pie crust circle and "cookies" until golden, about 10 minutes. 6. Let the pie crust cool. Carefully place the round piece atop the blueberry filling. Cut the pie into 8 servings, and serve in bowls with a scoop of ice cream and the small crust shapes. Garnish with fresh mint leaves.

Banana Pudding Cake

Prep time: 10 minutes | Cook time: 35 minutes | Serves 12

1 (18¼-ounce / 517-g) package vegan cake mix
1 (3½-ounce / 99-g) package instant vegan pudding mix
4 ounces (113 g) silken tofu
4 cups water, divided
¼ cup vegetable oil

3 small ripe bananas, mashed
2 cups powdered sugar, sifted
2 tablespoons unsweetened soy milk or almond milk
1 teaspoon vanilla extract
½ cup toasted and chopped walnuts

1. Treat a 1-quart or 6-cup Bundt or angel food cake pan with nonstick spray. Set aside. 2. Add the cake mix and pudding mix to a large mixing bowl; stir to mix. Make a well in the center and add the tofu and pour in 1 cup water, oil, and mashed bananas. 3. Beat on low speed until blended. Scrape bowl and beat another 4 minutes on medium speed. Pour the batter into the prepared pan. Cover tightly with a piece of heavy-duty aluminum foil. 4. Pour 3 cups water into the Instant Pot and insert the trivet. Lower the cake pan onto the rack. Lock the lid into place, press the Manual button, and adjust timer to 35 minutes. 5. When the timer beeps, quick-release pressure until float valve drops and then unlock lid. 6. Lift the cake pan out of the pot and place on a wire rack to cool 10 minutes, then turn the cake out onto the wire rack to finish cooling. 7. To make the glaze, mix together the powdered sugar, soy milk, and vanilla in a bowl. Drizzle over the top of the cooled cake. Sprinkle the walnuts over the glaze before the glaze dries.

Pear and Cranberry Crisp

Prep time: 10 minutes | Cook time: 5 minutes | Serves 6

3 large Anjou pears, peeled, cored and diced
1 cup fresh cranberries
1 tablespoon granulated sugar
2 teaspoons ground cinnamon
½ teaspoon ground nutmeg
½ cup water
1 tablespoon pure maple syrup

6 tablespoons melted unsalted butter
1 cup old-fashioned rolled oats
⅓ cup dark brown sugar
¼ cup all-purpose flour
½ teaspoon sea salt
½ cup toasted pecans (optional)
Vanilla ice cream, for serving (optional)

1. In the Instant Pot, combine the pears and cranberries and sprinkle with the granulated sugar. Let sit for a few minutes, then sprinkle with the cinnamon and nutmeg. Pour the water and maple syrup on top. 2. In a medium bowl, stir together the melted butter, oats, brown sugar, flour and salt. 3. Spoon the mixture on the fruit in the Instant Pot. 4. Secure the lid with the steam vent in the sealed position. Select Manual or Pressure Cook, and cook on high for 5 minutes. Use a quick release. 5. Spoon into individual bowls and serve hot. Top with pecans and vanilla ice cream (if using).

Chapter 9 Staples, Sauces, Dips, and Dressings

Chapter 9 Staples, Sauces, Dips, and Dressings

Thick and Rich Jackfruit Ragu

Prep time: 15 minutes | Cook time: 20 minutes | Serves 6

- 1 to 2 tablespoons olive oil (or dry sauté or add a little water/vegetable broth)
- 1 small onion, minced
- 4 cloves garlic, minced
- 2 small carrots, chopped small
- 1 medium stalk celery, chopped small
- 1 (20-ounce / 567-g) can jackfruit in brine (do not use the kind in syrup)
- 1 (28-ounce / 794-g) can tomato purée
- 2 tablespoons tomato paste
- 1 tablespoon balsamic vinegar
- 2 teaspoons dried oregano
- 1 teaspoon dried basil
- 1 bay leaf
- ½ teaspoon salt
- ¼ teaspoon dried rosemary
- ¼ teaspoon ground black pepper

1. Use the Sauté setting over normal, or medium heat, and heat the oil if using. Sauté the onion until transparent, 5 minutes. Then add the garlic, carrots and celery and sauté for 4 minutes more. 2. Rinse the jackfruit in a strainer and then smash it in your hands to get it to break into shreds. You can remove any large seedpods and discard. They will be obvious once you start smashing. 3. Add the jackfruit shreds, tomato purée, tomato paste, balsamic vinegar, oregano, basil, bay leaf, salt, rosemary and black pepper. Put the lid on and make sure the steam release handle is set to sealing, or closed; change to the Manual setting and set the timer for 10 minutes. 4. Allow the pressure to release naturally. You'll know when it's ready because the round silver pressure gauge will drop down. 5. Before serving, taste and add extra salt, pepper, herbs and balsamic vinegar if needed. Remove and discard the bay leaf. Serve over toasted bread, pasta or polenta.

Garden Salsa

Prep time: 10 minutes | Cook time: 5 minutes | Makes 6 to 8 cups

- 8 large tomatoes (I use multiple kinds of tomatoes in this, so if you're using any smaller tomatoes, just make sure the total amount is roughly the equivalent of 8 large tomatoes), roughly chopped
- 5 or 6 garlic cloves, finely diced
- 2 jalapeño peppers, seeded and diced
- 1 bell pepper, any color, diced
- 1 small red onion, diced
- 1 small yellow onion, diced
- 1 tablespoon ground cumin
- 3 to 4 teaspoons salt
- Generous ½ teaspoon freshly ground black pepper
- ½ teaspoon baking soda
- ¼ cup tomato paste
- 2 tablespoons freshly squeezed lime juice
- Chopped fresh cilantro leaves, to taste

1. In your Instant Pot, stir together the tomatoes, garlic, jalapeños, bell pepper, red onion, yellow onion, cumin, salt, pepper, and baking soda. Lock the lid and turn the steam release handle to Sealing. Using the Manual function, set the cooker to High Pressure for 5 minutes. 2. When the cook time is complete, let the pressure release naturally for 10 minutes; quick release any remaining pressure. 3. Carefully remove the lid and stir in the tomato paste, lime juice, and cilantro. Let cool completely before serving.

Cauliflower Sour Cream

Prep time: 5 minutes | Cook time: 3 minutes | Makes about 1 cup

- 2 cups cauliflower florets
- 2 cups water
- 3 tablespoons cashews (optional)
- 1 teaspoon nutritional yeast
- 1 teaspoon lemon juice
- ½ teaspoon apple cider vinegar
- 2 to 6 teaspoons cooking liquid, as needed
- Salt, to taste

1. Add the cauliflower, water and cashews (if using) to your Instant Pot and cook on high pressure for 3 minutes. 2. Let the pressure release naturally. 3. Drain, reserving the liquid for blending. 4. Add the cauliflower and cashews along with the nutritional yeast, lemon juice, apple cider vinegar and 1 teaspoon of the cooking liquid. Blend, scrape down the sides and add more cooking liquid if needed. Blend until smooth. Add salt to taste.

Cilantro-Lime Rice

Prep time: 10 minutes | Cook time: 8 minutes | Serves 4

- 2 tablespoons olive oil
- 1 cup long-grain white rice
- 1 garlic clove, minced
- 1¼ cups low-sodium chicken or vegetable broth, or water
- ¼ teaspoon fine sea salt (½ teaspoon if using water instead of broth)
- ¼ cup chopped fresh cilantro
- ½ teaspoon grated lime zest (optional)
- 2 teaspoons freshly squeezed lime juice

1. Select Sauté and adjust to heat to Medium. Add the oil to the inner cooking pot. When it shimmers and flows easily, add the rice and garlic and stir to coat the rice with the oil, cooking for about 1 minute, or until the garlic is fragrant. Add the broth and salt. 2. Lock the lid into place and turn the valve to Sealing. Select Pressure Cook or Manual and adjust the pressure to High. Set the time for 7 minutes. When cooking ends, carefully turn the valve to Venting to quick release the pressure. 3. Unlock and remove the lid. Add the cilantro, lime zest (if using), and lime juice. Stir very gently to combine. Put the lid back on the pot but do not lock it into place. Let the rice sit for 3 to 4 minutes. Fluff with a fork.

Fire-Roasted Tomato and Butternut Squash Sauce

Prep time: 15 minutes | Cook time: 10 minutes | Serves 4 to 6

2 (14½-ounce / 411-g) cans fire-roasted diced tomatoes	1 teaspoon pure maple syrup
1 cup water	1 tablespoon balsamic vinegar
1 yellow onion, diced	1 teaspoon dried oregano
3 cloves garlic, chopped	1 teaspoon dried thyme
3 cups peeled, seeded and cubed butternut squash	Pinch of crushed red pepper flakes
1 teaspoon salt, plus more to taste	½ teaspoon freshly ground black pepper, plus more to taste
	3 tablespoons tomato paste

1. In the Instant Pot, combine all the ingredients, except the tomato paste, and mix well. 2. Secure the lid with the steam vent in the sealed position. Press Pressure Cook until the display light is beneath high pressure. Use the plus and minus buttons to adjust the time until the display reads 10 minutes. 3. When the timer sounds, quick release the pressure. Remove the lid. 4. Stir in the tomato paste. Use an immersion blender to purée the sauce until smooth. Adjust the salt and pepper, if needed.

DIY Vegetable Stock

Prep time: 5 minutes | Cook time: 15 minutes | Serves 8 to 10

2 or 3 celery stalks	1 cup mushrooms
2 or 3 carrots	6 to 8 whole peppercorns
1 large onion (I like sweet or yellow; red is a bit too strong)	1 bay leaf
	8 cups water

1. In your Instant Pot, combine the celery, carrots, onion, mushrooms, peppercorns, bay leaf, and water, making sure the veggies are completely covered by water. Lock the lid and turn the steam release handle to Sealing. Using the Manual function, set the cooker to High Pressure for 15 minutes. 2. When the cook time is complete, let the pressure release naturally for 15 minutes; quick release any remaining pressure. 3. Carefully remove the lid. Strain the stock through a fine-mesh strainer into a large heatproof container. Use immediately or refrigerate in an airtight container for 3 to 4 days, or keep frozen for up to a year.

Peach Jam

Prep time: 15 minutes | Cook time: 10 minutes | Makes 4 cups

4 cups peeled and chopped peaches	1 teaspoon fresh lemon juice
4 cups granulated sugar	1 (1¾-ounce / 50-g) package dry pectin

1. Add the peaches, sugar, and lemon juice to the Instant Pot. Stir to combine. Lock the lid into place, press the Manual button, and adjust timer to 3 minutes. When the timer beeps, let pressure release naturally until float valve drops and then unlock lid. 2. Press the Sauté button on the pot and adjust setting to High. Stir in the pectin, and bring mixture to a rolling boil, stirring constantly. Continue to boil and stir 1 minute. 3. Skim off and discard any foam. Ladle into hot, sterilized glass containers or jars, leaving 1-inch headspace. Seal the containers or jars. (If you prefer, you can follow the instructions that came with your canning jars and process the preserves for shelf storage.) 4. Let cool at room temperature 24 hours before canning. Refrigerate up to 5 weeks or freeze up to 8 months.

Lentil Ragù

Prep time: 10 minutes | Cook time: 32 minutes | Makes for 1½ pounds pasta

2 tablespoons olive oil	and minced
1 large yellow onion, chopped	1 tablespoon dried basil
3 cups vegetable broth	1 teaspoon dried oregano
1 (14-ounce / 397-g) can diced tomatoes	½ teaspoon ground allspice
1 cup brown lentils	½ teaspoon table salt
½ cup green lentils	¼ teaspoon red pepper flakes
2 medium garlic cloves, peeled	3 tablespoons tomato paste

1. Press the Sauté button, abd set on Medium or Normal for 10 minutes. 2. Warm the oil in a 3-, 6-, or 8-quart cooker for a minute or two, then add the onion. Cook, stirring occasionally, until softened, about 5 minutes. Turn off the Sauté function. Stir in the broth, tomatoes, brown lentils, green lentils, garlic, basil, oregano, allspice, salt, and red pepper flakes. Secure the lid with the steam vent in the sealed position. 3. Press the button Chili/Beans, Pressure Cook or Manual, and set on High for 12 minutes with the Keep Warm setting off. 4. When the pot has finished cooking, turn it off and let the pressure return to normal naturally, about 25 minutes. Unlatch the lid and open the cooker. 5. Press the Sauté button, and set on Medium or Normal for 10 minutes. 6. Bring the sauce to a simmer, stirring constantly. Stir in the tomato paste until uniform, then continue cooking, stirring almost the whole time, until thickened, about 2 minutes. Turn off the Sauté function and remove the hot insert from the machine to stop the cooking.

Creamy Tomato and Basil Pasta Sauce

Prep time: 10 minutes | Cook time: 5 minutes | Makes for 2 pounds pasta

2 (28-ounce / 794-g) cans whole tomatoes, drained	leaves, roughly chopped
½ cup regular or low-fat evaporated milk	1 tablespoon fresh rosemary leaves, chopped (optional)
½ small yellow onion, chopped	½ teaspoon table salt
¼ cup loosely packed fresh basil	¼ cup heavy cream
	2 tablespoons tomato paste

1. Wash and dry your hands. Crush the canned tomatoes one by one into a 6-quart cooker. Add the evaporated milk, onion, basil, rosemary (if using), and salt. Stir well and lock the lid onto the pot. 2. Press the button Pressure Cook or Manual, and set on High for 5 minutes with the Keep Warm setting off. 3. Use the quick-release method to bring the pressure back to normal. Unlatch the lid and open the cooker. Stir in the cream and tomato paste. Either use an immersion blender to purée the sauce right in the pot, or pour the contents of the pot into a large blender, cover, and blend until smooth, scraping down the canister's inside at least once.

Butternut Peanut Sauce

Prep time: 10 minutes | Cook time: 8 minutes | Serves 6

1 tablespoon coconut oil
2 cloves garlic, crushed and minced
1 tablespoon fresh grated ginger
1½ cups butternut squash, peeled and cubed
1 cup vegetable broth
¼ cup low-sodium soy sauce
¾ cup natural peanut butter
¼ cup peanuts, chopped
1 teaspoon coconut sugar
1 tablespoon lime juice
1 tablespoon crushed red pepper flakes

1. Place the olive oil in the Instant Pot and choose the Sauté setting. 2. Once the oil is hot, add in the garlic, ginger and butternut squash. Sauté for 3 minutes. 3. Add in the vegetable broth and soy sauce. 4. Seal the cooker and, using the Pressure Cook option, cook on high for 5 minutes. 5. Use the quick release option to release the steam from the cooker. 6. Carefully open the lid and stir in the peanut butter, peanuts, sugar, lime juice and crushed red pepper flakes. 7. Transfer the sauce to a blender or food processor and pulse until creamy. 8. Serve immediately or store in the refrigerator until ready to use.

Game Day Black Bean Dip

Prep time: 15 minutes | Cook time: 35 minutes | Serves 12 to 16

2 cups dried black beans
1 large yellow onion, diced
6 garlic cloves, minced
2 serrano peppers, finely diced (and seeded for a mild version)
1 cup loosely packed fresh cilantro, roughly chopped
1 (14½-ounce / 411-g) can crushed fire-roasted tomatoes
2 cups low-sodium vegetable broth
2 tablespoons olive oil
3 tablespoons fresh lime juice (about 1½ limes), plus more for finishing
2 teaspoons kosher salt, plus more to taste
2 teaspoons ground cumin
1 teaspoon chili powder
1 teaspoon dried oregano
1½ teaspoons smoked paprika
½ teaspoon ground coriander
⅛ teaspoon cayenne pepper (optional)
Freshly cracked black pepper to taste
Optional Garnishes:
Chopped cilantro, red onion, avocado, and/or jalapeños
Salsa of choice or hot sauce

1. Place the black beans in a colander and rinse with water. Add the rinsed beans to the Instant Pot and top with the onion, garlic, serranos, cilantro, crushed tomatoes, vegetable broth, olive oil, lime juice, salt, cumin, chili powder, oregano, smoked paprika, coriander, cayenne (if using), and black pepper and stir to combine. 2. Select the Bean/Chili setting at high pressure and set the cook time to 35 minutes. 3. Once the 35-minute timer has completed and beeps, allow a natural pressure release for 10 minutes and then switch the Pressure Release knob from Sealing to Venting to release any remaining steam. 4. Open the pot and, using an immersion blender, blend the bean mixture until it is thickened and creamy. This should take about 2 minutes. (Alternatively, transfer the mixture to a food processor or blender, in batches if necessary, and blend until smooth and creamy.) 5. Taste for seasonings and spice, adding more salt as needed. Finish with a squeeze or two of lime juice. If you want the dip to be a bit spicier, add a few drops of hot sauce or ¼ cup spicy salsa. Serve with tortilla chips.

Garlic Red Sauce

Prep time: 5 minutes | Cook time: 20 minutes | Makes 2½ to 2¾ cups

4 medium (about 1 pound / 454 g) tomatoes, quartered
1 small sweet onion, peeled and quartered
⅓ cup strong hearty wine (like a Cabernet Sauvignon or Merlot), plus more as needed
½ cup water, plus more as needed
4 ounces (113 g) tomato paste
4 or 5 garlic cloves, or to taste, peeled
1½ teaspoons dried oregano
1 teaspoon dried basil
1 teaspoon salt
¼ teaspoon baking soda (this helps cut acidity without adding sugar)
Pinch red pepper flakes

1. Drop the tomatoes and onion into the Instant Pot. Add the wine, water, and tomato paste. Cover the veggies with the garlic, oregano, basil, salt, baking soda, and red pepper flakes. There is no need to stir; it's better to have everything mostly on top of the tomatoes than at the bottom of the pot. Lock the lid and turn the steam release handle to Sealing. Using the Manual function, set the cooker to High Pressure for 20 minutes. 2. When the cook time is complete, turn off the Instant Pot and let the pressure release naturally for 15 minutes; quick release any remaining pressure. 3. Carefully remove the lid. Using an immersion blender, create the red sauce of your dreams. Add a bit more water (or wine!) if you need to thin it.

Classic Barbecue Sauce

Prep time: 5 minutes | Cook time: 10 minutes | Makes about 4 cups

1 tablespoon oil
1 small onion, roughly chopped
3 garlic cloves, minced
1 cup tomato sauce
½ cup ketchup
¼ cup apple cider vinegar
¼ cup honey
2 tablespoons molasses
½ tablespoon kosher salt
¼ teaspoon freshly ground black pepper
1 teaspoon liquid smoke (optional)
Pinch of cayenne pepper (optional)

1. Preheat the pressure cooker on Sauté mode. When the display reads hot, add the oil. Add the onion and sauté until softened, 3 to 4 minutes. Add the garlic and cook for 1 minute. 2. Add the tomato sauce, ketchup, vinegar, honey, molasses, salt, pepper, and the liquid smoke and cayenne pepper (if using), scraping up any browned bits from the bottom with a wooden spoon and stirring them into the sauce. 3. Secure the lid and cook on High pressure for 10 minutes, then allow the pressure to naturally release, about 10 minutes. Open the vent at the top and remove the lid. Press Cancel. 4. Using an immersion or countertop blender, purée the sauce until smooth. Taste and adjust the seasonings, adding more salt, vinegar, honey, liquid smoke, or cayenne pepper as desired. If you'd like to thicken the sauce, select Sauté and simmer with the lid off, stirring frequently, until it reaches your desired consistency. 5. Store in an airtight jar in the refrigerator for up to 12 days or in the freezer (leave ½ inch headroom in the jar for expansion from freezing) for up to 6 months.

Za'atar Seasoning

Prep time: 2 minutes | Cook time: 5 minutes | Makes about 2 tablespoons

1 tablespoon white sesame seeds
1 tablespoon minced fresh thyme leaves
1 teaspoon ground sumac
(available at gourmet grocery stores, spice shops, or online)
¼ teaspoon coarse or flaked sea salt

1. In a small dry skillet, toast the sesame seeds, tossing occasionally, until golden, 3 to 5 minutes. Pour into a small bowl and add the thyme, sumac, and salt and stir to combine. Store in an airtight container in a cool, dry place.

Pumpkin Purée

Prep time: 5 minutes | Cook time: 10 minutes | Makes 2 to 3 cups

1 (2-pound / 907-g) pie pumpkin
1 cup water

1. Slice the pumpkin in half along its equator; remove the stem and seeds. 2. Pour the water into the Instant Pot and insert the steam trivet. Place the pumpkin, cut side down, on top of the trivet. 3. Secure the lid with the steam vent in the sealed position. Select Manual or Pressure Cook, and cook on high for 10 minutes. 4. Use a quick release, and make sure all the steam is released before taking off the lid. Using pot holders or tongs, carefully remove the pumpkin. 5. Gently scoop the flesh into a large bowl or food processor. Using an immersion blender or the food processor, pulse until smooth. 6. Store in the refrigerator for up to 1 week.

Nourishing Mushroom Gravy

Prep time: 10 minutes | Cook time: 26 minutes | Makes 3 cups

3 tablespoons grass-fed butter, ghee or avocado oil
2 yellow onions, sliced
8 ounces (227 g) white or cremini mushrooms, cleaned and halved
3 cloves garlic, chopped
1½ teaspoons chopped fresh sage
1½ teaspoons chopped fresh thyme
1 teaspoon sea salt
2 pieces precooked organic bacon (optional)
3 cups chicken or vegetable stock, or bone broth

1. Place your healthy fat of choice in the Instant Pot and press Sauté. Once the fat has melted, add the onions and sauté, stirring occasionally, for 5 minutes. Add the mushrooms and continue to sauté, stirring occasionally, for 7 minutes, or until the onions and mushrooms are light golden brown and caramelized. 2. Add the garlic and sauté, stirring with a wooden spoon, for 1 minute or until fragrant, making sure to scrape up any browned bits at the bottom of the pot. Press Keep Warm/Cancel and add the sage, thyme, salt, bacon (if using) and stock. 3. Secure the lid with the steam vent in the sealed position. Press Manual and set on High Pressure for 3 minutes. 4. Once the timer sounds, press Keep Warm/Cancel. Using an oven mitt, do a quick release. When the steam venting stops and the silver dial drops, carefully open the lid. 5. Carefully transfer the hot gravy into a blender, making sure to leave at least 3 inches of headspace as hot liquids expand in the blender. Cover with the blender lid and, wearing an oven mitt while holding the lid closed, blend on low speed until completely puréed, about 30 seconds. 6. Transfer the gravy back into the Instant Pot, then press Sauté and allow the gravy to simmer for 10 minutes to thicken. Once thickened, allow the gravy to sit and rest in the Instant Pot for about 15 minutes before serving. 7. Once the gravy has rested, it can be served immediately or stored for later use in an airtight glass container, such as a Mason jar, for up to 3 days.

Adobo Barbacoa Sauce

Prep time: 10 minutes | Cook time: 5 minutes | Makes about 2 cups

2 large dried guajillo chiles, stemmed and seeded
1½ cups hot water
2 teaspoons oil
½ onion, sliced
5 garlic cloves, smashed
2 teaspoons kosher salt, divided
¼ cup white wine
¼ cup vegetable stock
2 to 3 canned chipotle chiles in adobo sauce
1 tablespoon apple cider vinegar
1 teaspoon ground cumin
½ teaspoon dried oregano
½ teaspoon paprika
¼ teaspoon sugar or honey

1. Place the guajillo chiles in a shallow bowl and cover with the hot water for 15 minutes to rehydrate. 2. Meanwhile, preheat the pressure cooker on Sauté mode. When the display reads hot, add the oil to the pot and heat until shimmering. Add the onion, garlic, and 1½ teaspoons of salt and sauté until the onion is browned and softened, about 5 minutes. 3. Stir in the wine and deglaze the pot, scraping up the browned bits from the bottom with a wooden spoon and stirring them into the liquid. Add the stock and simmer until reduced by half, 3 to 4 minutes. 4. Carefully transfer the contents of the pot to a blender, along with the rehydrated chiles and ½ cup of their soaking liquid, the chipotles chiles, vinegar, cumin, oregano, paprika, sugar, and the remaining ½ teaspoon of salt. Blend until smooth. When cool, transfer to clean airtight jars, leaving about ½ inch headroom. 5. Store in the refrigerator for up to 12 days or in the freezer for up to 6 months.

Baked Potato

Prep time: 1 minute | Cook time: 15 minutes | Serves 4 to 6

1 cup water
4 to 6 medium Russet or Idaho potatoes, rinsed, scrubbed, with skins pierced
Optional Toppings:
Butter
Sour Cream
Chives
Bacon

1. Place the trivet in the Instant Pot and pour in the water. Arrange the pierced potatoes on the trivet. 2. Secure the lid, move the valve to the sealing position, and hit Manual or Pressure Cook on High Pressure for 15 minutes. When done, allow a 10-minute natural release followed by a quick release. 3. Using tongs, carefully transfer the potatoes to a plate, slice open, top as you wish, and serve!

Indian Simmer Sauce

Prep time: 10 minutes | Cook time: 31 minutes | Serves 4

- 2 tablespoons avocado oil or other neutral oil
- 3 large yellow onions, finely diced
- 2 cloves garlic, minced
- 1 (1-inch) knob fresh ginger, peeled and grated
- 1 teaspoon fine sea salt
- 4 teaspoons ground coriander
- 1 tablespoon ground cumin
- 1 tablespoon garam masala
- 1 tablespoon paprika
- ½ teaspoon cayenne pepper
- ½ teaspoon ground turmeric
- 1 cup water
- 1 (28-ounce / 794-g) can whole tomatoes

1. Select the Sauté setting on the Instant Pot, add the oil, and heat for 2 minutes. Add the onions, garlic, ginger, and salt and sauté until the onions soften, give up their liquid, and are just beginning to brown and stick to the pot, about 15 minutes. 2. Stir in the coriander, cumin, garam masala, paprika, cayenne, and turmeric and sauté for 1 minute more. Stir in the water, using a wooden spoon to nudge loose any browned bits from the bottom of the pot. Add the tomatoes and their liquid, leaving the tomatoes whole. 3. Secure the lid and set the pressure release to Sealing. Press the Cancel button to reset the cooking program. Then select the Manual or Pressure Cook setting and set the cooking time for 15 minutes at high pressure. (The pot will take about 10 minutes to come up to pressure before the cooking program begins.) 4. When the cooking program ends, let the pressure release naturally (this will take about 25 minutes). Open the pot and, using the wooden spoon, smash the tomatoes against the side of the pot to break them up into the sauce. Wearing heat-resistant mitts, remove the inner pot from the housing and let the sauce cool. 5. Set aside 2 cups of sauce for the chana masala and transfer the rest of the sauce to an airtight container and refrigerate for up to 3 days. To freeze the sauce, transfer 2-cup portions to quart-size ziplock plastic freezer bags and freeze for up to 4 months.

Italian Pot Roast Ragù

Prep time: 10 minutes | Cook time: 1½ hours | Makes for 2 pounds pasta

- 2 tablespoons olive oil
- 2 pounds (907 g) boneless beef chuck, trimmed of any large chunks of fat and cut in half
- 1 (28-ounce / 794-g) can whole tomatoes
- ½ cup frozen pearl onions
- ¾ cup light dry red wine
- 1 tablespoon drained and rinsed capers, chopped
- 1 medium garlic clove, peeled and minced
- 1 tablespoon dried rosemary
- 2 teaspoons dried oregano
- 1 bay leaf
- ½ teaspoon table salt
- ½ teaspoon ground black pepper

1. Press the Sauté button, and set on Medium or Normal for 20 minutes. 2. Warm the oil in a 6- or 8-quart cooker for a minute or two. Add the beef in two batches and brown, turning a couple of times. Make sure the first piece is well browned before transferring it to a bowl and adding the second one. At the end, both pieces of beef should be in the bowl. 3. Wash and dry your hands. One by one, squeeze the whole tomatoes over the pot, then add any remaining juice from the can. Add the pearl onions and stir well to scrape up all the browned bits on the bottom of the pot. Cook for 2 minutes, stirring often, just until the onions begin to brown lightly. Turn off the Sauté function. 4. Stir in the wine, capers, garlic, rosemary, oregano, bay leaf, salt, and pepper. Return the beef pieces and any juice in the bowl to the cooker. Secure the lid with the steam vent in the sealed position. 5. Press the button Pressure Cook or Manual, and set on High for 55 minutes with the Keep Warm setting off. 6. When the machine has finished cooking, turn it off and let its pressure return to normal naturally, about 30 minutes. 7. Unlatch the lid and open the cooker. Use a flatware tablespoon to skim off any excess surface fat. Find and discard the bay leaf, then use two forks to shred the meat. 8. Press the Sauté button, and set on High or More for 10 minutes. 9. Bring the sauce to a full simmer. Cook, stirring occasionally, until reduced to a fairly wet ragù, about 5 minutes. Turn off the Sauté function and set the lid askew over the pot for 5 minutes to blend the flavors.

Steamed Butternut or Spaghetti Squash

Prep time: 5 minutes | Cook time: 7 minutes | Makes about 5 cups

1 butternut or spaghetti squash, no larger than 3½ pounds (1.6 kg)

1. Pour 1½ cups water into the Instant Pot. Place the wire metal steam rack in the pot. 2. Trim off the stem end of the squash, cut the squash lengthwise into quarters, and scoop out and discard the seeds. Place the squash quarters on the steam rack in the pot, arranging the pieces in a single layer. 3. Secure the lid and set the pressure release to Sealing. Select the Steam setting and set the cooking time for 7 minutes at high pressure. (The pot will take about 10 minutes to come up to pressure before the cooking program begins.) 4. When the cooking program ends, perform a quick pressure release by moving the pressure release to Venting. Open the pot and, using tongs, transfer the squash to a plate or cutting board. Set aside until cool enough to handle, about 5 minutes. Use a spoon to scoop the flesh from the skin of the butternut squash, or a fork to separate the strands of the spaghetti squash. Discard the skin. 5. Use immediately, or let cool to room temperature, transfer to an airtight container, and refrigerate for up to 3 days. The texture of spaghetti squash tends to suffer when frozen, while pureed butternut squash freezes well, for up to 3 months.

Simple Adzuki Beans

Prep time: 2 minutes | Cook time: 10 minutes | Serves 4

- 1 cup adzuki beans
- 1½ cups water or vegetable stock
- 1 (3-inch) piece of kombu

1. Combine the beans, water, and kombu in the pressure cooker. Lock on the lid. Bring to high pressure; cook for 10 minutes. Let the pressure come down naturally. Let the beans sit in the pot for at least 10 minutes. Carefully remove the lid, tilting it away from you. 2. Taste a few beans to make sure they are thoroughly cooked. If not, bring back to pressure, cook for 2 minutes, and let the pressure come down naturally. Carefully remove the lid, remove the kombu (eat, set aside for stock, or compost), and serve.

Curried White Bean Dip

Prep time: 10 minutes | Cook time: 10 minutes | Serves 6

1 (15-ounce / 425-g) can cannellini beans, rinsed and drained	1 cup vegetable stock or water
2 cloves garlic, crushed and minced	¼ cup cashew butter
	1 tablespoon fresh grated ginger
1 tablespoon red curry paste	2 tablespoon fresh cilantro, chopped
	½ cup cashews, chopped

1. In the Instant Pot, combine the cannellini beans, garlic, red curry paste, and the vegetable stock or water. 2. Seal the cooker, and using the Pressure Cook option, cook on high for 10 minutes. 3. Use the quick release option to release the steam from the cooker. 4. Place the dip in a large sieve or on some cheese cloth placed over a bowl. Let it sit for 10 minutes to allow any excess water to drain off. 5. Place the dip in a bowl, add the remaining ingredients and stir. 6. Serve warm, or cover and place in the refrigerator until ready to serve.

Buttery Marinara Sauce

Prep time: 5 minutes | Cook time: 5 minutes | Makes for 1½ pounds pasta

2 (28-ounce / 794-g) cans diced tomatoes	and minced
2 medium yellow onions, peeled and halved	1 stick butter, cut into chunks
	1 teaspoon dried oregano
4 medium garlic cloves, peeled	½ teaspoon ground black pepper
	¼ teaspoon table salt

1. Stir all the ingredients in a 6-quart cooker. Secure the lid with the steam vent in the sealed position. 2. Press the button Pressure Cook or Manual, and set on High for 5 minutes with the Keep Warm setting off. 3. Use the quick-release method to return the pot's pressure to normal. Unlatch the lid and open the cooker. Fish out and discard the onion halves (or pieces, if they've come apart). Either use an immersion blender in the pot to purée the mixture into a sauce; or pour the mixture into a large blender, cover, and blend until smooth.

Fresh Tomato Marinara Sauce

Prep time: 10 minutes | Cook time: 40 minutes | Makes about 4 cups

1 tablespoon olive oil (or dry sauté or add a little water/vegetable broth)	2 tablespoons tomato paste
	1 tablespoon balsamic vinegar
1½ cups chopped onion	2 teaspoons dried basil
6 cloves garlic, minced	2 teaspoons dried marjoram or oregano
1 cup chopped bell pepper	
6 cups diced fresh tomatoes	1 teaspoon salt, or to taste

1. Use the Sauté setting over normal, or medium heat, and heat the oil (if using). Add the onion and sauté until transparent, 5 minutes. Then add the garlic and bell pepper and sauté for 3 minutes more. 2. Add the tomatoes, tomato paste, vinegar, herbs and salt to the onion mixture and stir to combine. Put the lid on and make sure that the steam release handle is set to sealing, or closed. Cook on Manual setting at high pressure and set for 30 minutes. 3. Carefully move the pressure valve to release the pressure manually. If there's too much liquid, switch back to the Sauté setting and heat until the extra liquid evaporates. 4. You can leave it as is, but I like to blend it with an immersion blender or in a regular blender. 5. Taste and season as needed. Store in the fridge for up to a week or freeze in meal-size portions in resealable plastic bags.

Garlic Marinara Sauce

Prep time: 5 minutes | Cook time: 25 minutes | Serves 4 to 6

½ cup extra-virgin olive oil	1 tablespoon Italian seasoning
1 very large Spanish (or yellow) onion, diced	1 tablespoon oregano
	1 tablespoon parsley
30 cloves garlic, 6 minced, 24 sliced into slivers	1½ teaspoons granulated sugar
	1 to 2 tablespoons seasoned salt
1 (28-ounce / 794-g) can crushed tomatoes	2 teaspoons black pepper
	1 bunch fresh basil leaves, rinsed
1 (28-ounce / 794-g) can whole peeled tomatoes	
2 cups vegetable or garlic broth	1 (6-ounce / 170-g) can tomato paste
½ cup dry red wine	

1. Place the olive oil in the Instant Pot and then hit Sauté and adjust to the More or High setting. Heat the oil about 3 minutes. 2. Add the onion and sauté until slightly translucent, about 3 minutes. Add the garlic and sauté for 5 minutes longer, until lightly browned. 3. Pour in the crushed and peeled tomatoes, followed by the broth, wine, Italian seasoning, oregano, parsley, sugar, seasoned salt, and black pepper and stir to combine. Top with the basil leaves but do not stir them in. 4. Secure the lid, move the valve to the sealing position, and hit Keep Warm/Cancel followed by Manual or Pressure Cook on High Pressure for 10 minutes. Quick release when done. 5. Remove the lid and use a potato masher to lightly crush the plum tomatoes to the desired chunkiness. Stir in the tomato paste, and let stand for 10 to 20 minutes longer, until slightly thickened.

Cranberry Apple Sauce

Prep time: 10 minutes | Cook time: 3 minutes | Serves 2

1 to 2 apples, peeled, cored, and cut into chunks	1 teaspoon cinnamon
	½ cup maple syrup or honey
10 ounces (283 g) cranberries, frozen or fresh, preferably organic	¼ cup lemon juice
	¼ teaspoon sea salt

1. Combine all of the ingredients in the Instant Pot. 2. Close and lock the lid. Select the Manual setting and set the cooking time for 1 minute at High pressure. 3. Once cooking is complete, use a natural release for 15 minutes, and then release any remaining pressure manually. Open the lid. 4. Using a wooden spoon, mash the fruit a bit. 5. Select Sauté and simmer for 1 to 2 minutes to evaporate some water, stirring occasionally. 6. Once the sauce begins to thicken, press the Cancel button to stop the Sauté function. 7. Pour into clean jars and refrigerate.

Tabasco Sauce

Prep time: 10 minutes | Cook time: 1 minute | Makes 2 cups

18 ounces (510 g) fresh hot peppers or any kind, stems removed and chopped
3 teaspoons smoked or plain salt
1¾ cups apple cider

1. Combine all of the ingredients in the Instant Pot. 2. Select Manual and cook at High pressure for 1 minute. 3. Once timer goes off, allow to naturally release for 15 minutes, and then release any remaining pressure manually. Uncover the pot. 4. Using an immersion blender, purée the mixture. 5. Pour into clean and sterilized bottles and refrigerate.

Gingery Spinach, Scallion, and Sesame Sauce

Prep time: 10 minutes | Cook time: 4 minutes | Makes 3 cups

1 teaspoon sesame seeds
2½ cups finely chopped scallions
1 tablespoon grated fresh ginger
½ cup vegetable stock or water
1 cup unsweetened nondairy milk
2 cups frozen chopped spinach
1 teaspoon grated lemon zest
2 tablespoons fresh lemon juice
3 tablespoons tahini
1 to 2 teaspoons tamari, to taste
Salt and freshly ground black pepper

1. Set the Instant Pot to Sauté. Add the sesame seeds and dry sauté for 1 minute. Add 1½ cups of the scallions and the ginger and dry sauté another minute, adding the stock as soon as the mixture starts to stick. Stir well. Add the milk. 2. Lock the lid on the cooker. Bring to high pressure; cook for 1 minute. Quick release the pressure. Remove the lid, carefully tilting it away from you. 3. Add the frozen spinach; do not stir. Lock the lid on the cooker. Bring to high pressure and cook for 1 more minute. Quick release the pressure. Remove the lid, tilting it away from you. 4. Transfer the contents of the cooker to a blender or food processor, always taking precaution with hot liquids. Add the remaining 1 cup scallions, the lemon zest and juice, tahini, and tamari. Blend until smooth. Add salt and pepper to taste. 5. The sauce will keep for up to 5 days in the refrigerator and can be frozen for up to 1 month.

Fiery Arrabbiata Sauce

Prep time: 10 minutes | Cook time: 18 minutes | Makes about 7 cups

2 (28-ounce / 794-g) cans whole peeled San Marzano tomatoes
2 tablespoons extra-virgin olive oil, plus more for finishing
½ medium yellow onion, diced
1 small carrot, diced
4 garlic cloves, chopped
1 to 2 teaspoons crushed red pepper flakes, to taste (1 teaspoon for moderate heat, 2 teaspoons for spicy)
½ cup fresh basil, chopped, plus 2 tablespoons, finely slivered
1 sprig fresh oregano or 1 teaspoon dried oregano
¼ teaspoon kosher salt (½ teaspoon if using fresh tomatoes)
Freshly cracked black pepper
2 tablespoons tomato paste
1½ teaspoons reduced-sodium tamari or soy sauce (optional)
1 tablespoon high-quality balsamic vinegar

1. Pour the canned whole tomatoes into a large bowl (with the sauce) and crush the tomatoes with your hands by squeezing them through your fingers until no large pieces remain. 2. Select the Sauté setting on the Instant Pot and let the pot heat up for a few minutes before adding the olive oil. Once the oil is hot, add the onion and carrot. Cook until the vegetables are mostly softened, about 4 minutes. 3. Add the garlic and pepper flakes. Cook for 1 minute, stirring frequently to prevent burning. 4. Select the Cancel setting and pour in the crushed tomatoes, the ½ cup chopped basil, the oregano, salt, and black pepper to taste. Stir gently to combine all of the ingredients. Spoon the tomato paste on top but do not stir, to prevent burning. 5. Secure the lid and set the Pressure Release to Sealing. Select the Pressure Cook setting at high pressure and set the cook time to 10 minutes. 6. Once the 10-minute timer has completed and beeps, perform a quick pressure release by carefully switching the Pressure Release knob from Sealing to Venting. 7. Open the pot, remove the oregano sprig, and stir in the tamari (if using) and balsamic vinegar. Using an immersion blender, blend the sauce until it has a thick, chunky texture. (Alternatively, blend the sauce in batches in a high-powered blender. Be sure to remove the center cap from the blender lid to vent steam, but cover the hole with a kitchen towel.) Taste for seasonings and adjust accordingly. 8. When ready to serve, add the remaining 2 tablespoons basil and, if desired, a drizzle of extra-virgin olive oil. 9. Serve the sauce immediately, or allow the sauce to cool to room temperature, transfer to airtight containers, and refrigerate for up to 1 week. You can also freeze the sauce for up to 6 months. To reheat, warm the sauce gently in a saucepan, stirring until heated through, adding water as needed to thin.

DIY Poultry Seasoning

Prep time: 2 minutes | Cook time: 0 minutes | Makes scant 6 tablespoons

2 tablespoons dried sage
2 tablespoons dried thyme
1 tablespoon dried marjoram
2 teaspoons celery seed

1. Mix the sage, thyme, marjoram and celery seed together. Store in an airtight container for about 3 months.
Almond Ricotta
Prep time: 2 minutes | Cook time: 0 minutes | Makes about 2 cups

2 cups raw, slivered almonds, soaked overnight (Trader Joe's recommended)
½ cup water
2 tablespoons extra-virgin olive oil
½ teaspoon truffle salt

1. Drain and rinse the soaked almonds. Transfer to a blender or food processor and add ½ cup water, olive oil, and the truffle salt. 2. Blend, slowly adding up to ½ cup more water as needed until the mixture resembles ricotta cheese in texture. This may take more blending than you first expect, at least 5 minutes. Continue scraping down the sides of the bowl with a rubber spatula until it's completely smooth and creamy without any bits of crunchy nuts. 3. Taste and add more salt and oil if desired. Transfer to an airtight container and keep in the refrigerator for up to 1 week or use immediately in your favorite recipes.

Ginger Carrot Miso Butter

Prep time: 2 minutes | Cook time: 3 minutes | Makes about 2 cups

1 pound (454 g) carrots (about 6 carrots)
½ cup low-sodium vegetable broth
3½ tablespoons white or yellow miso paste
1½ tablespoons pure maple syrup
3½ tablespoons coconut oil, melted
½ teaspoon ground ginger or 1 teaspoon finely grated or minced fresh ginger
Freshly cracked black pepper, to taste

1. Peel and dice the carrots into ½-inch pieces. You should end up with 3 to 3½ cups carrots. 2. Place the carrots in the Instant Pot and add the vegetable broth. 3. Secure the lid and set the Pressure Release to Sealing. Select the Steam setting at high pressure and set the cook time to 3 minutes. 4. Once the 3-minute timer has completed and beeps, perform a quick pressure release by carefully switching the Pressure Release knob from Sealing to Venting. 5. Open the pot. There will be some vegetable broth remaining. Don't drain this liquid, as it will help bring the butter together. If you are using an immersion blender, leave the carrots and cooking liquid in the pot and add the miso, maple syrup, coconut oil, ground ginger, and pepper to taste. Blend all of the ingredients together until you have a smooth and spreadable texture. This process will take 2 to 3 minutes. 6. If you are using a food processor, transfer the carrots and the cooking liquid to a food processor and add the miso, maple syrup, coconut oil, ginger, and pepper. Blend until you have a completely smooth purée. 7. Store the miso butter in an airtight container in the fridge for up to 1 week.

Black Beans

Prep time: 10 minutes | Cook time: 25 minutes | Serves 4

1 pound (454 g) dried black beans, rinsed and sorted
1 large green bell pepper, seeded and chopped
1 medium onion, chopped
1 teaspoon dried oregano
1 bay leaf
4 ounces (113 g) salt pork, cut into 1-inch pieces, or 1 ham hock (optional)
1 (14-ounce / 397-g) can diced tomatoes, drained
4 cups chicken or vegetable broth
¼ cup distilled white vinegar
1 teaspoon granulated sugar
2 teaspoons fine sea salt (optional)

1. Rinse the beans and discard any that float. Combine the beans, bell pepper, onion, oregano, bay leaf, pork (if using), tomatoes, and broth in the inner cooking pot. The liquid should cover the beans by about 1½ inches. Add water, if needed, to achieve this. 2. Lock the lid into place and turn the valve to Sealing. Select Manual or Pressure Cook and adjust the pressure to High. Set the time for 25 minutes. When cooking ends, let the pressure release naturally for 10 minutes, then turn the valve to Venting to quick release the remaining pressure. 3. Unlock and remove the lid and taste the beans for doneness. If done, use a fork to press the beans against the side of the pot to mash them. This will thicken the liquid. Stir in the vinegar, sugar, salt (if not using pork or ham)

Oil-Free Chickpea Sliceable Cheese

Prep time: 2 minutes | Cook time: 9 minutes | Makes about 3 cups

2 cups water
1½ cups cooked chickpeas
2 tablespoons nutritional yeast
2 teaspoons sea salt
1½ teaspoons lactic acid
½ teaspoon granulated onion
½ teaspoon granulated garlic
3 tablespoons tapioca starch
2 tablespoons kappa carrageenan

1. In the jar of a strong blender, combine the water, chickpeas, nutritional yeast, salt, lactic acid, granulated onion and garlic. Blend well. 2. Add the tapioca starch and kappa carrageenan, and blend for 5 to 10 seconds until smooth. 3. Pour the mixture into a large saucepan or your Instant Pot on Sauté. Bring to a simmer over medium heat, whisking continually. Continue cooking, whisking continuously, for about 7 to 9 minutes, until the mixture has thickened nicely and is very glossy. 4. Pour the cheese into a container that can hold a minimum of 2 cups in volume. I like small loaf pans or glass bowls. 5. If properly cooked, the cheese will start to set right away. Allow the cheese to set at room temperature for 30 minutes. Then cover and refrigerate the cheese to finish setting for 3 to 4 hours. 6. If the cheese doesn't set up properly that means you haven't cooked it long enough. If this happens to you, throw it back into the saucepan and cook for a few minutes more! It will remelt and then you can pour it back into the mold for it to solidify. 7. Remove the cheese from the mold and serve. Store leftovers in the fridge. The cheese should last 10 to 14 days in the fridge.

Clam Sauce

Prep time: 10 minutes | Cook time: 5 minutes | Makes 4 cups

4 tablespoons butter
2 tablespoons olive oil
½ cup finely chopped onion
8 ounces (227 g) fresh mushrooms, chopped
2 garlic cloves, minced
2 (10-ounce / 283-g) cans whole baby clams
½ cup water
¼ cup sherry
2 teaspoons lemon juice
1 bay leaf
¾ teaspoon dried oregano
½ teaspoon garlic salt
¼ teaspoon white pepper
¼ teaspoon Italian seasoning
¼ teaspoon black pepper
2 tablespoons chopped fresh parsley
Hot cooked pasta
Grated Parmesan cheese (optional)
Additional lemon juice (optional)
Minced parsley (optional)

1. Select Sauté setting on a 6-quart electric pressure cooker. Adjust for medium heat; add butter and oil. When hot, cook and stir onion 2 minutes. Add mushrooms and garlic; cook 1 minute longer. Press Cancel. 2. Drain clams, reserving liquid; coarsely chop. Add clams, reserved clam juice and the next 9 ingredients to pressure cooker. Lock lid; close pressure-release valve. Adjust to Pressure Cook on high 2 minutes. Quick-release pressure. 3. Discard bay leaf; stir in parsley. Serve with pasta. If desired, serve with grated Parmesan cheese and additional lemon juice and parsley.

Beurre Blanc

Prep time: 5 minutes | Cook time: 10 minutes | Makes 1 cup

2 cups dry white wine
1 tablespoon minced shallot
2 cups cold vegan margarine, cut into cubes
1 teaspoon salt

1. Press the Sauté button on the Instant Pot and adjust setting to Low. Heat the wine and shallots and bring to a simmer. Let the wine reduce to half. 2. Whisk in the cubes of margarine gradually, adding a few at a time to create an emulsion. 3. Once all the margarine has been whisked into the sauce, lock the lid into place. Press the Manual button and adjust timer to 5 minutes. When the timer beeps, quick-release pressure until float valve drops and then unlock lid. 4. Season with salt and serve.

Butternut Basil Red Sauce

Prep time: 10 minutes | Cook time: 20 minutes | Makes 4 to 4½ cups

1 small butternut squash, peeled and cubed (2 to 3 cups)
2 medium or 3 small tomatoes, quartered
2 garlic cloves, peeled
¼ to ½ cup water (not necessary if your tomatoes are juicy)
4 ounces (113 g) tomato paste
1 bay leaf
1 teaspoon salt
½ teaspoon freshly ground black pepper
¼ teaspoon baking soda (this helps cut acidity without adding sugar)
Pinch red pepper flakes
½ cup fresh sweet basil leaves, torn
1 to 2 tablespoons fresh Italian parsley leaves

1. In your Instant Pot, combine the squash, tomatoes, garlic, and water (if using). Top with the tomato paste, bay leaf, salt, pepper, baking soda, and red pepper flakes. There is no need to stir. 2. Lock the lid and turn the steam release handle to Sealing. Using the Manual function, set the cooker to High Pressure for 20 minutes. 3. When the cook time is complete, let the pressure release naturally for 10 to 15 minutes; quick release any remaining pressure. 4. Carefully remove the lid—your kitchen should smell amazing! Let the sauce cool for a few minutes (use mitts or tongs to remove the inner pot). Discard the bay leaf, and add the basil and parsley. Using an immersion blender, blend the sauce until smooth. There may still be a few small intact pieces of basil.

Restaurant-Style Hummus

Prep time: 5 minutes | Cook time: 40 minutes | Makes 3½ to 4 cups

8 ounces (227 g) dried chickpeas (about 1 cup plus 2 tablespoons)
1 teaspoon baking soda
2 teaspoons kosher salt, plus more to taste
¾ cup tahini
6 tablespoons fresh lemon juice
(about 2 small lemons)
4 garlic cloves, roughly chopped
1½ teaspoons ground cumin
8 to 12 tablespoons ice water
Optional Garnishes:
Extra-virgin olive oil, smoked paprika, chopped Italian flat-leaf parsley

1. Add the dried chickpeas to the Instant Pot and cover with 6 cups water. Stir in the baking soda and 1 teaspoon of the salt. 2. Secure the lid and set the Pressure Release to Sealing. Select the Pressure Cook setting at high pressure and set the cook time to 40 minutes. 3. Once the 40-minute timer has completed and beeps, allow a natural pressure release for 15 minutes and then switch the Pressure Release knob from Sealing to Venting to release any remaining steam. 4. Open the pot. The chickpeas should be very tender. Drain the chickpeas in a colander (discard the cooking liquid). 5. Transfer the chickpeas to a food processor and blend for 2 minutes until you have a thick paste-like purée, scraping down the sides with a silicone spatula as needed. 6. To the food processor, add the tahini, lemon juice, garlic, cumin, and the remaining 1 teaspoon salt. With the motor running, stream in the ice water, 1 tablespoon at a time, until the hummus is thick yet smooth and creamy. Taste for seasonings and add more salt, lemon juice, garlic, or cumin as needed. If the hummus is still too thick for your liking, add a tablespoon or two more of ice water. 7. Transfer the hummus to a serving bowl and cover with plastic wrap to keep it from drying out. Ideally, let it rest for 30 minutes before serving. If desired, drizzle a generous amount of extra-virgin olive oil on top of the hummus and garnish with chopped parsley and smoked paprika. Store leftovers in the fridge in an airtight container for up to 1 week. Let the hummus come to room temperature before serving.

Homestyle Applesauce

Prep time: 10 minutes | Cook time: 7 minutes | Makes about 6 cups

¼ cup water
4 pounds (1.8 kg) unpeeled organic apples, cored and roughly chopped
1 tablespoon ground cinnamon
1 teaspoon vanilla extract
¼ teaspoon kosher salt
¼ teaspoon nutmeg (optional)

1. Add the water to your pressure cooker, then add the apples, cinnamon, vanilla, salt, and nutmeg (if using). Secure the lid and cook on High for 7 minutes, then allow the pressure to naturally release, about 5 minutes. Open the vent at the top and remove the lid. Press Cancel. 2. Using an immersion blender, or in batches using a countertop blender, carefully blend the applesauce to the desired texture. It will thicken more when it cools. Spoon into clean glass jars, leaving about ½ inch headroom. 3. Store in the refrigerator for up to 10 days or in the freezer for 8 to 10 months.

Plain Applesauce

Prep time: 5 minutes | Cook time: 10 minutes | Makes about 5 cups

4 pounds (1.8 kg) apples
1 cup water

1. Peel the apples, core them and cut into chunks. Add to your Instant Pot with the water and cook on high pressure for 10 minutes. 2. Let the pressure release naturally. 3. Drain the water, or use a slotted spoon to remove the apples from the liner and put in a food processor or blender. Blend until smooth. 4. Keep what you will use in the refrigerator for up to 5 days and freeze the rest in the sizes you typically use it.

Italian Ragù Sauce

Prep time: 10 minutes | Cook time: 22 minutes | Makes 3 cups

1 tablespoon olive oil
1 small yellow onion, peeled and diced
1 medium carrot, scrubbed and diced
1 stalk celery, diced
2 slices bacon, diced
½ pound (227 g) ground pork
½ pound (227 g) ground beef
4 cloves garlic, peeled and minced
4 ounces (113 g) dry red wine
1 (15-ounce / 425-g) can tomato sauce
½ cup beef broth
1 teaspoon salt
½ teaspoon ground black pepper
¼ cup whole milk

1. Press the Sauté button on the Instant Pot. Heat oil 30 seconds. Add onion, carrot, and celery to pot. Stir-fry 3 minutes until onions are tender. Add bacon, pork, and beef, and heat 5 minutes until meat is no longer pink. Add garlic and heat for an additional minute. Add red wine and stir for 2 minutes, allowing alcohol to burn off. 2. Add tomato sauce, beef broth, salt, and pepper to pot and stir to combine. Lock lid. 3. Press the Manual or Pressure Cook button and adjust cook time to 10 minutes. When timer beeps, let pressure release naturally until float valve drops and then unlock lid. Stir in milk. 4. Use immediately or store lidded in refrigerator and use within 3 days or in the freezer for up to 4 months.

Green Tomato Chutney

Prep time: 10 minutes | Cook time: 12 minutes | Makes 5 cups

2 pounds (907 g) green tomatoes, stemmed and diced
1 white onion, peeled, quartered lengthwise, and thinly sliced
2 medium red bell peppers, seeded and diced
¼ cup dried currants
2 tablespoons grated fresh ginger
¾ cup firmly packed dark brown sugar
¾ cup dry white wine
Pinch sea salt

1. Put all ingredients in the Instant Pot and stir to combine. Lock the lid into place, press the Manual button, and adjust timer to 12 minutes. When the timer beeps, let pressure release naturally until float valve drops and then unlock lid. 2. Transfer the chutney to an airtight container and refrigerate overnight before serving. It can be stored in a covered container in the refrigerator 2 months.

Homemade Elderberry Syrup

Prep time: 5 minutes | Cook time: 15 minutes | Makes about 2 cups

2 cups water
½ cup dried elderberries
2 tablespoons chopped and peeled fresh ginger
2 tablespoons lemon juice
1 whole cinnamon stick
1 teaspoon lemon zest
½ cup liquid sweetener, such as maple syrup, agave nectar or date syrup

1. Add the water, elderberries, ginger, lemon juice, cinnamon stick and lemon zest to your Instant Pot. 2. Cook on High Pressure for 15 minutes and let the pressure release naturally. Use a potato masher to smash the berries. 3. Use a fine-mesh strainer to strain out the berries and spices. Add the sweetener and mix well. Store in the fridge for up to 3 months.

Simple Cashew Cream

Prep time: 2 minutes | Cook time: 0 minutes | Makes 1 cup

1 cup raw cashews, soaked overnight or in hot water for at least 1 hour
½ cup water
½ teaspoon sea salt

1. Drain the soaked cashews, then rinse and drain again. Place in the blender with ½ cup water and salt. 2. Blend until very smooth and creamy. Use immediately, or store in an airtight container in the refrigerator for up to 4 days.

Pinto Beans

Prep time: 5 minutes | Cook time: 50 minutes | Serves 6

8 bacon slices, cut into small pieces (optional)
1 tablespoon olive oil (if not using bacon)
1 onion, finely chopped
1 garlic clove, minced
1 pound (454 g) dry pinto beans
4 cups beef, chicken, or vegetable broth
½ teaspoon ground cumin
1 teaspoon fine sea salt
½ teaspoon ground black pepper

1. Combine the bacon or oil, onion, and garlic in the inner cooking pot. Select Sauté and adjust the heat to Medium. Sauté, stirring occasionally, for 5 minutes. 2. Rinse the beans and discard any that float. Add the beans, broth, cumin, salt, and pepper to the pot and stir well. 3. Lock the lid into place and turn the valve to Sealing. Select Manual or Pressure Cook and adjust the pressure to High. Set the time for 45 minutes. When cooking ends, let the pressure release naturally for 30 minutes, then turn the valve to Venting to quick release the remaining pressure. Unlock and remove the lid.

Dal Dip

Prep time: 5 minutes | Cook time: 10 minutes | Serves 4

1 tablespoon sesame oil
2 cloves garlic, minced
1 cup diced carrot
1 (1-inch) piece ginger root, minced or grated (about 2 teaspoons)
½ teaspoon cumin
½ teaspoon fennel seeds
1 cup diced fresh tomato
1 cup dried red lentils
2¼ cups water
2 tablespoons lemon juice

1. In an uncovered pressure cooker, heat the oil on medium-high. Add the garlic, carrot, and ginger root and sauté for 2 minutes. Add the cumin, fennel seeds, tomato, lentils, and water. Stir to combine. 2. Cover and bring to pressure. Cook at high pressure for 5 minutes. Allow for a natural release. 3. Remove the lid. Stir in the lemon juice. Transfer to a food processor or high-speed blender and pulse quickly. This should not take more than 10 seconds. Refrigerate for at least 2 hours but overnight is best. Serve cold.

Creamy Curry Sauce

Prep time: 5 minutes | Cook time: 8 minutes | Serves 4

2 tablespoons coconut oil
1 cup onion, chopped
3 cloves garlic, crushed and minced
1 tablespoon fresh grated ginger
1 tablespoon serrano peppers, minced
2 tablespoons cumin
1 tablespoon curry powder

1 teaspoon cinnamon
1 teaspoon coriander
2 cups tomatoes, chopped
2 cups coconut milk
1 cup vegetable broth
½ cup soy yogurt
½ cup fresh cilantro, chopped

1. Place the olive oil in the Instant Pot and select the Sauté setting. 2. Once the oil is hot, add in the onion, garlic, ginger, serrano pepper, cumin, curry powder, cinnamon and coriander. Sauté the mixture for 5 minutes, or until fragrant and the onions are tender. 3. Add the tomatoes, coconut milk and vegetable broth to the cooker. 4. Seal the cooker and, using the Pressure Cook option, cook on high for 3 minutes. 5. Use the natural release option to release the pressure. 6. Carefully open the lid and add in the soy yogurt and cilantro. 7. Transfer the mixture to a blender or food processor and purée until smooth. 8. Serve immediately or store in the refrigerator until ready to use.

Red Hot Enchilada Sauce

Prep time: 10 minutes | Cook time: 10 minutes | Makes 3 to 4 cups

6 garlic cloves, peeled
2 poblano peppers, chopped
2 tomatoes, chopped
1 or 2 canned chipotle peppers in adobo sauce
½ red onion, chopped
½ cup vegetable stock
1 tablespoon adobo sauce from the can

1 teaspoon chili powder (I use a nice New Mexico blend), plus more as needed
1 teaspoon ground cumin
1 teaspoon salt
1 teaspoon apple cider vinegar
½ teaspoon smoked paprika
8 ounces (227 g) tomato paste

1. In your Instant Pot, combine the garlic, poblanos, tomatoes, chipotles, red onion, stock, adobo sauce, chili powder, cumin, salt, vinegar, and paprika. Stir well. Spoon the tomato paste on top, without mixing it in. Lock the lid and turn the steam release handle to Sealing. Using the Manual function, set the cooker to High Pressure for 10 minutes. 2. When the cook time is complete, turn off the Instant Pot and let the pressure release naturally until the pin drops. 3. Carefully remove the lid. Using an immersion blender. There may still be a few small intact pieces of basil.

Pumpkin Pie Spice

Prep time: 2 minutes | Cook time: 0 minutes | Makes 4 to 5 tablespoons

3 tablespoons ground cinnamon
1½ tablespoons ground ginger

1 teaspoon freshly grated or ground nutmeg
1½ teaspoons ground cloves

1. In a small bowl, mix together the cinnamon, ginger, nutmeg, and cloves, stirring to combine thoroughly.

Appendix 1 Measurement Conversion Chart

MEASUREMENT CONVERSION CHART

VOLUME EQUIVALENTS (DRY)

US STANDARD	METRIC (APPROXIMATE)
1/8 teaspoon	0.5 mL
1/4 teaspoon	1 mL
1/2 teaspoon	2 mL
3/4 teaspoon	4 mL
1 teaspoon	5 mL
1 tablespoon	15 mL
1/4 cup	59 mL
1/2 cup	118 mL
3/4 cup	177 mL
1 cup	235 mL
2 cups	475 mL
3 cups	700 mL
4 cups	1 L

VOLUME EQUIVALENTS (LIQUID)

US STANDARD	US STANDARD (OUNCES)	METRIC (APPROXIMATE)
2 tablespoons	1 fl.oz.	30 mL
1/4 cup	2 fl.oz.	60 mL
1/2 cup	4 fl.oz.	120 mL
1 cup	8 fl.oz.	240 mL
1 1/2 cup	12 fl.oz.	355 mL
2 cups or 1 pint	16 fl.oz.	475 mL
4 cups or 1 quart	32 fl.oz.	1 L
1 gallon	128 fl.oz.	4 L

WEIGHT EQUIVALENTS

US STANDARD	METRIC (APPROXIMATE)
1 ounce	28 g
2 ounces	57 g
5 ounces	142 g
10 ounces	284 g
15 ounces	425 g
16 ounces (1 pound)	455 g
1.5 pounds	680 g
2 pounds	907 g

TEMPERATURES EQUIVALENTS

FAHRENHEIT (F)	CELSIUS (C) (APPROXIMATE)
225 °F	107 °C
250 °F	120 °C
275 °F	135 °C
300 °F	150 °C
325 °F	160 °C
350 °F	180 °C
375 °F	190 °C
400 °F	205 °C
425 °F	220 °C
450 °F	235 °C
475 °F	245 °C
500 °F	260 °C

Appendix 2 Recipes Index

A

acorn squash
Seitan-Stuffed Acorn Squash — 62

adzuki bean
Citrus-Infused Sweet Bean Paste — 90
Simple Adzuki Beans — 104

all-beef hot dog
Chili Dog Soup — 77

all-purpose flour
Berries and Cream Breakfast Cake — 15
Raspberry-Almond Breakfast Cake — 17
Lava Cake — 87

almond butter
Flourless Brownies — 93

almond flour
Refined-Sugar-Free Blueberry Pie — 97

almond milk
Chickpea-Flour Egg Bites with Roasted Red Peppers — 8

Anasazi bean
Anasazi Bean and Winter Vegetable Stew — 81

apple
Creamy Winter Squash Soup — 74
Cinnamon-Vanilla Applesauce — 89
Cinnamon Apples — 93
Pear and Sweet Potato Applesauce — 88
Plain Applesauce — 108
Homestyle Applesauce — 108
Butternut and Apple Mash — 63
Basic Vegetable Broth — 80
Apple Dumplings — 86
Fruit Compote — 96
Cranberry Apple Sauce — 105

apple cider
Tabasco Sauce — 106

Arborio rice
Maple Pecan Breakfast Risotto with Chia Seeds — 13

artichoke heart
Chicken Oreganata — 47

asparagus
Lemony Asparagus with Gremolata — 62
Creamy Asparagus Soup with Basil — 76

avocado
Carnitas Tacos with Avocado Crema — 26

B

baby back pork rib
Spice-Rubbed Apricot-Glazed Ribs — 29

baby bella mushroom
Mushroom and Goat Cheese Frittata — 15

baby clam
Clam Sauce — 107

baby spinach
Creamy Eggs Florentine — 8
Middle Eastern Lentil and Spinach Soup — 80
Navy Bean, Spinach, and Bacon Soup — 83

baby white potato
Best-Ever Pot Roast — 23

bacon
Loaded Mashed Cauliflower — 66
Beef Bourguignon — 21
Chicken-Bacon Stew — 40
Blue Cheese Pancetta Mussels — 59
Creamy Bacon-Corn Casserole — 70

banana
Double Chocolate Banana Bread — 14
Bananas Foster — 91
Banana Pudding Cake — 98
Chocolate-Berry Bread Pudding — 95

basmati rice
Easy Beef Biryani — 30

beef
Beef and Pasta Casserole — 21
Beefy Mexican Casserole — 26
Beef and Broccoli Casserole — 27
Mama's Meatballs — 27
Easy Taco Casserole — 23
Chili Dog Soup — 77
Corned Beef and Cabbage — 33

beef bottom round
Color Beef and Potato Curry — 22

beef bottom round roast
Sauerbraten-Style Pot Roast — 20
Streamlined Bollito Misto — 32

beef brisket
Jewish Brisket — 24
Mexican Shredded Brisket Salad — 29

beef chuck
Italian Pot Roast Ragù — 104

beef chuck roast
Beef Roast with Asian Black Bean Sauce	26
Simple Shredded Beef	22
Shredded Beef Burritos	24
Smoky Shredded Beef Tacos	31
All-American Pulled Beef	28

beef short rib
Korean Short Ribs	20
Easy Boneless Beef Short Ribs	30

beef shoulder roast
Beef Pot Roast and Potatoes	33

beef-round steak
Beef Burgundy in a Pinch	23

beet
Balsamic and Allspice–Pickled Beets	66
Sweet and Sour Beet Salad	67
Orange Juice Beets	71

bell pepper
Italian Sausage and Peppers Hoagies	21
Chi-Town Italian Beef and Peppers	28
Chow-Chow Relish	71

berry
Pearberry Crisp	95

Bibb lettuce
Asian Lettuce Wraps	24

biscuit
Pull-Apart Cinnamon Bread	17

Bisquick
Blueberry Cinnamon Coffee Cake	10

black bean
Coconut-Gingered Black Bean Brownies	91
Game Day Black Bean Dip	102
Black Beans	107
Easy Taco Casserole	23
Spicy Chicken Chili	80

blackberry
Blackberry Crisp	96

black-eyed pea
Creamy Black-Eyed Peas	70
Ground Turkey Stew with Black-Eyed Peas	79

blueberry
Lemony Blueberry Buckle Dessert Sauce	88
Blueberry Cinnamon Coffee Cake	10
Blueberry Dijon Sprouted Wheatberry Salad	71
Refined-Sugar-Free Blueberry Pie	97

bottom round roast
French Dip Soup	77

bread
Caramelized Onion, Mushroom and Spinach Strata	12

bread crumb
Cajun Fish Cakes	50
Tilapia Fish Cakes	50

breakfast sausage link
Sausage and Cheddar Egg Muffins	14

breakfast sausage pattie
Sausage and Egg Sandwiches	14
Cheesy Hash Brown Casserole	18

broccoli
Mixed Vegetables with Peanut Sauce	68
Fast Salmon with Broccoli	50
Vegetable Chowder	78

broccoli raab
Veggie Queen's Broccoli Raab with Shiitake Mushrooms	68

brown lentil
Middle Eastern Lentil and Spinach Soup	80
Lentil Ragù	101

brown sugar
Lava Cake	87

buckwheat groat
Buckwheat and Bulgur Porridge	7

bulgur
Spice Trade Beans and Bulgur	73

bulgur wheat
Buckwheat and Bulgur Porridge	7

bulk Italian sausage
Kidney Bean and Sausage Soup	76

butternut squash
Butternut and Apple Mash	63
Creamy Butternut Spinach Soup	82
Butternut Peanut Sauce	102
Steamed Butternut or Spaghetti Squash	104
Butternut Basil Red Sauce	108
Butternut Squash Chickpea Tagine	75
Creamy Winter Squash Soup	74
Fire-Roasted Tomato and Butternut Squash Sauce	101

button mushroom
Pepperoni Pizza Stew	83

cabbage
Chow-Chow Relish	71
Corned Beef and Cabbage	33
Buttery Sour Cream Cabbage	65
Braised Savoy Cabbage	69

C

cake flour
Cherry Chocolate Poke Cake	90
calamariUmami Calamari	49

cannellini bean
Curried White Bean Dip	105
Shrimp and White Bean Soup	77

carrot
Carrot Purée	62
Basic Vegetable Broth	80
Ginger and Spice Carrot Soup	80
Lentil Minestrone	79
Ginger Carrot Miso Butter	107
Pork Chili Verde	33
Root Veggie Tagine	62
Jamaican-Style Yellow Split Pea Soup	81
Tofu and Miso Soup	75
Instant Pot Miso Soup	75
Split Pea Soup with Old Bay Croutons	84
Dark Vegetable Stock	82
Spring Split Pea Soup	84
Thick and Rich Jackfruit Ragu	100
DIY Vegetable Stock	101
Fiery Arrabbiata Sauce	106

cashew
Blueberry Cheesecake	86
Simple Cashew Cream	109

catfish
Catfish Bites with Creamy Slaw	57

cauliflower
Cheesy Cauliflower Au Gratin	61
Crustless Veggie Potpie	67
Loaded Cauliflower Soup	83
Cauliflower Sour Cream	100
Thai Green Curry Chicken and Cauliflower	45
Loaded Mashed Cauliflower	66

Cheddar cheese
Carolina Shrimp and Cheddar Grits	58
King Ranch Chicken Soup	82
Macaroni and Cheese Soup	84

Cheddar cheese sauce
Cheesy Potato Soup	83

cherry tomato
Eggplant, Tomato and Chickpea Tagine	67
Steamed Fish	53

chicken
Faux-Tisserie Roasted Chicken Dinner	44
Spicy Chicken Chili	80

chicken breast
Salsa Chicken Tacos	36
Spicy Lime Chicken	36
Black Bean Chicken Nachos	37
Chicken Penne Puttanesca	35
Orange Chicken	38
Shredded Chicken with Marinara	41
Sweet and Tangy Thai Bash Orange Chicken	41
Lemon Chicken with Basil	38
Sweet and Sour Chicken	44
Chicken Tikka Masala	37
Chipotle Chicken Fajita Lettuce Cups	39
Curried Chicken Couscous Casserole	39
Caprese Chicken Bowl	41
Forgotten Jambalaya	42
Sicilian-Style Braised Bone-in Chicken Breasts	39
Chicken Oreganata	47
Thai Green Curry Chicken and Cauliflower	45
Spicy Sichuan Steamed Chicken	43
Carolina-Style Vinegar BBQ Chicken	43
Buffalo Chicken	45
Chicken alla Diavola	46
Thai-Inspired Pulled Chicken Breasts	46
Vietnamese-Style Chicken and Glass Noodle Soup	78
King Ranch Chicken Soup	82
Chicken Potpie Soup	74

chicken drumstick
Chicken Chile Verde	35

chicken leg
Korean Gochujang Chicken Legs	46

chicken thigh
Autumn Apple Chicken	36
Chicken Potato Casserole	35
Creamy Southwest Chicken	36
Chicken Scarpariello	37
Apricot Chicken	38
Huli Huli Chicken Thighs	38
Easy Pesto Chicken and Red Potatoes	36
French Cider and Mustard-Braised Chicken	43
Chicken-Bacon Stew	40
Greek Chicken	42
Lemon Mustard Chicken with Potatoes	45
Chicken Nachos	42
Smothered Chicken with Mushrooms	42
Pulled Chicken with Chipotle Chilies	41
Southern-Style Braised Bone-in Chicken Thighs	40
Sticky Sesame Chicken	39
Persian Chicken	44
Senegalese Braised Chicken with Onions and Lime	45

chickpea
Butternut Squash Chickpea Tagine	75
Restaurant-Style Hummus	108
Oil-Free Chickpea Sliceable Cheese	107
Sweet Potato Curry Pot	61
Spice Trade Beans and Bulgur	73

chickpea flour
Chickpea-Flour Egg Bites with Roasted Red Peppers	8

chocolate
Fudgy Brownies	92
Double Chocolate Banana Bread	14

chocolate chip
Turtle Brownie Pudding	89

chocolate sandwich cookie
Cookies and Cream Cheesecake	94

chocolate sandwich cookie
Peanut Butter Cup Cheesecake	90

chuck roast
Chi-Town Italian Beef and Peppers	28
Best-Ever Pot Roast	23

chuck roast or brisket
Roma Vieja	74

clam
Red Clam Sauce	51

coconut milk
Chocolate-Covered-Strawberry Breakfast Quinoa	15
Maple Pecan Breakfast Risotto with Chia Seeds	13
Spiced Green Lentil and Coconut Milk Soup	79
Salted Date Caramel Sauce	88
Coconut Ginger Pork	25
Coconut Curry Sea Bass	52
Coconut Poached Halibut	56
Shrimp Curry	57
Mango Cardamom Tapioca Pudding	87
Flan in a Jar	91
Coconut-Gingered Black Bean Brownies	91
Mango-Coconut Custard	92
Sticky Rice and Fresh Fruit	93
Creamy Curry Sauce	110

coconut sugar
Flourless Brownies	93
Walnut Brownie Sundaes with Coconut Caramel Sauce	94

cod
Cajun Fish Cakes	50
Curried Cod with Tomatoes and Okra	51

coffee
Pumpkin Spiced Latte Oats	16

condensed coconut milk
Walnut Brownie Sundaes with Coconut Caramel Sauce	94

corn
Two-Corn Chowder with Green Chili and Scallions	68
Creamy Bacon-Corn Casserole	70

corn tortilla
Chipotle Huevos-Less Rancheros	13

Cornish hen
Cornish Hens with Ginger-Cherry Glaze	35

couscous
Curried Chicken Couscous Casserole	39

crab
Crustless Crab Quiche	11
Crab Bisque	83

crab leg
Steamed Crab Legs	54

cranberry
Cozy Fruit Compote	10
Cranberry-Orange Sauce	65
Cranberry Apple Sauce	105
Pear and Cranberry Crisp	98

crawfish tail
Crawfish Étouffée	54

cream cheese
Banana Cheesecake	91
Peanut Butter Cup Cheesecake	90
Pumpkin Cheesecake	89
Mini Pumpkin Cheesecakes	89
Cookies and Cream Cheesecake	94

cream cheese frosting
Berries and Cream Breakfast Cake	15

cremini mushroom
Caramelized Onion, Mushroom and Spinach Strata	12
Wild Rice and Mushroom Stew	81
Nourishing Mushroom Gravy	103
French Cider and Mustard-Braised Chicken	43
Spicy Beef and Broccoli Zoodle Soup	79

crescent roll
Apple Dumplings	86

crouton
French Dip Soup	77

D

deli ham
Breakfast Hash	15
Denver Omelet Frittata	12

demi baguette
Eggs in a Boat	12

dry red wine
Spiced Red Wine-Poached Pears	86

dry white wine
Beurre Blanc	108

duck breast
Italian Duck	43

E

Earl Grey Tea
Steel-Cut Oats Cooked with Earl Grey Tea	16

egg
Zesty Egg White Bites	9
Coddled Eggs with Garlicky Kale	9
Denver Omelet Frittata	12
Sausage and Cheddar Egg Muffins	14
Bacon and Chive Egg Muffins	11
Sausage and Egg Sandwiches	14

Soft-Boiled Eggs with Truffle San and Prosciutto	17
Flan in a Jar	91
Chocolate Cake with Peanut Butter Ganache	87
Mexican Eggs in Purgatory with Chorizo	7
Huevos Rancheros	7
Creamy Eggs Florentine	8
Spanish Tortilla with Red Bell Pepper Sauce	10
Ham and Egg Casserole	11
Peanut Butter Bread Pudding	9
Crustless Crab Quiche	11
Eggs in a Boat	12
Tex-Mex Breakfast	13
Ham and Swiss Muffin Frittatas	13
Smoked Salmon and Pumpernickel Egg Casserole	16
Southwestern Breakfast Casserole	11
Mushroom and Goat Cheese Frittata	15
Tasty Potato Hash	66
Mustard Potato Salad	66
Mini Crustless Pumpkin Pies	86
Butterscotch Pudding	89
Banana Cheesecake	91
Pumpkin Flans	88
Mexican Chocolate Gelatin Pudding Cups	96

egg noodle
Tuna Noodle Casserole	49

eggplant
The Best Damn Ratatouille	64
Miso-Dressed Eggplant	64
Eggplant Spread	69
Eggplant, Tomato and Chickpea Tagine	67
Chinese Braised Pork and Eggplant	25

elbow macaroni
Macaroni and Cheese Soup	84

elderberry
Homemade Elderberry Syrup	109

F

fennel
Cream of Fennel Soup	81

fingerling potato
Beef Pot Roast and Potatoes	33

flank steak
Beef Gyro Bowls	25
Beef Bourguignon	21

flaxseed milk
Savory Oat Porridge	16

flour tortilla
Smoky Shredded Beef Tacos	31

G

Gala apple
Autumn Apple Chicken	36

garlic
Garlic Marinara Sauce	105

ginger beer
Pork Belly Braised in Ginger Beer	21

gingersnap
Pumpkin Cheesecake	89

gingersnap cookie
Mini Pumpkin Cheesecakes	89

glass noodle
Vietnamese-Style Chicken and Glass Noodle Soup	78

green bean
Sesame Green Beans	63
Chik'n Lentil Noodle Soup	75

green lentil
Lentil Minestrone	79
Spiced Green Lentil and Coconut Milk Soup	79

green split pea
Split Pea Soup with Old Bay Croutons	84
Spring Split Pea Soup	84

green tomato
Green Tomato Chutney	109

grouper
Louisiana Grouper	57

Gruyère cheese
Delectable Swiss Fondue	63

H

haddock
Cheddar Haddock	51

halibut
Coconut Poached Halibut	56

ham
Ham and Egg Casserole	11
Tex-Mex Breakfast	13
Ham and Swiss Muffin Frittatas	13

hash brown
Cheesy Hash Brown Casserole	18

heavy cream
Mexican Chocolate Gelatin Pudding Cups	96

heavy whipping cream
Spiced Peaches with Cinnamon Whipped Cream	88

hominy
Two-Corn Chowder with Green Chili and Scallions — 68

hot pepper
Tabasco Sauce — 106

Italian sausage
Sausage and Kale Soup — 73
Toscana Soup — 80
Chicken Scarpariello — 37
Italian Sausage and Peppers Hoagies — 21

jasmine rice
Lentil Stew — 84

kabocha squash
Steamed Kabocha Squash — 65

kale
Garlicky Kale and Potatoes — 71
Polenta and Kale — 71
Coddled Eggs with Garlicky Kale — 9
Sausage and Kale Soup — 73
Toscana Soup — 80

kidney bean
Beef and Beans — 26
Kidney Bean and Sausage Soup — 76

L

lamb leg
Spoon Lamb — 32
Irish Stew — 76

lemon
Lemony Asparagus with Gremolata — 62

lentil
Lentil Stew — 84

linguine
Mussels Fra Diavolo with Linguine — 52
Quick Shrimp Scampi — 55

linguini
Shrimp Linguini with Spinach Pesto — 49

long-grain white rice
Cilantro-Lime Rice — 100
Beef Gyro Bowls — 25
Crawfish Étouffée — 54

M

mahi-mahi
Ginger-Glazed Mahi-Mahi — 55

Maine lobster tail
Perfect Lobster Tails with Lemon-Butter Sauce — 53

mango
Sweet Coconut Rice with Mango — 87
Mango-Coconut Custard — 92
Mango Cardamom Tapioca Pudding — 87

maple syrup
Homemade Elderberry Syrup — 109

maraschino cherry
Cherry Chocolate Poke Cake — 90

Medjool date
Blueberry Cheesecake — 86
Salted Date Caramel Sauce — 88

Mexican-blend shredded cheese
Beefy Mexican Casserole — 26

milk
Creamy Asparagus Soup with Basil — 76
Pumpkin Pie Cups — 96
Vegan Yogurt — 17

mushroom
DIY Vegetable Stock — 101
Smothered Chicken with Mushrooms — 42
Wild Rice Soup — 78
Clam Sauce — 107

mussel
Mussels in White Wine Sauce — 56
Steamed Mussels in White Wine — 57
Mussels Fra Diavolo with Linguine — 52
Blue Cheese Pancetta Mussels — 59
Steamed Mussels with Peppers — 54
Seafood Paella — 51

N

navy bean
Navy Bean, Spinach, and Bacon Soup — 83

oat
Butter-Toasted Steel-Cut Oats with Dried Apples — 8
Peanut Butter and Jelly Oatmeal — 12
Cinnamon Roll Oatmeal — 8
Peanut Butter Crunch Granola Bars — 10
Pumpkin Spiced Latte Oats — 16
Steel-Cut Oats Cooked with Earl Grey Tea — 16
Peaches and Cream Steel-Cut Oatmeal — 16
Savory Oat Porridge — 16
Raisin Nut Oatmeal — 18
Blackberry Crisp — 96

O

oat groat
Sweet Potato Spice Breakfast Oat Groats — 14

okra
Curried Cod with Tomatoes and Okra — 51

onion
Cream of Fennel Soup — 81
Garden Salsa — 100

Classic Barbecue Sauce — 102
Fresh Tomato Marinara Sauce — 105

oyster
Oysters-in-the-Shell — 53

oyster mushroom
Thai Red Curry — 69

P

Parmesan cheese
Cheddar Haddock — 51

parsnip
Empty-the-Root-Cellar Curry — 66

pasta
Beef and Pasta Casserole — 21

pea
Chicken Potpie Soup — 74

peach
Crumbly Oat Stuffed Peaches — 92
Spiced Peaches with Cinnamon Whipped Cream — 88
Cinnamon Stuffed Peaches — 95
Peach Jam — 101
Peaches and Cream Steel-Cut Oatmeal — 16
Peach-Raspberry Crisp — 97

peanut butter chip
Chocolate Cake with Peanut Butter Ganache — 87

pear
Spiced Red Wine-Poached Pears — 86
Fruit Compote — 96
Poached Pears with Spiced Pomegranate Sauce — 95
Pearberry Crisp — 95
Stout-Poached Pears — 94
Pear and Cranberry Crisp — 98

pecan
Sweet Potatoes with Pecans — 65

penne pasta
Chicken Penne Puttanesca — 35

pepperoni
Pepperoni Pizza Stew — 83

pineapple
Huli Huli Chicken Thighs — 38
Sweet and Sour Pork — 29

pinto bean
Huevos Rancheros — 7
Pinto Beans — 109

plum
Baked Plums — 95

poblano pepper
Chicken Chile Verde — 35

polenta
Creamy Polenta — 68
Creamy or Crispy Parmesan Polenta — 70
Polenta and Kale — 71

popcorn kernel
Flea Market Kettle Corn — 63

pork
Asian Lettuce Wraps — 24
Italian Ragù Sauce — 109
Mama's Meatballs — 27

pork baby back rib
Memphis-Style Ribs — 22

pork belly
Pork Belly Braised in Ginger Beer — 21

pork butt
Coconut Ginger Pork — 25
Carnitas with Pickled Red Onions — 32

pork chop
Chinese Braised Pork and Eggplant — 25

pork chorizo
Mexican Eggs in Purgatory with Chorizo — 7

pork loin chop
Pork Chops — 30

pork loin roast
Teriyaki Pork Roast — 24
Sweet and Sour Pork — 29

pork rib
Sicilian Meat Sauce — 25

pork sausage
Southern Pork-Sausage Gravy — 20

pork shoulder
Smoked Pork Shoulder — 20
Mole Carnitas — 22
Braised Pork with Ginger and Star Anise — 31
Pork Ragu with Green Olives and Warm Spices — 28
Pork and Beans — 31
Coriander-Braised Pork with Oregano and Feta — 27
Pork and Tofu Soup with Miso and Cabbage — 82

pork shoulder roast
Carnitas Tacos with Avocado Crema — 26

pork sirloin roast
Pork Chili Verde — 33

pork tenderloin
Garlic-Herb Pork Loin — 27

potato
Better Syracuse Potatoes — 61
French Fries — 64
Tasty Potato Hash — 66
Vegetable Chowder — 78
Shrimp Boil — 58

prosciutto
Soft-Boiled Eggs with Truffle San and Prosciutto — 17

pumpkin
Curried Pumpkin Bisque — 76
Pumpkin Flans — 88
Pumpkin Purée — 103

pumpkin purée
Mini Crustless Pumpkin Pies — 86
Pumpkin Pie Cups — 96

Q

quinoa
Chocolate-Covered-Strawberry Breakfast Quinoa — 15

R

radish
Mexican Shredded Brisket Salad — 29

raspberry
Raspberry Curd — 91
Raspberry-Lemon Curd — 97
Peach-Raspberry Crisp — 97
Raspberry-Almond Breakfast Cake — 17
Chocolate Cake with Dark Chocolate Ganache — 93

red bell pepper
Green Tomato Chutney — 109

red lentil
Red Lentil Curry Soup — 74
Curried Lentil Soup — 78
Dal Dip — 109

red potato
Easiest Rosemary Potatoes — 61
Mustard Potato Salad — 66
Cheesy Potato Soup — 83
Beef and Broccoli Casserole — 27
Easy Pesto Chicken and Red Potatoes — 36
Lemon Mustard Chicken with Potatoes — 45
Faux-Tisserie Roasted Chicken Dinner — 44

Roma tomato
Vegetable Tian — 70

round steak
Beef and Beans — 26

russet potato
"Baked" Potatoes — 62
Fluffy Garlic Mashed Potatoes — 65
Baked Potato — 103
Garlicky Kale and Potatoes — 71
Irish Stew — 76
Hash Browns — 7
Ham and Caramelized Onion Home Fries — 9
Spanish Tortilla with Red Bell Pepper Sauce — 10

Chicken Potato Casserole — 35

S

salmon
Smoked Salmon and Pumpernickel Egg Casserole — 16
Fast Salmon with Broccoli — 50
Honey Garlic Salmon — 50
Salmon with Pecan Coating — 55
Teriyaki Salmon — 53
Dilly Ranch Salmon — 52
Teriyaki Salmon Salad — 52
Dijon Salmon — 54
Salmon with Lemon Sauce — 56
Chipotle-Lime Salmon — 58
Salmon with Citrus Horseradish-Mustard Aioli — 58
Poached Salmon with Horseradish Sauce — 56

San Marzano tomato
Fiery Arrabbiata Sauce — 106

scallion
Gingery Spinach, Scallion, and Sesame Sauce — 106

scallop
Seafood Paella — 51
Sea Scallops with Cherry Sauce — 51

sea bass
Coconut Curry Sea Bass — 52

seitan
Seitan-Stuffed Acorn Squash — 62

shell pasta
Mini Tuna Casseroles — 55

shiitake mushroom
Dark Vegetable Stock — 82
Veggie Queen's Broccoli Raab with Shiitake Mushrooms — 68

short rib
Spiced Short Ribs — 30

shrimp
Shrimp Creole — 55
Quick Shrimp Scampi — 55
Seasoned Steamed Shrimp — 49
Spicy Buttery Shrimp — 57
Carolina Shrimp and Cheddar Grits — 58
Shrimp Curry — 57
Coconut-Lime Shrimp — 54
Shrimp Boil — 58
Shrimp and White Bean Soup — 77
Shrimp Linguini with Spinach Pesto — 49

smoked sausage
Forgotten Jambalaya — 42

snap pea
Coconut-Lime Shrimp — 54

snow pea
Beef Roast with Asian Black Bean Sauce — 26

soba noodle
Chik'n Lentil Noodle Soup — 75

spaghetti squash
One-Pot Turkey Bolognese with "Spaghetti" — 40

spinach
Gingery Spinach, Scallion, and Sesame Sauce — 106
Italian Duck — 43
Creamy Butternut Spinach Soup — 82

squid
Tasty Squid — 56
Mediterranean Squid — 53

strawberry
Lower-Sugar Strawberry Chia Jam — 11

sweet corn
Mom's Corn Chowder — 73
Tiger Prawns Paella — 50

sweet potato
Sweet Potato Curry Pot — 61
Gingered Sweet Potatoes — 63
Sweet Potatoes with Pecans — 65
Root Veggie Tagine — 62
Spicy White and Sweet Potatoes — 69
Sweet Potato Spice Breakfast Oat Groats — 14
Southern-Style Braised Bone-in Chicken Thighs — 40
Mixed Vegetables with Peanut Sauce — 68
Pear and Sweet Potato Applesauce — 88

sweet rice
Sticky Rice and Fresh Fruit — 93

Swiss cheese
Delectable Swiss Fondue — 63

T

taco shell
Salsa Chicken Tacos — 36

tiger prawn
Tiger Prawns Paella — 50

tilapia
Almond Tilapia — 50
Tilapia Fish Cakes — 50
Lemon Pepper Tilapia "Bake" — 53

tofu
Chipotle Huevos-Less Rancheros — 13
Tofu and Miso Soup — 75
Instant Pot Miso Soup — 75
Tofu or Chickpea Shakshuka — 18
Pork and Tofu Soup with Miso and Cabbage — 82

tomatillo
Turkey Chili Verde — 77

tomato
Tofu or Chickpea Shakshuka — 18
Veggie Stewed Tomatoes — 64
Garden Salsa — 100
Fire-Roasted Tomato and Butternut Squash Sauce — 101
Lentil Ragù — 101
Creamy Tomato and Basil Pasta Sauce — 101
Garlic Red Sauce — 102
Fresh Tomato Marinara Sauce — 105
Garlic Marinara Sauce — 105
Creamy Curry Sauce — 110
Buttery Marinara Sauce — 105
Red Hot Enchilada Sauce — 110
Sicilian Meat Sauce — 25
Apricot Chicken — 38
Caprese Chicken Bowl — 41
Pulled Chicken with Chipotle Chilies — 41
Umami Calamari — 49
Red Clam Sauce — 51
Shrimp Creole — 55
Steamed Mussels in White Wine — 57
Mediterranean Squid — 53
Louisiana Grouper — 57
The Best Damn Ratatouille — 64
Red Lentil Curry Soup — 74
Game Day Black Bean Dip — 102
Indian Simmer Sauce — 104
Butternut Basil Red Sauce — 108
Black Beans — 107
Dal Dip — 109
Italian Pot Roast Ragù — 104

tomato paste
Garlic Red Sauce — 102
Red Hot Enchilada Sauce — 110

tomato purée
Thick and Rich Jackfruit Ragu — 100
Chicken Tikka Masala — 37

tomato sauce
Classic Barbecue Sauce — 102
Italian Ragù Sauce — 109

top round
Easy Beef Biryani — 30

top sirloin steak tip
Spicy Beef and Broccoli Zoodle Soup — 79

tortilla chip
Black Bean Chicken Nachos — 37

tuna
Tuna Noodle Casserole — 49
Mini Tuna Casseroles — 55

turkey
Turkey Chili Verde — 77
Ground Turkey Stew with Black-Eyed Peas — 79
One-Pot Turkey Bolognese with "Spaghetti" — 40

turkey bacon
Buttery Sour Cream Cabbage — 65

turkey breast
Thanksgiving Turkey and Gravy	38
DIY Turkey Lunchmeat	44

turkey cutlet
Turkey Rice Soup	73

turkey sausage
Turkey Sausage and Cabbage	37

turkey tenderloin
Lemon and Ginger Pulled Turkey	46

turnip
Anasazi Bean and Winter Vegetable Stew	81

V

vanilla almond milk
Raisin Nut Oatmeal	18

vegan cake mix
Banana Pudding Cake	98

vegan margarine
Beurre Blanc	108

vegan white bread
Chocolate-Berry Bread Pudding	95

W

wheat berry
Blueberry Dijon Sprouted Wheatberry Salad	71

white bean
Pork and Beans	31

white bread
Peanut Butter Bread Pudding	9

white fish
Steamed Fish	53

white mushroom
Beef Burgundy in a Pinch	23

white onion
Curried Lentil Soup	78

white potato
Color Beef and Potato Curry	22

white rice
Sweet Coconut Rice with Mango	87

whole milk
Butterscotch Pudding	89

whole wheat bread
Southwestern Breakfast Casserole	11

whole wheat hamburger bun
Carolina-Style Vinegar BBQ Chicken	43

whole wheat pastry flour
Chocolate Cake with Dark Chocolate Ganache	93

wild rice
Wild Rice Soup	78
Wild Rice and Mushroom Stew	81

winter squash
Thai Red Curry	69

Y

yellow beet
Empty-the-Root-Cellar Curry	66

yellow cornmeal
Cornmeal Mush	13

yellow onion
Indian Simmer Sauce	104
Ham and Caramelized Onion Home Fries	9
Jewish Brisket	24
Senegalese Braised Chicken with Onions and Lime	45
Curried Pumpkin Bisque	76
Nourishing Mushroom Gravy	103
Buttery Marinara Sauce	105

yellow potato
No-Drain Mashed Potatoes	69
Breakfast Hash	15

yellow split pea
Jamaican-Style Yellow Split Pea Soup	81

Yukon Gold potato
Mashed Yukon Gold Potatoes	67

Yukon gold potato
Crustless Veggie Potpie	67
Spicy White and Sweet Potatoes	69

Z

zucchini
Vegetable Tian	70

Made in the USA
Las Vegas, NV
28 November 2022